WHAT ARE YOU SEARCHING FOR? LET SYDNEY OMARR® HELP YOU FIND IT!

Your Sun sign reveals an astonishing balance of traits and characteristics, a wealth of energy and potential just waiting to be tapped. Although your sign is not your automatic destiny, it can provide the map you need to go where you want in life.

The best way for this to happen is for you to learn how to communicate with your "guardian spirit" and heed its advice. Now America's foremost astrologer offers his sage advice on how you can do just that. Your journey has already begun. . . .

SYDNEY OMARR'S®

Spirit Guides

WITH TRISH MACGREGOR

A SIGNET BOOK

SIGNET
Published by New American Library, a division of
Penguin Group (USA) Inc., 375 Hudson Street,
New York, New York 10014, U.S.A.
Penguin Books Ltd, 80 Strand,
London WC2R 0RL, England
Penguin Books Australia Ltd, 250 Camberwell Road,
Camberwell, Victoria 3124, Australia
Penguin Books Canada Ltd, 10 Alcorn Avenue,
Toronto, Ontario, Canada M4V 3B2
Penguin Books (N.Z.) Ltd, Cnr Rosedale and Airborne Roads,
Albany, Auckland 1310, New Zealand

Penguin Books Ltd, Registered Offices:
80 Strand, London WC2R 0RL, England

First published by Signet, an imprint of New American Library,
a division of Penguin Group (USA) Inc.

First Printing, September 2003
10 9 8 7 6 5 4 3 2 1

PUBLISHER'S NOTE
While the authors have made every effort to provide accurate telephone numbers and
Internet addresses at the time of publication, neither the publisher nor the authors as-
sume any responsibility for errors, or for changes that occur after publication.

Contents

Introduction

If you ask ten people to define "spirit," you'll get ten different answers that run the gamut from what you drink to things that go bump in the night. In popular culture, two extremes come to mind—the religious version of spirits and guardian angels and the Hollywood version. The first version depicts an ethereal being with beautiful wings and an aura of goodness; the second is along the lines of Nicolas Cage as an angel who falls so madly in love with physician Meg Ryan that he forgoes immortality to become human.

From ethereal beings to handsome leading men, each of us has some concept of what a spirit or angel is. One of the most common ideas is that a spirit is what haunts a place—as in the movie *Ghost* or Stephen King's classic *The Shining*. In many popular depictions, spirits are viewed as evil; Shirley Jackson's "The Haunting of Hill House" is such a story.

But the spirit of spirit communication is generally viewed as benevolent, capable of transmitting information and guidance to the living. In spiritualist beliefs, the spirit—simply called Spirit—communicates through a medium. A medium is a psychic individual who "hears" messages from the dead and passes those messages on to the rest of us. Think John Edward in *Crossing Over,* the TV show that exhibits Edward's mediumistic talents. In other belief systems, spirits are called guardian angels, guides, the higher self. Regardless of the term used, the experience of spirit communication contradicts the adage that what you see is what you get, that what you see is, in fact, all there is.

People as diverse as Charles Lindbergh, Carl Jung, and Emanuel Swedenborg all had experiences with spiritual guides. Author and medium Jane Roberts wrote a number of books channeled through a "personality essence" who called himself Seth. Author and medium James Van Praagh, like John Edward, communicates with his guides in front of live TV audiences. Author and psychiatrist Brian Weiss writes movingly of "the masters" in *Many Lives, Many Masters,* his groundbreaking book on reincarnation. Edgar Cayce, often referred to as the most documented psychic of the twentieth century, gave thousands of readings throughout his life while he was in a trancelike sleep. In this state, he drew on the higher knowledge of guides who were able to diagnose illnesses and prescribe remedies and, in some cases, cures.

We may not all be Cayces, but each of us is capable of contacting our guardian spirits. Desire and need are probably the most important prerequisites. You really have to want to embark on this particular journey. Sometimes, this kind of desire is triggered by a crisis or a major life turning point—the death of someone you love, the looming reality of your own mortality, being fired from a job, a birth, a divorce, a marriage. Sometimes, it's simply a hunger to find out about the afterlife. For each of us, the event that launches the search differs.

Once the desire is there, firmly rooted, there are certain techniques and disciplines that help create the internal conditions for this kind of communication. If you're a physical individual, then yoga, tai chi, or something as simple as a walk through the woods can be conducive. If you're the mental type, meditation and visualization will put you in the right frame of mind for spiritual communication. Intuitive individuals may find it easier to request dreams in which their spirit guides speak to them.

ASTROLOGY & SPIRIT COMMUNICATION

The role of the stars is to provide guidelines for your particular Sun sign that will facilitate your ability to communicate with your guardian spirits. In fact, it all starts with your Sun sign and the sign that lies 180 degrees away from it. If you're an Aries, then your polar opposite sign is Libra. If you're a Taurus, your polar opposite sign is Scorpio, and so on around the zodiac.

Your Sun sign and its opposite create an astonishing balance of traits and characteristics where each sign supplies what the other lacks. The energy of this kind of polarity is enfolded in who we are and is always available to us. Once we learn how to tap this energy, to hear its unique voice, and to heed the advice that it offers, our lives function more smoothly.

The planet Neptune is also important in spirit communication. At one end of the spectrum, Neptune represents our illusions, our blind spots, our methods of escapism. For some of us, the escapism manifests as addiction to foods, alcohol, drugs, sex, glamour. But Neptune also symbolizes the ways we disconnect from our ego and merge with what psychologist Carl Jung called the collective mind. It represents our spiritual lives, our thirst for a larger perspective. The sign of your natal Neptune and its placement in your birth chart can provide tremendous insight into your capacity for spirit communication and how it's most likely to manifest for you.

Neptune won't break any records for speed as it travels through the zodiac. It takes an average of fourteen years to get through a single sign, so its impact is considered to be "generational." For example, anyone born between December 25, 1955, and January 4, 1970, has Neptune in Scorpio. They won't all be merging with the collective in the same way. Some, in fact, may not be merging with the collective at all. But most people born with Neptune in Scorpio find that ego boundaries dissolve through intense experiences and emotions. Appendix 1 will tell you what sign your Neptune is.

How to Use This Book

If you know your birthday, you can use this book. Everything else you might need for a deeper understanding of the material is provided. Part 1 of the book is an overview.

In Part 2 of the book, each Sun sign chapter is arranged in the same way: an introduction to the qualities of the sign; a description of the polarity axis and how to use the strength of your polarity in this exploration; the quest; the journey; meeting your guides; the map for your journey; and the grail.

The quest is the point at which you begin; the grail is what you find. Everything in between is how to get there. In other words, the Sun sign sections constitute a kind of road map for your journey.

Part 3 explores Neptune and its role in spirit communication. Part 4 is about the town of Cassadaga, a Spiritualist community that is more than a century old and is open to the public. All of its residents communicate with spirits in one form or another. Here, we meet Hazel West, a medium who has lived in this odd little town for more than twenty years. Hazel describes her experiences with spirit communication and offers guidelines for spirit communication that anyone can use, regardless of their Sun sign or spiritual beliefs.

So let's get started.

PART ONE

❋

Spirits & the Stars

1. Restless Souls

Each soul comes to his own truth in a personal,
unique way and at the proper time.

—JAMES VAN PRAAGH

A BIT OF HISTORY

Most ancient cultures shared not only a belief in spirits, but a belief that the living could communicate with the dead.

Paleolithic cave art often depicts animal figures, which may have been used as totems to symbolize certain spirits or served as magical symbols to invoke the protection of these spirits. The ancient Sumerians, who lived in the fourth millennium B.C., held fervent beliefs in ghosts and created many intricate rituals intended to protect and exorcise these restless and allegedly malevolent spirits.

The ancient Egyptians were obsessed with the afterlife. They believed that the spirit—the *ka*—survived, which was why bodies were mummified and offerings of food were left in the tombs of the pharoahs.

The belief in spirits and ghosts was so pervasive in ancient Rome that the dead were constantly appeased. Every daily act had a corresponding spirit and name. If these particular spirits weren't pacified in some way, there were invariably repercussions. Not surprisingly,

3

signs and portents were seen in the most common occur-rences, and the practice of magic and divination flour-ished. Astrology was one of the most popular forms of divination in ancient Rome, and the people who prac-ticed it were often revered and given special privileges.

In ancient Greece, the most powerful communication with the spirit world happened through the oracle of Del-phi. Here, the oracle's chief priestess, the Pythia, sat on a three-legged chair over a chasm that emitted what were probably toxic fumes. It was believed that when she went into trance, foaming at the mouth and spewing words that made no sense, she was speaking for the spirits and the gods.

Alexander the Great was a big believer in oracles. He not only revered the oracle at Delphi, but consulted ora-cles in other lands throughout his numerous journeys.

In modern times, the belief that the living can and do communicate with the dead can be traced to 1848, in a small cottage in Hydesville, New York, where the Fox family lived. John and Margaret Fox and two of their daughters, Margaret and Kate, had moved into the house in December 1847. The place was reputedly haunted. Strange noises and rappings could be heard at night, which kept the family awake.

On the night of March 31, about three nights after the family had moved into the house, young Kate heard the noises and responded by snapping her fingers and called out, "Mr. Splitfoot. Do as I do." She then clapped her hands several times.

The pattern of her clapping was instantly duplicated. Her sister then joined in and demanded that "Splitfoot" do what she did. Her four claps were immediately an-swered with four claps. Mrs. Fox asked the invisible guest to rap out the ages of all of her seven children, which it did, with a pause between each one to individualize them.

Mrs. Fox began to question the rapper. Was it a human being? There was no response. She then asked it to rap twice if it was a spirit. It rapped twice—and the Spiritualist movement was born.

The Foxes devised a simple method of communicating with their resident spirit. One rap meant yes and two raps meant no. Using this code, they learned that the spirit was that of a peddler who had been murdered in the house some years before and had been buried beneath it.

The Foxes began inviting neighbors and friends into the house to witness these odd conversations with the peddler's spirit, and news got around quickly. At one point, John Fox suggested digging under the house to look for the peddler's remains and had no shortage of volunteers. They didn't get far before they struck water and had to stop. Five months later, however, they resumed their digging. Five feet down, they uncovered a plank, and under that, buried in charcoal and quicklime, they found hair and bones.

Fifty-six years later, the rest of the skeleton was found when workmen were trying to restore a wall that had fallen down about a yard from the cellar. Near the skeleton was a peddler's tin box. The story was reported in the *Boston Journal* on November 23, 1904.

Once other people heard about the rappings, life for the Fox sisters got progressively stranger. What began as rappings in the house soon manifested in other ways— gurgling noises, sounds like that of a body being dragged across the floor—and the family finally moved out of the house.

Even after they moved out, the sisters continued to

communicate with the rapper. They would recite the alphabet until the rapper responded to a particular letter. In this way, they received their first spelled-out message: "Dear friends, you must proclaim this truth in the world. This is the dawning of a new era; you must not try to conceal it any longer. When you do your duty God will protect you and good spirits will watch over you."

The first Spiritualist meeting was held on November 14, 1849, in Rochester, New York, where the sisters demonstrated their ability. Reaction was mixed. Skeptics formed two different committees to investigate the sisters, but neither committee found any evidence of fraud. Within a year, the sisters were famous, and Spiritualism had become a full-blown movement with mediums cropping up all over—in New York, Philadelphia, the Midwest, even in Europe.

The oldest Fox sister, Leah, joined the demonstrations and became the first professional medium, giving private séances for money. Within a short time, the other two sisters started doing the same thing. In New York in 1850, Horace Greeley, editor of the *Tribune,* had a sitting with the sisters and was convinced they were the real thing.

In April 1851, Margaret Fox supposedly confessed to fraud in a letter that was published by one of her relatives. It had absolutely no impact whatsoever on the popularity of Spiritualism. Margaret, like her other two sisters, continued to do sittings. In the late 1850s, Margaret and Leah both withdrew temporarily from public life when they got married. Kate, however, continued with her work and began to produce "spirit forms" at her séances.

In 1861, Kate was hired by a rich New York banker, Charles Livermore, to conduct séances exclusively for him. His wife had died a year earlier and he wanted desperately to contact her. Kate conducted more than four hundred séances for Livermore, most of them in his home, and witnessed by other people. Doors and windows were locked, and precautions were taken to prevent any fraudulence.

The spirit forms that Kate allegedly produced weren't identifiable until the forty-third séance, when the banker recognized his dead wife, Estelle. She continued to materialize through Kate, and her shape became more substantial as time went on. But communication was rarely verbal; it was conducted through raps and a kind of automatic writing, in which a sitter would hold Kate's hand while she wrote on cards that Livermore placed in front of her. The handwriting supposedly matched that of Livermore's dead wife.

At séance 388, Estelle announced she wouldn't be back and apparently kept her word. Kate's stint with Livermore ended shortly afterward. To show his gratitude, Livermore sent her to England, where she met and conducted séances with other renowned mediums. In 1888, Margaret Fox publicly confessed that the whole thing had been fraudulent. She and her sister Kate, she said, had made the raps by dropping an apple on the floor. Later on, they learned how to snap the joints of their fingers and toes so perfectly that they avoided detection. Two months later, Kate Fox also confessed to fraud. But even these confessions failed to deter Spiritualism's faithful thousands.

Less than a year later, Margaret Fox retracted her confession. She said that she was having financial difficulties at the time, which led to speculation that she and her sister had hoped to gain monetarily from their confessions. In 1890, Leah died. Kate died two years later, and Margaret a year after that. By then, though, there were many mediums in the United States and Europe, and some of them were far more impressive than the Fox sisters.

Daniel Dunglas Home, born in Scotland in 1833, was investigated by the best debunkers and scientists of the day. Despite his astonishing feats during séances, he was never found to use trickery or engage in fraud. These feats included the appearance of disembodied hands, levitation, rooms that shook with thunder, and the ability to grow taller while "under spirit guidance." His séances were performed before royalty and aristocracy, and impressed the likes of Elizabeth Barrett Browning and Napoleon.

In 1885, William James investigated a well-known Boston medium named Leonora Piper. Although she wasn't as flamboyant as some of her peers—no levitations or materializations—James found her to be impressive. Through her spirit guide, Phinuit, she excelled at providing information that was unknown to her and anyone present and which later was established as known to the dead person when that individual was alive.

When James's other commitments forced him to give up his investigation of Mrs. Piper, he recommended that Dr. Richard Hodgson take over his study of the medium. Hodgson was a member of the Society for Psychical Research, and during his long study of Piper's abilities he became convinced of her abilities.

The case that was most convincing involved George Pelham, a pseudonym for a New York attorney, George Pellew, who had given up law to become a writer. Hodgson knew Pelham, who was an utter skeptic when it came to contact with the spirit world and the soul's survival of death. Pelham promised Hodgson that if he died first, he somehow would contact him. Strangely enough, Pelham died not long afterward, in a fall from a horse.

A month later, Hodgson took a friend of Pelham's to see Piper. The man used a pseudonym—John Hart—and was unknown to Piper. After she went into trance, her spirit guide came through and announced that someone named "George" was present. George gave John Hart's real name, mentioned a couple named Howard, and gave their daughter, Katherine, a message. The Howards, when told the message for their daughter, realized it was a reference to a conversation that Pelham had with Katherine years earlier. Hodgson wasn't fully convinced, but continued to observe Piper. Over the next six years, Pelham spoke to 150 people. Thirty of them had been friends when he was alive and he identified all of them. When Pelham's parents attended one of Piper's séances, they also used pseudonyms and yet, when Pelham came through Piper, he greeted them as his parents.

What was unique about Mrs. Piper, at least for that time, was that her mediumship lacked the flamboyance that marked Spiritualism during its heyday. Nothing was rapped out, there were no tilting tables, materializations, or levitations. The information related by her guides was usually clear, accurate most of the time, and the quality of the evidence was superior to that offered by many other mediums.

ARTHUR FORD

One of the fascinating chapters in the annals of spirit communication concerned stage magician Harry Houdini and medium Arthur Ford.

Houdini spent much of his life exposing mediums. Yet, before he died, he and his wife, Beatrice, agreed that if the soul survives death, he would somehow communicate in the code they had used in their mind-reading act. He had a similar agreement with his mother, and her death, in fact, was part of what triggered Houdini's search.

Houdini died in 1926. Two years later, the spirit guide of celebrated medium Arthur Ford—an entity who called himself Fletcher—announced during a séance that Houdini's mother was present. Fletcher said that the word Houdini and his mother had decided upon was "forgive." When the message was conveyed to Beatrice, she agreed it was the code that Houdini and his mother had selected.

In a later séance, Fletcher came through to say that Houdini himself—whose real name was Ehrich Weiss—was present and wanted to send his wife the ten-word message they had agreed upon. The message, Houdini said, was to be taken to Beatrice, and he wanted her to follow the plan they had discussed before he had died. The message read:

> *Rosabelle . . . answer . . . tell . . . pray-answer . . .*
> *look . . . tell . . .*
> *answer-answer . . . tell*

When Beatrice heard the message, she requested a Ford séance in her home. Fletcher asked if the message she'd been given was correct and she said that it was. Fletcher then asked her to explain what Rosabelle meant to her. It was the song she was singing the night that Houdini met her. Fletcher explained that the words of Houdini's code, which he and his wife used in their mind-reading act, actually made up the first ten letters of the alphabet. It broke down as:

1. Pray: A
2. Answer: B
3. Say: C

   4. Now: D
   5. Tell: E
   6. Please: F
   7. Speak: G
   8. Quickly: H
   9. Look: I
  10. Be quick: J

So, using this code, Fletcher said, and applying it to the Rosabelle message, *answer* represents B, *tell* stands for E. Since *pray-answer* is hyphenated, it represents the numbers 1 and 2 together, which form the number 12. The twelfth letter of the alphabet is L. The word *look*, according to the Houdinis' code, stands for the letter I, the second *tell* in the Rosabelle message is another E, and *answer-answer* equals number 22, or the letter V. The final *tell* is another E. BELIEVE. Even though Beatrice Houdini said at the time that the message was the one she and her husband had agreed upon, she later retracted that statement. No one is quite sure why, although it may have had something to do with Ford's flamboyant style.

But Ford's reputation was cemented. He became one of the most prominent mediums of his time. In the late 1960s, he was again propelled into the spotlight when he spoke for the dead son of Bishop Pike, the former Episcopalian bishop of California. Pike's son had committed suicide a year earlier, and the séance, broadcast on Toronto TV, was a sensation. Pike later said he felt as if he had actually spoken with his deceased son.

After the deaths of both Ford and Pike, however, doubts arose about the authenticity of the séance. Ford was known for his theatrics and flamboyance, and considerable speculation arose that the whole thing may have been nothing but a clever ploy.

THOMAS EDISON

Edison didn't just invent the lightbulb. Around 1920, eight years before Ford's spirit guide tackled the Houdini code, Edison revealed that he was working on an apparatus that would allow the dead and the living to communicate. This announcement was made in the esteemed magazine *Scientific American,* and because Edison was unquestionably the greatest inventor of the day, people listened.

"I don't claim that our personalities pass on to another existence or sphere. I don't claim anything because I don't know anything . . . But I do claim it is possible to construct an apparatus which will be so delicate that if there are personalities in another existence or sphere who wish to get in touch with us . . . this apparatus will at least give them a better opportunity . . ."

Skeptics, of course, pointed out that Edison was seventy-three years old at the time and thoughts of his own mortality no doubt influenced his thinking. He died without completing his electronic medium.

EILEEN GARRET

It was the equivalent of a floating ocean liner, complete with salons, staterooms, and even a promenade. It was the British R101, the largest dirigible ever built, and it left for its maiden voyage on October 4, 1930, bound for India. But early in the morning of October 5, it ran into a thunderstorm and crashed into a hillside north of Paris. It burned and left little more than a skeleton, killing most of the fifty-four passengers.

Two days later, during a séance at the National Laboratory of Psychical Research in London, medium Eileen

Garret, psychic investigator Harry Price, and journalist Ian Coster were attempting to contact the spirit of Arthur Conan Doyle. But when Garret went into trance, a voice came through that identified itself as Flight Lieutenant H. Carmichael Irwin, captain of the doomed airship.

In a voice filled with grief, he proceeded to describe the final moments of the dirigible's flight, using technical terms to describe the flaws in the dirigible's design. When the story ran, it was read by a man involved in the dirigible's construction. He was astonished at the detail that had been given, much of it confidential, with more than forty technical terms.

Before the official inquiry into the crash, a major from the Ministry of Aviation sat in on a séance with Garret and questioned the spirit of one of the crew. The technical information that was given was verified during the official inquiry. While the accuracy of the information that the séance provided is astonishing in itself, the incredible part of this story is that investigating officials actually attended a séance in search of information about what happened! This would be the equivalent of some high-ranking official of the FAA interrogating the spirit of the captain of an air disaster.

EDGAR CAYCE

Cayce wasn't a medium, at least not in the same tradition as Garret or Ford. And yet, he saw and spoke to spirits for most of his life. Even as a youngster in Kentucky, where he was born, he was considered strange and was shunned by other children and adults alike. One of the oddest things that Cayce did as a boy was to sleep with his head on a spelling book, and the next morning he could spell every word in it, even though he was a poor speller.

By the time Cayce was in his early twenties, he could put himself into a trancelike sleep and, provided with nothing more than a name, was able to diagnose health ailments and to prescribe remedies, even, in some cases, cures. Between 1901 and 1944, he gave more than fourteen thousand such readings, most of them carefully recorded and logged by Cayce's longtime assistant, Gladys Davis. During his readings, Cayce always spoke in the plural—"we"—suggesting that a consortium of souls were in attendance.

In the years since Cayce's death, his sons and his grandson have perpetuated his work. The Association for Research and Enlightenment, located in Virginia Beach, where Cayce lived much of his adult life, is open to the public. In its library are Cayce's many readings, containing information on health, astrology, reincarnation, the Aquarian Age, Atlantis, birth, and life and death.

Cayce's birth chart is shown in the Star Charts of the Appendices.

JANE ROBERTS

During the 1970s, Jane Roberts was often referred to as an Elmira, New York, housewife. This rather simplistic description hardly scratches the surface of this complex and determined woman who was an artist, writer, and one of the most extraordinary mental mediums of the twentieth century.

Like Leonora Piper, Roberts wasn't into showmanship. She didn't seek media attention. Her mediumistic abilities initially began to manifest in a heightened creative state of mind one night when "a fantastic avalanche of radical, new ideas burst into my head with tremendous force, as if my skull were some sort of receiving station turned up to unbearable volume." In late 1963, she and her husband, Robert Butts, experimented with a Ouija board. When the marker began to spell out coherent messages, they became intrigued and continued their experiments.

Quite soon, Roberts was anticipating the marker's answers before they were spelled out and, one night, simply stood up and began speaking as Seth. Seth described himself as "an energy personality essence no longer focused in physical existence." But even Roberts seemed confused at times about whether Seth was a spirit guide in the spiritualistic sense, a fragment of her own personality, or something else altogether.

"The 'spirit guide' designation may be a handy symbolic represent of this idea, and I'm not saying that spirit guides do not exist," Roberts wrote in the introduction of *The Nature of Personal Reality*. "I am saying that the idea deserves greater examination, for the spirit guide may represent something far different than we think."

Whatever Seth was, he spoke through Roberts for nearly twenty years, dictating a vast amount of information about the nature of reality. Roberts's husband used a kind of shorthand to transcribe the sessions, as they were termed, and today all of the Seth material—including unpublished information—has a permanent home at Princeton University.

Roberts's chart can be found in the Star Charts of the Appendices.

MEDIUMS IN THE 21ST CENTURY

Today's mediums bear little resemblance to the mediums who plied their craft during the heyday of Spiritualism. These individuals don't tilt tables in darkened rooms or materialize spirits or decipher rappings. They are ordinary people whose abilities allow them to access information in nontraditional ways. Like you, they are seekers.

Take James Van Praagh. He looks ordinary enough, has a likable demeanor, doesn't do anything to call attention to himself. He could be your neighbor, your grocer. He has a sense of humor. You know that he has bad days when everything goes wrong—his car won't start, his hard drive crashes, he has run out of milk. But when he talks about life and death, about spirits and his communication with the dead, he shines. A certainty enters his voice, an *authenticity* that resonates intuitively for whoever is listening.

Van Praagh's first book, *Talking to Heaven,* hit the top of *The New York Times* bestseller list. His subsequent books have all been bestsellers. He travels worldwide, spreading the word about the survival of the soul. He has appeared on numerous TV talk shows and is a sought-after speaker.

At a recent conference in Fort Lauderdale, Florida, put on by the Omega Institute, Van Praagh teamed up with past-life researcher, author, and psychiatrist Brian Weiss, and the two of them captivated an audience for an hour. There weren't any parlor tricks. This wasn't show biz. This was a group of spiritual seekers with a lot of questions, which Van Praagh and Weiss answered.

John Edward is also a medium and a writer. He is younger than Van Praagh, but his resume, if he had one, probably would be similar. Psychic as a kid. Some weird experiences as a teenager. Somewhat skeptical of his abilities as he was growing up. Heard voices. You get the idea here. This is the modus operandi of a medium in the making. John Edward now has several bestselling books and his own TV show on the Sci-Fi channel. *Dateline* recently followed him around, interviewing him, watching him at a workshop, commenting on how he worked and what he said. Edward, like Van Praagh, came across as an ordinary guy with a genuine and extraordinary talent.

Char Margolis, author of *Questions from Earth, Answers from Heaven,* opens her book with a chapter heading that reads: "I Talk to Dead People for a Living." She has been a psychic for twenty-five years. Although the media calls her a *psychic intuitive,* she thinks of herself as "your most affordable long-distance carrier to the other side." Like Edward, she was psychic as a child and grew up in a family that didn't discourage or chastise her when she saw or heard things that other people didn't.

She's good at getting initials and names of people who are both living and dead, so good, in fact, that Sally Jesse Raphael called her "the alphabet soup psychic." On one recent show where she appeared with Van Praagh, Sylvia Brown, and several other psychics, her specificity with initials and names was impressive.

In countless neighborhoods and towns, there are mediums and psychics who may not write bestselling books or appear on TV talk show circuits, yet who practice their crafts quietly, bringing messages from the dead and solace to the living. They have committed to a search, developed their own abilities, and shown the rest of us what is possible. If at some point you decide to have a reading with a psychic or medium, don't stop at the first road sign for psychic readings that you see. Ask around, get a referral from a friend. If you can't find someone, refer to the resource guide in Appendix 2. The psychics and mediums listed in the resource guide are reputable, and their charges are reasonable.

Mediumship in the twenty-first century isn't about showmanship; it's about a search for truth. It's about learning how to pierce the barrier between this world and another world so that we all ultimately come to understand that death isn't the end of life, that it's just another state of being, a transition from matter to spirit.

And in that spirit, the adventure begins.

2. The Afterlife

. . . it appears that this reality and the next are different in degree, but not in kind.

—MICHAEL TALBOTT

We talk about guides, spirits, souls—all of them dead. So where, exactly, are they?

In the movie *What Dreams May Come,* husband and father Robin Williams is killed in a car accident. He comes to in a place that is very much like our world, but with some glaring differences. The colors are brighter and more vivid; he moves as soon as the desire to do so enters his mind; communication is through thought. Every desire and thought, in fact, is materialized instantly, and the reality he experiences is sculpted from his deepest beliefs. He doesn't really believe he's dead, however, until he seeks out his family and realizes that although he can see and hear them, they aren't even aware of his presence.

In many ways, the movie's depiction of the afterlife fits what many mediums and psychics describe.

Medium George Anderson, author of *Lessons from the Light,* says that the souls with whom he communicates have described the hereafter as "a perfect summer day . . . Since we enter the hereafter with only our earthly reality as our reference point, we have to be introduced into this new reality one step at a time . . . For as long as we need it, the hereafter will be for us a reflection of life on earth—with the exception that everything is perfect and glowing with the energy of the Infinite Light and its peaceful environment."

In the movie, once Williams realizes he is dead, he quickly learns there is no lapse of time between a thought and its manifestation. If he wants to get somewhere, he only has to think himself there. If he wants a book, it materializes instantly. Whatever he thinks, whatever he desires, is instantly *there.* James Van Praagh, in his bestseller *Reaching to Heaven,* writes, "Everything is created with thought, and all a spirit needs to do is learn how to breathe life into its thought and a dream is realized."

The afterlife isn't limited by the physical laws that bind us on earth. Gravity? No such thing. Speed? Forget it. Transportation, communication, desires: it's all done by thought. His description of the afterlife parallels many elements of *What Dreams May Come,* from the brilliant colors to the incredibly fragrant air to the exquisite gardens and the "schools of knowledge housed in extraordinary buildings created with materials unfamiliar to our earthly minds."

At one point in the movie, Williams goes to one such building to find out when his wife is due to pass over. This hall of records, as it seems to be, bears an uncanny resemblance to Edgar Cayce's description of the akashic records. These "records written on time and space," as Cayce described them in readings, contain everything about every soul that has ever lived or will live. Every thought, action, and deed, every event: Williams discovers that his wife died before she was supposed to, that she was so bereft over his death she committed suicide.

In the book upon which the movie was based, author Richard Matheson describes the place where Williams's wife resides in terms that, although horrifying, are understood to be a product of her own beliefs. Screenwriter Ron Bass, however, depicts this place as pretty similar to the Catholic version of hell.

Van Praagh describes a "dark land." The air stinks, the light is dim, shadowy figures dart about, some of them missing limbs. "The atmosphere in this region resembles a scene right out of a Dickens novel," he writes. "Spirits in such a dark realm harbor mental attitudes of hate, malice, and the need for control over others; they are ruled by the lowest elements of the physical world." Think murderer, rapist, child and animal abuser. Think *bad person.* "A soul remains in this darkened hole until all of its lowest desires are lived out."

Williams descends into this terrible place in search of his wife. The cinematography during this part of the movie can make even the seasoned movie fanatic somewhat uncomfortable. The house where Williams's wife lives looks very much like the house the two of them had when they were alive, except that it is incredibly bleak. Dead trees surround the house. The grass is brown and ugly. A kind of permanent twilight permeates the air.

Inside the house, the situation is even worse. No light. Leaks. Complete neglect. Williams finds his wife sitting in the dark, apparently drowning in an ocean of self-pity. If he can't get through to her somehow, this is the state in which she will spend eternity.

"Only when it (a soul) comes into spiritual awareness can it move to the upper portions of the astral plane," writes Van Praagh.

Van Praagh's descriptions are similar to Seth's, but Seth goes into much more detail. In *Seth Speaks,* he has this to say about death: "There is no separate, indivisible, specific point of death. Life is a state of becoming, and death is a part of this process of becoming."

Too theoretical. But Seth doesn't leave it there. "The boredom and stagnation of a stereotyped heaven will not for long content the striving consciousness. There are teachers to explain the conditions and circumstances. You are not left alone, therefore, lost in mazes of hallucinations. You may or may not realize that you are dead in physical terms."

Seth contends that each individual's experience of death and the hereafter is largely dependent upon that individual's belief system during his or her life. If a person believes his or her consciousness begins and ends with his physical body, then he may cling to it after death, not understanding that he is dead. Williams goes through a period like this in the movie. But as Seth points out, there are always teachers nearby who are willing to assist people in grasping that they are dead. He calls these individuals an "honorary guard" and says they are made up of spirits as well as people who are traveling out of body. "These people are particularly helpful because they are still involved with physical reality, and have a more immediate understanding of the feelings and emotions involved at your end."

These out-of-body helpers bear a striking resemblance to what other consciousness pioneers have discovered. In 1958, businessman Robert Monroe began having spontaneous out-of-body experiences, which he later documented in *Journeys Out of the Body* and two other books. His experiences led him to establish the Monroe Institute, a research facility devoted to the exploration of states of consciousness not ordinarily available to the human mind and their practical application.

Monroe was essentially a pioneer who mapped inner dimensions, what Van Praagh calls "the astral world." Toward the end of his life, Monroe began to chart the area just beyond the borders of the physical world, where souls enter and depart physical life. In doing this, he picked up "signals" from people who had recently died but didn't know they were dead. In his out-of-body state, Monroe was able to assume different "forms" and used this ability to aid these people in realizing they were dead, often by appearing to them as a parent, relative, or trusted friend. His task was to take them to wherever they were supposed to go. "Each phased out when we encountered the radiation of a belief system with which they resonated," Monroe writes in *The Ultimate Journey*.

As a result of these experiences, he developed the Lifeline program, in which participants who have been through at least one other program at the institute are taught how to help recently departed souls get to where they are supposed to be.

Author Bruce Moen, a graduate of several programs at the Monroe Institute, now teaches "soul retrieval" workshops around the country. His three books, beginning with *Voyages into the Unknown,* are especially insightful about life in the hereafter and should be read by anyone embarking on a path of spirit communication. He uses Monroe's terminology, in which levels of consciousness are assigned names. Focus 10, for instance, is known as "mind awake, body asleep." Focus 12 is a state of expanded awareness. Focus 15 is "no time." This is a level of consciousness "which opens avenues of the mind that offer vast opportunities for self-exploration beyond the constraints of time and place," writes Moen in *Voyages into the Unknown.*

Before Monroe passed on, he had mapped focus levels

up to Focus 27, a place he called the Reception Center or the Park. Monroe described it as a place designed to ease the shock of transition out of physical reality. In *The Ultimate Journey,* Monroe recounts his journeys to Focus 27 to visit his wife after she died and say it was too emotionally wrenching. After two visits, he never went back, at least not while he was alive.

The belief systems that Monroe mentions fall in Focus 24, 25, and 26. Van Praagh refers to these areas as well. Once you die, says Van Praagh, ". . . you will be attracted to a state of being where everyone thinks, behaves, and lives the same as you. Therefore, you will find yourself on the same level with other spirits with similar belief systems."

Seth, the entity for which mystic and author Jane Roberts spoke, insists there is no single after-death reality; everyone's experience is different. There are, however, certain generalized dimensions into which the after-death experience will fall. "There is an initial stage for those who are still focused strongly in physical reality, and for those who need a period of recuperation and rest. On this level there will be hospitals and rest homes."

In another level of afterlife reality, there are training centers where the nature of reality is explained to souls who need this kind of explanation. Here, too, are educational centers that offer certain types of instruction to souls who have chosen to reincarnate.

In the movie *Defending Your Life,* Albert Brooks is killed in a car accident and finds himself in Judgment City, where he must—literally—defend the life he has just left. This idea of judgment by some higher power or authority (God) is curiously absent in the descriptions of the afterlife provided by most psychics and mediums.

If, however, you have a strong belief in heaven or hell,

in being "judged," then initially that may be what you experience. While these beliefs can be very limited in the time immediately after death, in some ways they are useful, says Seth, because they lead the individual to expect some sort of spiritual evaluation and review.

During the review period in the afterlife, counsel is always available to any soul that wants or needs advice. The decision to return and the circumstances of that return are always left to the soul's free will.

"A soul decides how fast or how slowly it wants to advance," writes Van Praagh, echoing what Seth says. Some souls remain on the other side until they feel they are completely ready for another life with difficult challenges. Other souls are enthusiastic to return. Seth contends there's no time schedule for reincarnating, ". . . yet it is very unusual for an individual to wait for anything over three centuries between lives, for this makes the orientation very difficult, and the emotional ties with earth have become weak."

Guides and guardian angels that we have during physical life may be souls of people we have loved in this life, who have passed on, or the souls of people with whom we were connected in other lives. These guides may also be other parts of our multidimensional higher self.

Psychic medium Renie Wiley has had the same group of guides for most of her life. "They've been with me since I was old enough to walk and talk." She hears them as inner voices, each voice distinct, each energy separate.

Some years ago, she used to work with police in several South Florida counties on cases that usually involved homicide or missing children. When she worked with police, she always requested an object that belonged to the victim—jewelry or clothing for an adult, a toy or clothing for a child. This enabled her to tune in on the victim's energy, and then her guides would communicate with her about the victim. But because Wiley is empathic—she feels what the victim feels—this type of work was especially painful for her, particularly when she was working on cases that involved kids. "My guides couldn't do anything to mitigate the pain I experienced when I tuned in on a child who had died of abuse."

Char Margolis notes that people who are empathic—whether they're psychic or doctors, nurses, and others in the healing profession—tend not to take care of themselves because they're so busy taking care of others. "They become repositories for others' negative energy," she writes in *Questions from Earth, Answers from Heaven.* "Then they don't take the time to clear the energy out of their systems and they get sick."

She advises that anyone who works intuitively should protect themselves by visualizing a white light around themselves "and send the negative emotion back where it came from." Other protective measures include saying a prayer, requesting that the only energy which will touch you will be for your highest good, smudging an area first with sage or some other cleansing herb.

THE ROLE OF INTUITION IN SPIRIT COMMUNICATION

Intuition is what psychics and mediums use to bridge the gap between the physical world and the world of spirit. There's nothing mysterious about it. It's simply the ability to access information in nontraditional ways. All of us have intuition and, as with any talent, the more we use it, the stronger it gets.

"When I tune in on someone," says intuitive Millie Gemondo, "I usually focus on something, maybe their birth date, maybe something else. Once I tune in on that, I get visions of things and it rolls out, right off my tongue. It's as if I see a TV screen and on that screen information about the person flashes off and on, in and out. Even if what I receive doesn't make sense to me, it may make sense to the other person. I have to trust what I receive and not interpret it."

Intuitive information comes to us in a variety of ways—through hunches or gut feelings, through dreams, through coincidences or synchronicities, through creative endeavors, even through what our bodies sense. Gail, a hairstylist, described how her body sensed her father's presence after he had died. He had been diagnosed with Alzheimer's and was eventually put into a nursing home. During this time, she and her husband moved and her father expressed regret that he'd never gotten to see her new house. The morning after his death, she was standing in the kitchen, fixing a pot of coffee, when she suddenly caught movement out of the corner of her eye and felt something brush against her shoulder. She thought it was a bug and quickly looked down to brush it off, and then it hit her. Her father was finally visiting her new house!

"When you walk by a spirit," writes intuitive Char Margolis, "a lot of times there's a coldness or a warm or chill breeze will blow through the room for no apparent reason . . ."

John Edward, writing in his book *One Last Time,* compares psychic energy to radio waves. "Even without the radio on, the air is filled with invisible signals from countless radio stations operating on various frequencies. All you have to do to receive them is to flick the radio on and tune the dial. When I do a reading, I flick on my own switch and wait for the program to come on." In other words, Edward tunes in intuitively.

YOUR GUIDES

Mediums and psychics contend that we all have guides and guardian angels, souls on the other side that look after us out of love and compassion. They may be people we have loved who have died, they may be people we have known in other lives. Whatever they are, they are as close as our need, our curiosity, our questions.

They speak to us through whatever means they can find. Mediums. Dreams. A song on the radio. A line in a movie. A phrase in a book. Old photos. Even straight pins, as in the following example.

Linda and Megan have known each other for more than thirty years. They were college roommates and still talk about the year that Linda's grandmother moved in with them.

Linda's grandmother had a grand old house on the Hudson River. She loved to sew, and in her house there were always straight pins found in odd places. Shortly after she died, Linda's mother—who doesn't sew—began to find straight pins around her house. Now and then she even found straight pins marking certain passages in books that just happened to be passages that her deceased mother-in-law had loved. She would mention these incidents to Linda in a casual way—*Oh, Nana has been here again* . . .

Neither Linda nor Megan sewed. Between them, they didn't even own a straight pin. Yet, within months of the grandmother's death, they started finding straight pins around their apartment. They realized that Linda's grandmother had moved in with them and used to joke about it. *Hey, she's spying on us.*

Her presence wasn't intrusive. If anything, it was protective, comforting, a point of stability in their chaotic college lives. Linda's grandmother stuck around for about a year, until both women had moved.

Years later, Megan went to St. Augustine with Linda and her parents. They were standing in the St. Augustine fort, in line with other tourists, inside this historic place that had no furniture, just cold stone walls and the ghosts of the past. Suddenly, Linda's mother looked down and smiled.

"Hey, look what I found," she said, and stooped over to pick up a straight pin. "Nana's here with us."

There are several ways to become acquainted with your own guides and angels.

- Request a dream in which they appear or communicate with you.
- Quiet time. Set aside some time during the day when you won't be disturbed. Relax, quiet your thoughts, shut your eyes. Request that your guides appear. You may get a specific image, you may just get lights or shapes. The image isn't as important as what you feel. Talk to your guide, even if it appears as an animal. Listen to what it says. Does the advice seem sound? During this exercise, you may want to have an object nearby that holds personal meaning for you. It can be anything—a piece of jewelry, a statue, a talisman of some sort, a gem, a crystal. You can light incense or aromatic oils. Do whatever creates an atmosphere of calm and relaxation.
- Meditation. It isn't for everyone. Some people are simply too restless to meditate. But if you find that you enjoy it, then by all means meditate. It's one of the best ways to contact your guides.
- Physical exercise. Quite often, physical exercise can stimulate spirit communication, perhaps because the

left brain is busy making sure your body is doing what it's supposed to do. Hiking, walking, swimming are all excellent conduits.

- Once you feel certain you actually have contacted your guide or guides, ask them for help in deepening your intuition and keeping you centered.
- Trust that the answers you seek are within your capacity to find.

BELIEFS

Seth had a lot to say about the role of beliefs in creating reality here—and there. "A belief in demons is highly disadvantageous after death, as it is during physical existence. A systematized theology of opposites is also detrimental. If you believe, for example, that all good must be balanced by evil, then you bind yourself into a system of reality that is highly limiting, and that contains within it the seeds of great torment."

A core belief is one that we usually adopt from parents, teachers, or other authority figures when we're very young. It becomes a belief that we hold about the nature of reality, about how things work in the world, and it inadvertently influences everything we do and think. Examples of core beliefs are:

- It's a dog-eat-dog world.
- Money doesn't grow on trees.
- I'm not good enough (or smart enough or good-looking enough).
- There isn't enough.
- If it *can* go wrong, it *will* go wrong.
- Rich people aren't nice.

- Everyone else comes first.
- Being selfish is bad.
- Money is evil.
- I'm fat.
- I'm skinny.
- I'm not worthy.
- People are out to get me.
- I'm unlovable.
- The world is filled with demons and evil people.
- Sex is bad.

Do you recognize any of these statements as beliefs that you hold?

Over time, our core beliefs become so ingrained in who we are that we don't realize they even exist. If, for instance, you saw or heard things when you were a child and your family made fun of you, then you learned that to see or hear things that other people don't is harmful or bad—and that may have become one of your core beliefs. But any belief about the nature of reality is just that—a belief—and beliefs can be changed. Once the belief is changed, your reality changes.

Medium George Anderson tells a harrowing story about how his family reacted to his experiences when he was a child. Anderson saw and heard spirits from the time he was quite small and, of course, told his parents about his experiences. They replied that he should stop talking about all that nonsense. He stopped telling them about it, but the experiences didn't stop. When Anderson relayed to a neighborhood friend the message he'd received from the kid's grandmother, the boy's parents were angry and terrified. Anderson realized that for his own safety it was best not to say anything to anyone about his experiences.

During a high school discussion about the French Revolution, Anderson had a vision that the Dauphin, Louis XVII of France, had been smuggled safely to England. "The fallout from that one statement and spontaneous admission of my ability was disastrous," Anderson writes in *Lessons from the Light.* Other students made fun of him, and the school guidance counselor called in his parents and suggested psychiatric help.

Anderson's parents took him to Catholic Charities, an intervention center for families in crisis. He was tested, put on various types of medication, but no conclusions were reached. "I was diagnosed with paranoid schizophrenia and it was suggested that I be admitted to the Central Islip State Hospital 'for a rest,' because the visions I saw and my inability to fit in indicated to them proof of 'episodic psychotic behavior.' " The upshot of all this was that Anderson came very close to being admitted to a state hospital for nothing more than the fact that he saw and heard things that other people didn't.

As a result of this experience, Anderson learned to trust his visions and voices. His *beliefs* about himself changed. Later in life, he was able to empathize with people who came to him in such desperate need of help and confirmation that their loved ones still lived on.

"The experiment that would transform your world," said Seth, "would operate upon the basic idea that you create your own reality according to the nature of your beliefs, and that all existence was blessed, and that evil did not exist in it. If these ideas were followed individually and collectively, then the evidence of your physical senses would find no contradiction. They would perceive the world and existence as good."

It sounds like a positive way to begin not only this particular journey, but the journey that is life.

3. Who Are You?

In general terms, channeling is any expression of the vibration you are. If you are a dancer, you are channeling the vibration of expression of the dance you portray. If you are an artist, the medium becomes the conduit for the channeling of artistic effect.

—EDMOND H. WOLLMAN

When we think of ourselves, we usually do so in terms of physical, emotional, intellectual, and spiritual attributes. We think of the whole package, the complex bundle of our fundamental selves. We think in terms of our *identities*. In astrological terms, this identity is encompassed in our Sun sign.

Every Sun sign, like every birth chart, is a kind of blueprint of traits and talents, a schematic of *potential*. Or, to borrow a word from Carl Jung, it's an *archetype*. Like any archetype, a Sun sign depicts the broad strokes of personality characteristics and potential. We are such complex creatures, however, and endowed with free will to boot, that some traits in each of us remain dormant and not all potential is fulfilled.

Keep in mind, too, that none of us is only our Sun sign. In eastern astrology, in fact, the importance of the Moon is given equal billing. In addition to the Sun and the Moon, there are eight planets, the Ascendant (Rising sign), the Moon's nodes, angles, and other points in a chart that all have some say in who we are astrologically. Our free will interacts with all of these components so that a birth chart becomes a living, breathing entity rather than a still-life portrait.

In terms of spirit communication, your Sun sign describes the communication method that may work best for you. It represents your quest. Are you interested in this for self-knowledge? To satisfy some deep curiosity? Do you hope to ultimately make contact with a loved one who has died? What's your ultimate goal? Do you *have* an ultimate goal?

If the beginning point is the quest, then the end point is the grail. In legend, the grail is supposedly the cup from which Christ drank at the Last Supper. Some variations of the legend say that Joseph of Arimathea brought the grail to the crucifixion of Christ and caught his blood in the cup. Joseph later carried the cup into some other country, and his descendants subsequently took it to Glastonbury Abbey in England or to a castle in Spain. Parsifal, the last of the grail kings, then supposedly took the cup with him to India, where it vanished forever.

Carl Jung, like mythologist Joseph Campbell, interpreted the grail legend as the embodiment of man's search for personal meaning in life. For our purposes, the grail is what you find through your journey into spirit communication. The quest and the grail are inexorably linked.

At the end of this chapter, the quest and the grail of spirit communication are illustrated through the life of psychic Edgar Cayce. Before that, though, let's go through a few basics.

Most of us know our Sun signs. But just in case there's any doubt, find your birth date and Sun sign in Table 1.

Table 1: Sun Signs		
Dates	*Signs*	*Symbols*
March 21–April 19	Aries	♈
April 20–May 20	Taurus	♉
May 21–June 21	Gemini	♊
June 22–July 22	Cancer	♋
July 23–August 22	Leo	♌
August 23–September 22	Virgo	♍
September 23–October 22	Libra	♎
October 23–November 21	Scorpio	♏
November 22–December 21	Sagittarius	♐
December 22–January 19	Capricorn	♑
January 20–February 18	Aquarius	♒
February 19–March 20	Pisces	♓

THE ELEMENTS

All signs are grouped according to elements.

The elements, of course, are fire, air, earth, water—a tidy division that puts three signs with each element. An element describes a sign's basic approach to life. It's like a certain spectrum of color. When we think of blues, for instance, we think of air. The red spectrum is fire, the browns are earth, and the greens are water.

Fire Signs—Action: Aries, Leo, Sagittarius. They are impulsive, enthusiastic, adventurous, action-oriented, fearless, passionate. They are the doers of the zodiac, the folks who are out there fighting for causes, seeking change, trying to correct injustices, discovering new worlds. They're great at starting projects, but unless their passion is sustained, they may not finish what they start.

In terms of spirit communication, the fire signs are the least likely candidates for meditation. They tend to be spiritual pioneers. Psychic mediums Millie Gemondo and Renie Wiley are fire signs.

Earth Signs—Practical: Taurus, Virgo, Capricorn. They are just what they sound like: grounded, stable, focused, prudent, and security-minded. They don't sweep through life, like fire signs. They are more dilatory in their approach, careful and often fastidious. They finish what fire signs begin, or they cultivate the ideas that fire signs have seeded. They can be stubborn, always strive for practicality, and long after the fire signs have burned out, they're still in the running.

When earth sign individuals delve into spirit communication, they tend to be committed. Authors and mediums Jane Roberts and James Van Praagh are earth signs.

Air Signs—Mental: Gemini, Libra, Aquarius. They are intellectual, studious, social, the communicators of the zodiac. They love ideas and enjoy talking about ideas with other people. They are studious, diligent in their quest for information. They are networkers. In terms of spirit communication, they are the most likely to be part of a group studying the topic. They may excel at automatic writing, communication through dreams and altered states of consciousness, clairaudience, and clairvoyance.

Author Whitley Streiber is an air sign. Due to the unusual nature of his writings and interests (UFOs, aliens), one might argue that he isn't really communicating with spirits. But the truth is that we *don't know*. What does seem certain, however, is that Streiber has had numerous experiences in altered states of consciousness that certainly don't fit into consensus reality. Like Robert Monroe, Streiber is an explorer, but he approaches these explorations in a true air sign fashion—through *communication.*

Water Signs—Emotions: Cancer, Scorpio, Pisces. They are intuitive, sensitive, emotional. They are able to connect at deep levels with the personal and collective unconscious. When they are able to express and systematize what they learn at these levels, they can be extraordinary teachers. Their imaginations and intuitions are finely tuned. They live within inner worlds that the rest of us might consider strange.

In terms of spirit communication, their main challenge is balance. Because these individuals are so naturally intuitive, it's easy for them to become so immersed in spirit communication that their daily lives get lost. Edgar Cayce was a water sign.

THE QUALITIES OR MODALITIES

Are you set in your ways? Do you hold rigid opinions?

Are you adaptable? Are you sometimes too willing to change your point of view to fit someone else's?

Are you quick to act? Are you sometimes too rash and impulsive?

These questions all address the quality or modality of the signs, the ways in which they use energy. There are three modalities—cardinal, mutable, fixed—with four signs assigned to each of them.

Cardinal Signs: Aries, Cancer, Libra, Capricorn: Think of them as initiators, the people who get things moving. They tend to move in a singular direction, with a singular goal. Although they take detours on their particular paths, they rarely lose sight of where they would like to be. Yes, each one acts within the boundaries of its element. But each also tailors life and experience through the specific lens called trailblazer.

Among the mediums whose charts are found in the Star Charts section of the Appendices, the only cardinal Sun sign is psychic intuitive Noreen Renier. Jane Roberts and James Van Praagh, for instance, both have Capricorn Rising. The Rising sign (Ascendant)—how other people see them, the self they present to the rest of the world—gives them incredible focus, drive, and ambition. Renie Wiley has a Capricorn Moon, which gives her the emotional and intuitive stamina this type of work seems to demand at times, and also has Aries Rising, which indicates she has experimented with numerous methods in her psychic mediumship.

Fixed Signs: Taurus, Leo, Scorpio, Aquarius: They know what they believe, they defend those beliefs, and they don't change those beliefs unless they are thoroughly convinced the new belief is truer or better than the old one. Stubborn? Absolutely! Fixed signs generally don't adapt well to change. What they lack in flexibility, however, is compensated for in their steady movement toward a goal.

Among the mediums in the Star Charts, Jane Roberts was a double fixed sign—Sun and Moon in Taurus— Millie Gemondo has a fixed Ascendant in Taurus, and Edgar Cayce had a fixed Moon in Taurus.

Mutable Signs: Gemini, Virgo, Sagittarius, Pisces. They are adaptable, love change, and thrive in new situations. Instead of resisting a problem, like a fixed sign, mutable sign individuals find a way around the problem or they simply adapt to it. They are easily bored and need constant change to flourish.

Cayce (Pisces Sun), Millie Gemondo and Renie Wiley (Sagittarius Sun), and James Van Praagh (Virgo Sun) are all mutable signs.

Even though this is primarily a Sun sign book, other planets are mentioned from time to time. Below and on the next page, Table 2 summarizes the attributes of the other planets and points in a horoscope.

Table 2: Planetary Traits		
Planet	*Symbol*	*Traits*
Sun	☉	Vitality, general health, who you are, ego
Moon	☽	Emotions, intuition, how you nurture, mom or her equivalent
Mercury	☿	Mind, intellect, logic, reason, self-expression
Venus	♀	Love, friendship, creative & artistic talents
Mars	♂	Energy, self-assertion, self-confidence, aggression
Jupiter	♃	Luck, capacity for optimism & generosity, expansion, serendipitous experiences, growth
Saturn	♄	The system, rules & regulations, discipline, accomplishment
Uranus	♅	The rebel, unexpected change, sudden insights, genius
Neptune	♆	The dreamer, psychic ability, imagination, spiritual inclinations, dissolves boundaries

Table 2: Planetary Traits (cont.)

Planet	Symbol	Traits
Pluto	♀,♇	Death, regeneration, rebirth, obsessions, transformation at the deepest levels, power
North Node	☊	A karmic point, not a planet. Personal growth, direction for spiritual evolution
South Node	☋	Directly opposite North Node. Habits, karmic patterns established in previous lives, what you must release to grow and evolve

Four points on a chart

Rising Sign	Asc	The face you present to others, your physical appearance, who you appear to be
Descendant	Des	Directly opposite Ascendant (Rising sign). Describes approach toward marriage & relationships
Midheaven	MC	Highest point on a chart. Your approach to your career & profession, your public self
Imum Coeli	IC	Lowest point on a chart, directly opposite MC. Your attitude toward home, family, the parent who nurtured you

THE POLARITIES

Up and down. Black and white. Happy and sad. We live in a world of opposites. Applied to astrology, every Sun sign has an opposite sign, and together the two create an axis of energy known as a polarity.

Polarities always have different but compatible elements and the same quality or modality. The characteristics that one sign lacks, the other sign has, so the energy is available because a sign and its polarity are inexorably linked.

In terms of spirit communication, your Sun sign describes your approach, and its opposite sign describes the best route to accomplishing your goals. Edgar Cayce, a Pisces, approached spirit communication by going into a trance so deep that he appeared to be asleep. It allowed him the deepest access to his guides. But he called on the service-oriented nature of his polarity, Virgo, to use the information to help other people.

Or take an individual with an Aries Sun, a cardinal fire sign. Aries is typically a loner, a doer, active, competitive. Libra, the polar opposite, is a cardinal air sign, much more social and people-oriented than Aries. To develop communication with his spirit guides, Aries would benefit from some type of work with another person or a group of people who share the same goal and interest.

In each of the Sun sign sections, the polarity for each sign is explored. Table 3 on the next page lists the polarities.

Table 3: Polarities	
Aries	Libra
Taurus	Scorpio
Gemini	Sagittarius
Cancer	Capricorn
Leo	Aquarius
Virgo	Pisces

CAYCE'S QUEST & HIS GRAIL

To illustrate how these various astrological elements function, let's look at the life of Edgar Cayce.

Edgar Cayce was born with Sun in Pisces. At its basest expression, a Pisces Sun can indicate a propensity for addiction, escapism, and an ambivalence that can drive everyone around them crazy. But at its highest expression, it exemplifies everything that Cayce was—a humble man with an extraordinary gift that touched thousands while he was alive and millions since he died in 1945.

Cayce was a religious man—not just spiritual, but religious. This is also in keeping with the potential of Pisces. In the various biographies that have been written about Cayce, his religious beliefs were depicted as the bedrock of who he was. These beliefs collided several times with the expanded worldview that his readings eventually gave him and perhaps, at the heart of it, may explain why Cayce was able to read for people only while in a trance so deep it was like sleep. In fact, Jess Stearn's biography of Cayce is entitled *The Sleeping Prophet*.

One such collision in belief systems happened when the concept of reincarnation entered Cayce's readings.

He initially balked at the very idea and was afraid it deviated too widely from the Bible. But he eventually was able to reconcile the idea with his religious beliefs and to incorporate past-life readings successfully into his work. This ability to adapt is typical of mutable signs.

Cayce's diagnostic abilities actually surfaced when he was about twenty-three years old and lost his voice. He was newly engaged to Gertrude, who would become his future wife. The loss of his voice delayed the marriage and his work, especially when the voice condition persisted month after month, despite expert help.

Finally, a hypnosis enthusiast named Al Layne put Cayce under hypnosis and asked him to explain the problem. Cayce, in a voice that was normal and resonant, explained there was partial paralysis of the muscles around the vocal cords and directed Layne to give Cayce a hypnotic suggestion that would increase the blood circulation around the vocal cords for twenty minutes. Cayce's voice returned.

Layne was so impressed that he offered himself as Cayce's next subject. While he was asleep, Cayce gave Layne a full medical diagnosis, and in a few months his health improved dramatically. Cayce was astonished and terrified at what he had done and didn't want to continue. But when his voice began to go again, he turned to Layne once more.

Pretty soon, Layne was having Cayce diagnose other people. Although Cayce was astonished at what was happening, he didn't attach anything spiritual to it. He just wanted to forget about it and didn't even like to discuss it with his family. But word got around town, and the reaction was mixed. Some people were skeptical, others marveled at the young man's ability, and still others made fun of him.

The first case that convinced Cayce this was to be his life's work was that of a six-year-old girl who lived in Hopkinsville, the daughter of the former superintendent of schools. For two years, she had had as many as twenty convulsions a day and was basically a vegetable. She'd seen numerous experts, who told her parents that the only thing they could do was keep her comfortable until she died.

Cayce, in trance, diagnosed her ailment as due to congestion at the base of the brain. He prescribed a treatment, followed up as needed, and within three months, she was in perfect health.

In *A Seer Out of Season: The Life of Edgar Cayce,* author Harmon Hartzell Bro, who knew Cayce, had this to say about the seer's ability: "He could not use it to exploit others, nor to help others gain advantage over their fellows. It deserted him if he tried. Instead, he had to use it for those with real needs, who would invest themselves and grow personally as they explored and applied his counsel."

Cayce didn't consider himself a *medium* and didn't think of himself as someone who communed with the dead. Perhaps, because of his religious beliefs, the idea of such a label made him uncomfortable. But in light of metaphysical and scientific research in the nearly sixty years since Cayce's death, it's obvious that he was able to connect with a higher power of some sort. The name we give that higher power—spirits, the dead, God, saints, whatever—becomes a moot detail in light of the information he was able to impart.

And maybe that's really the point about guides and guardian angels and spirit communication. Perhaps the label we assign the source is less important than the information we obtain.

Cayce's psychic gifts were so considerable that he constantly struggled against the intrusion of other people's thoughts and feelings upon his own. "Sometimes after church," wrote Bro, "he would describe the discarnates whom he had seen sitting in empty rows of his Sunday school class, listening. Others came to his home . . ." On numerous occasions, while the rest of the family was upstairs in bed, Cayce answered the door and for a long time he could be heard talking to whoever was there, but without any responses from the other person. The visitor was usually someone who recently had died, Cayce said, and who needed direction and guidance in the afterlife state.

Bro witnessed one of these encounters himself. "One Sunday afternoon while sitting alone with him, I watched the door of the library open and close, though nobody came in. Cayce laughed at me for not perceiving the dead person who had entered and my worries about my wits were only a little relieved when his wife called down to ask who had entered, since she had heard footsteps on the walk."

If his quest can be summarized simply, it might be that despite financial problems and profound skepticism from the society and time in which he lived, Cayce embraced his abilities, thus allowing them to develop fully, and used them to help whoever came to him. What he found, his grail, was that he was of service to thousands of people who needed answers and help.

4. The Birth Chart

The place . . . or medium of realization is neither mind nor
matter, but that intermediate realm of subtle reality
which can only be adequately described by the symbol.

—CARL JUNG

UNDERSTANDING A BIRTH CHART

A birth chart is a symbolic map of the potential with
which you're born. So let's take a deeper look at
a chart.

As the Sun and planets travel across the sky, they follow a path (called the ecliptic) that surrounds the earth.
This path is divided into twelve signs, and every day the
earth spins past these signs as it rotates on its axis. The
sign that is rising when you're born is called your Rising
sign (or Ascendant). Your time of birth determines the
degree and sign of your Ascendant, which is why the
exact time of birth is so important.

Since we went into Cayce's life in the previous chapter,
let's take a look at his birth chart. It's in the Star Charts
of the Appendices. In the center of Cayce's birth chart
lies his birth data. The horizontal line to the left of center
is his Rising sign—Leo at 24 degrees and 29 minutes
(24♌29). This puts his Descendant—exactly opposite the
Ascendant, or rising sign—at 24 degrees and 29 minutes
Aquarius (24♒29). His MC (Midheaven) at the top of

the chart is 18 degrees and 59 minutes Taurus (18 ♉ 59). And his IC (Imum Coeli, or Nadir), at the bottom of the chart, is 18 degrees and 59 minutes of Scorpio (18 ♏ 59). What all this means is that a birth chart isn't just a circle drawn on a piece of paper and sliced into twelve unequal parts. It represents the position of the stars in the sky at the moment you drew your first breath.

In a birth chart, the Rising, Descendant, MC, and IC are the four most important angles. Any planets at or within four or five degrees of these angles are especially significant. In Cayce's chart, those planets would be Uranus (♅) in the 12th house, but within three degrees of his Rising; Pluto (♀) in the 10th house; and the Moon (☽) in the 9th house.

Those twelve unequal slices of the circle are called houses. Think of them as symbolic of a process of unfoldment from birth to death. They represent our experiences of people, situations, and events. They constitute a map.

The line that divides one house from another is called a cusp. The cusp of Cayce's 2nd house is Virgo at 22 degrees and 40 minutes (22 ♍ 40), the cusp of the 3rd house is Libra at 21 degrees and 1 minute (21 ♎ 01), and so on around the zodiac, one sign following the other.

When reading a birth chart, you have to imagine that you're "on top of the planet" and looking down, at least if you're in the northern hemisphere. That's why east (the eastern horizon) is on the left, west is on the right, south is at the top, and north is at the bottom. Just remember that planets rise on the left side (east) of the chart and set on the right side (west). At noon, the Sun is at the MC (Midheaven); at midnight it's at the IC (Nadir).

The first six houses, which lie under the horizon, are

related to our subjective experience, the intangible reality of our inner lives, our deepest secrets, our most private emotions. If a person has the majority of his planets under the horizon, it doesn't necessarily mean he's an introvert. It indicates, though, that everything he experiences is filtered through a subjective lens, a feeling state.

With the majority of planets above the horizon, as in Cayce's chart—eight out of ten in houses seven through twelve—life is more public, less subjective. A person's evolving identity is marked by events rather than by subjective states.

The vertical line that divides the middle of the chart, known as the MC/IC axis, divides the circle into east and west. Think of the eastern houses—1, 2, 3, 10, 11, 12—as symbolic of freedom, the power of our free will. With a preponderance of planets on this side of the chart, self-determination is what makes things happen.

Houses 4, 5, 6, 7, 8, 9—the western houses—have a sense of destiny about them. Here we encounter boundaries, limits, certain commitments we have agreed to before we were born. Cayce has eight planets on the western side of his chart. His biographies certainly portray a man seized by a sense of destiny. True to this hemisphere, Cayce had to sort out the threads of events and encounters in his early life to grasp the context of his destiny.

So what do these houses mean, anyway?

THE HOUSES

1st House. The woman enters the room and conversations stop. Eyes turn in her direction. Is she a beautiful woman? Is she someone famous? Is she well-dressed? No one can say for sure. It doesn't matter. The woman herself projects the image that she is beautiful and famous and well-dressed. *She projects a presence, a charisma.* And that's really what the Ascendant and 1st house are all about. Image. How we project who we are and how other people see us.

The Ascendant and 1st house also describe, to some extent, our physical appearance, our general health, our early childhood conditioning. Planets in the 1st house describe people, experiences, and events that play prominent roles in shaping our early selves.

In the 1st house, Cayce had only the South Node in Virgo (☋10♍36)—a clear indication that in his life as Cayce he was supposed to release the focus on himself and reach for the 7th house North Node, signifying partnership with others.

2nd House. The woman who entered the room is an art collector. She is rich. She owns an original Picasso, an original Van Gogh, sculptures and paintings by contemporary artists who are on their way up. In a room filled with artists, she is Someone. Even in a room filled with business investors, she is Someone. Her collections and her money define her values and her self-worth. That's the nature of the 2nd house.

Planets in the 2nd house describe people, experiences, and events that play a part in what we value. These planets also describe how we earn and spend money and our attitudes toward our material possessions.

3rd House. Years ago, Marshall McLuhan wrote, "The medium is the message." He was referring to the medium we use to communicate, which really fits the 3rd house. Writing, speaking, dancing, art: all of these are ways to communicate. But the 3rd house also describes the people with whom we communicate, the atmosphere in which that communication takes place, and what we do on a daily basis.

The 3rd house also represents our neighborhood buddies, our brothers and sisters, our relatives in general. It's the place we hang out on holidays, the people whom we call to say happy birthday. It's our day-to-day *stuff*.

Planets in the 3rd house describe the events, experiences, and people that figure into our communication process.

4th House. In the movie *The Haunted,* based on a novel by British author James Herbert, a skeptic investigates a house that is reputedly haunted. He falls in love with a young woman who lives in the house with her two brothers and a nanny. He has many strange experiences in this house, disturbing dreams, a sense that his life is shifting. He even sees the sister whom he lost as a child in a drowning accident. The longer he stays in this house, the less distinct the boundary becomes between what is real and what is imagined.

Welcome to the 4th house, where the unconscious is alive and well. In the 4th house, it's always midnight, dark, spooky, unsettling. The trick is to make this spooky stuff visible, understandable. The skeptic in *The Haunting* actually does this by the end of the movie, when he discovers that all of the inhabitants of the house—except for the nanny—are ghosts and have been dead for a very long time.

The 4th house also symbolizes our home, our family and nurturing parents, our ancestral roots, the deepest psychic connections between our personal worlds—and the collective, whatever it might be. Planets here describe the elements of this strange and most subjective of worlds.

Notice that Cayce has no planets in houses 1 through 4.

5th House. What are your greatest pleasures in life? Kids? Art? Gambling? Playing the stock market? Travel? Books? Love affairs? The 5th house describes the pleasures that sustain us throughout our lives. And these pleasures are as individual and unique as a fingerprint.

The 5th house describes our children, especially the first-born, our creative thrust, and our capacity for playfulness. Notice that Cayce has two planets in the house—Jupiter in Capricorn ($\u2643$ 02 $\u260d$ 03) and Mars in Capricorn ($\u2642$ 11 $\u2643$ 14).

Jupiter indicates that he met the right people at the right time, through serendipitous experiences. The placement is naturally lucky and suggests that Cayce's life expanded tremendously through his children. Both of his sons, in fact, perpetuated Cayce's work after his death. Mars in the 5th house usually indicates an enjoyment of competitive sports and athletics, which didn't fit Cayce. But Mars in Capricorn shows, among other things, ambition that can take you into public life and sufficient energy to get you there, certainly true of Cayce.

6th House. Your phone rings in the middle of the night. It's your neighbor. The plumbing in her basement has sprung a massive leak and the basement if flooding. You drive over to her house with your tools and your skills and fix the leak, then help her clean up the mess. This captures the essence of the sixth house—services performed through some skill you possess, without any thought of compensation.

The 6th house represents our particular skills, our daily work and work environment, and our day-to-day health.

7th House. You're in college. You're assigned to read *Gone With the Wind* by next week. It really annoys you, all those pages to read when you've got five million other things to do. You resist, you dig in your heels. But one night it happens. You decide you'll read the first page. If it doesn't seize you, you'll buy a synopsis or rent the movie. You read the first page. And the second. And before the night is over, you're deep inside the Civil War. You *become* Scarlett, you walk in her shoes. And by dawn, it's over and you're in tears.

First and foremost, the 7th house is about seeing the world through another person's eyes. It's the house of marriage, partnerships, commitment, intimacy.

Cayce's 7th house is full: the North Node, Mercury, Saturn, and Venus are all there in Pisces. To evolve spiritually, he must work in partnership with others, delving deeply into his own soul and psychic abilities (North Node in Pisces). Communication with his wife was of prime importance, and their union was based on deep psychic bonds. His thought processes were colored by intuitive impressions, and he gleaned information through psychic means (Mercury in Pisces). Saturn in Pisces demands practical use of psychic abilities; Cayce certainly excelled in that area. Venus in Pisces in the 7th house indicated great sensitivity to others and a compassionate and romantic nature.

8th House. You wake suddenly from a sound sleep and see your mother standing at the foot of your bed. Then she vanishes. You immediately call home, two thousand miles away, and discover that your mother died at the exact moment you saw her standing at the foot of your bed.

The 8th house is known as the house of death. But it's

actually about more than that. The 8th house smacks of destiny, fate, any powerful and inexplicable experience or event that involves death, rebirth, sexuality, or instincts. It's also the house of joint resources—your spouse's finances, taxes, insurance.

Notice that Cayce's Sun in Pisces is in his 8th house. The Sun here, especially in mystical Pisces, increases interest and involvement in metaphysics, particularly in life after death. Quite often, the Sun here also portends fame after death. Cayce was famous during his lifetime, but his legacy since his death in 1945 has grown considerably.

9th House. You're born on a reservation, under the hot glare of the Arizona sun. Dust blows everywhere. You taste it in your food, feel it in your clothing. But your family life is rich with mysteries and rituals that connect you to your ancestral spirits. Your worldview is defined by your life on the reservation.

Then, when you're eighteen, you're awarded a scholarship to a university on the east coast. You see the ocean for the first time. There's no dust in your food, only the lingering sweetness of the salt air. Your connection to your ancestral spirits still sings in your blood, but the song is more distant now, a whisper. You discover philosophy, the spiritual history of other cultures, and your worldview expands accordingly. You are still a Native American, but your model of reality has expanded.

The 9th house describes your worldview and the texture of your higher perceptions. It encompasses higher education, philosophy, spiritual beliefs, foreign cultures, and travels. Cayce's chart has both the Moon and Neptune in the 9th house, in Taurus. The 9th house is one of the most psychic placements for Neptune and one of the most spiritual placements for the Moon. Cayce

wasn't much of a foreign traveler, but his inner travels
certainly took him places where others hadn't gone before.

A 9th house Moon close to the Midheaven is one indi-
cator of possible fame.

10th House. *What are you going to be when you grow
up?* What this question is really asking is how are other
people going to perceive you when you're an adult? Just
as the 4th house describes your most private self, the
10th house, its opposite, identifies your most public self,
your role in the social scheme of the time and society in
which you live.

The closer a planet is to the Midheaven, the more
significant it is. Look at Cayce's chart. Pluto is conjunct
to the MC (Midheaven) within three degrees. This is
about transformation at the deepest levels through his
public role.

11th House. Where are we going and what are we
going to do when we get there? Even more to the point,
how are we going to get from *here* to *there?* Goals and
ambitions, dreams, life strategies: that's what the 11th
house is about. Traditionally, it's called the house of
friends. But these friends are different from our close
friendships in the 7th house. The 11th house friends are
people with whom we share a common interest. If you're
a writer, then you seek out other writers. If you're into
bridge, then perhaps you belong to a bridge club.

Cayce has no planets in the 11th house.

12th House. The year gets off to a tough start. In January, the man's marriage falls apart. In March, he loses
his house. In June, one of his parents passes away. By

August, he is unemployed. This is the stuff of the 12th house, which is why it once was called the house of sorrows. So how does the man react to these experiences? Does he become a drunk? An addict? A thief? Or does he seek to understand this repetitive pattern of loss and try to break it?

The 12th house is about the personal unconscious and how we deal with issues over which we have little or no control. We can take the escapist route, or we can use the adversity in a positive way. As always, the choice is up to us.

Cayce had one planet in the 12th house—Uranus in Leo. It suggests a sudden change in how others see him, a particular brilliance that comes about through unexpected illness or confinement, and a rebellion against existing standards. It looks as if that part fits Cayce's life like a glove.

WHERE YOUR SUN FALLS

If you know your approximate birth time, it's possible to estimate the house in which your Sun sign falls. Remember, though, this is only an estimate.

At the end of this book, after the Star Charts, make a copy of the blank horoscope chart. Then use Table 4 on the next page to find the house in which your Sun falls. In using the chart, the Ascendant (Rising sign) represents when the Sun rises, the Descendant when the Sun sets. The MC is approximately noon, the IC is approximately midnight. You start numbering at the Ascendant and move clockwise into houses 12, 11, 10, and so on around the chart.

Once you locate the house in which your Sun sign falls, read the descriptions of the Sun through the houses. These descriptions are based on polarities.

Table 4: Where Your Sun Lies	
If you were born between	*then your Sun falls in house #*
5–7 a.m.	1
7–9 a.m.	12
9–11 a.m.	11
11 a.m.–1 p.m.	10
1–3 p.m.	9
3–5 p.m.	8
5–7 p.m.	7
7–9 p.m.	6
9–11 p.m.	5
11 p.m.–1 a.m.	4
1–3 a.m.	3
3–5 a.m.	2

SUN THROUGH THE HOUSES

Sun 1st House. Partnership in your psychic and spiritual adventures is vital. Discuss your experiences, be open about them, and don't be too concerned about what other people think. A partnership can be something as simple as consulting a psychic or medium about your experiences, or sharing them with your significant other, friends, or family.

Sun 2nd House. You benefit from workshops, books, and any other information or resources available to you concerning afterlife communication, near-death experiences, and reincarnation. Your journey is sure to lead you into much deeper areas about the nature of reality.

Sun 3rd House. Because you embarked on this particular quest, your philosophical and spiritual beliefs are completely overhauled and reinvented. Consider writing about your experiences for ordinary people who, like you, have questions that desperately need answers.

Sun 4th House. Your personal discoveries in this area may bring you into conflict with the authority figures in your life. But what you learn will enrich your life so deeply that it won't matter. You may even find a new career or profession as a result of these experiences.

Sun 5th House. These experiences will answer some wish or dream that you have. They will bring you into contact with people of like mind who are asking the same questions. There is a strong creative drive behind your quest. Honor it. Jane Roberts's Taurus Sun was in the 5th house.

Sun 6th House. By learning to trust your experiences in afterlife and spirit communication, you will reclaim a part of yourself you have disowned. As a result, you may end up working in some capacity with people who are near death and need your knowledge and wisdom.

Sun 7th House. You may have had experiences in early childhood with spirit communication, or grown up in a household where these types of experiences were accepted. If your open attitude toward such experiences persisted, then it won't be a problem in your intimate relationships. It's important that your significant other holds beliefs that are similar to yours.

Sun 8th House. It's important that you share what you learn through these experiences with other people. But even more to the point, these experiences must have an impact on what you personally value. They must make a difference to you on an emotional and spiritual level, otherwise it's all just so much hot air. Cayce's Pisces Sun was in the 8th house. So is James Van Praagh's Virgo Sun.

Sun 9th House. You don't have any problem with the philosophical and spiritual implications of afterlife communication. The challenge for you lies in expressing these experiences with siblings, friends, neighbors. The issue here is self-expression.

Sun 10th House. Your exploration of afterlife communication may bring you into conflict with the spiritual beliefs that have grounded you for most of your life. But if you learn nonresistance, the benefits you attain will be enormous personally and professionally.

Sun 11th House. The temptation is to sit around with your buddies and talk talk talk about all this fascinating stuff. The challenge is to somehow use what you learn creatively, to enrich your life, and to redefine what brings you the most pleasure.

Sun 12th House. The farther the Sun lies in the 12th house, the more challenging it will be for you to be forthright about what you learn. You prefer keeping it all bottled up in your private life, perhaps sharing your deep interest with just a few friends. The payoff comes when you use what you learn in your daily work life.

The only way you'll know the exact position of your Sun sign, of course, is to have a computerized chart drawn up. But in lieu of that, read the next section.

Your Rising Sign

If you're interested in figuring out your Rising sign, see Appendix 3. This will be only an approximation, however. If you have a computer or access to the Internet, you can get a free chart on a number of astrology Web sites. One of the best is at www.alabe.com. Make sure you have your exact time of birth. Another good site is www.astrology.com/, where you can get a free birth chart and other information as well.

PART TWO

❀

Spirit Guides &
Your Sun Signs

5. Aries the Ram ♈

Everything comes to us in its own time.

—JAMES VAN PRAAGH

March 21–April 19
Cardinal Fire
Ruled by Mars

THE SYMBOL

The ram stands poised and proud on the mountaintop. His head is held high, his stance is that of the independent loner, firm and unyielding. Everything about him makes it clear he won't surrender the mountain without a fight. Pity the fool who thinks it's just show. Down go the horns, tension rippling through that powerful body, and the ram charges.

Welcome to the world of Aries, warrior and pioneer, whose life reads like the *Star Trek* motto: Boldly going where no man (or woman) has gone before. He thrives on competition. It infuses his passion, seizes it, and rouses his most primal instincts. At the heart of his competitive spirit lies a strong, fierce will that rises to any challenge, obstacle, or desire. It is his most valuable resource for shaping his life. When his will seems insuffi-

63

cient for the task, he simply batters his way through whatever is keeping him from what he wants.

His insistence on doing things his way sometimes runs to extremes and extends to other people. Just because *he* wants to do something a particular way, he assumes that everyone else wants to do it that way, too. Or since *he* believes something to be true, he figures everyone around him also believes that thing to be true as well. Imagine how he feels when he discovers this may not be the case. *What?* he rails. *Of course it's true. Of course it's the only way to do it. How can you not see that?* Once he's finished ranting, he marches out, indignant and disgusted. Fortunately, these tirades rarely last long and are forgotten soon afterward—forgotten by Aries, but perhaps not forgotten by the recipients of the anger or argument.

Despite the bravado, the risk taking, the incredible, often consuming energy of Aries, what he's really about is individuation. *Who am I separate from everyone else?* This battle cry carries him from birth to death.

STRENGTH IN OPPOSITES: ARIES/LIBRA POLARITY

Okay, some straight talk. Aries is so combative at times it's as if he were born with a chip on his shoulder. His impatience is legendary and usually manifests itself when someone doesn't understand what he's saying or doesn't do something the way he wants it done.

Just let me do it, he snaps, then later wonders why the person keeps a respectful distance or acts cold toward him.

This combativeness and impatience lead to arguments, especially if Aries is challenged about what he says, thinks, or does, and at some point the arguments collapse into pettiness. When this pattern begins to drive away the people who love him, Aries reacts in one of two ways: he blames other people or he tackles the pattern in order to change it.

If he chooses the latter, then this is usually the point where his spiritual journey begins. It can take any number of forms, but will always be in keeping with the basic nature of Aries—action, inspiration, pioneering, doing doing doing. He must embark on this journey in a way that will sustain his interest and passion and without isolating himself unnecessarily, not an easy task for Aries unless he draws on the strength of Libra—his polarity.

Where Aries is combative, Libra seeks harmony. Where Aries slams through obstacles, Libra works through them or around them, using whatever tools are at his disposal to bring resolution in a peaceful way. Where Aries is a loner, Libra needs intimate relationships. Where Aries leads, Libra has no special need to lead anyone. Where Aries is often inconsiderate of others, Libra is constantly fretting about how not to offend anyone. Where Aries is independent, Libra is social.

So if, as a starting point, Aries can embark on his journey with one other person or with a group of like-minded seekers, something that Libra would do, the journey will unroll much more smoothly. But how, exactly, does that translate into everyday life?

Jenny, an Aries, says the beginning of her spiritual journey happened as the result of an impulse to attend a gathering of people at a friend's home. The group, the friend said, was "exploring new ideas." At the time, Jenny was widowed, her kids were grown, and she was looking for something but didn't even know what it was. She figured she had nothing to lose.

There were about twenty people at that first gathering.

They ranged in age from teens to a retired eighty-year-old Russian professor. Most of them were strangers to each other, and yet, at the beginning of the informal meeting, they joined hands and the Russian professor recited a short prayer, first in Russian, then in English. "Then we meditated for a few minutes and after that, we went around the circle and each of us reported what, if anything, we had received."

Because she was an Aries, meditation wasn't something that particularly appealed to her. But this meditation was short, relaxing, and she was flooded with images. Afterward, when people in the circle reported what they had gotten during meditation, Jenny was surprised that others in the group had experienced images similar to those she had seen.

Even though she considered herself an independent loner and had never done anything like this with a group before, she returned week after week. Her spiritual journey had begun by drawing on the energy of Libra, by *becoming more social, more open to working within a group.*

THE QUEST

In a nutshell, Aries, your quest is this: *To connect with the deeper part of yourself so that you transcend your present beliefs about who you are.*

Allow your innate courage and drive to be directed inward for a period of time. In fact, give yourself a time limit for this experiment, if that makes you feel better. A month, perhaps. Or two weeks. Select a time frame you feel you can live with and to which you can commit. Make it realistic. Be honest with yourself. If your life is already jammed to the hilt and you barely have time to breathe, don't commit to something that simply becomes one more mountain to climb, one more obstacle to get out of the way.

THE JOURNEY

No bags to pack for this trip! In fact, the only prerequisites are an open mind and a willingness to try something a bit different.

Find a group of like-minded individuals with whom you can undertake this exploration. If, for instance, you're a writer who seeks to connect with your spiritual guides so that you can deepen the quality of your writing—as well as your life—then join a writers' group. If you can't find a group in your area, then create one. Or create an online group. This should appeal to your Aries drive for action. Regardless of the kind of group you create, however, do it with the understanding that you are *not* in charge; everyone is equal.

If a group of some kind isn't possible, then find at least one other person willing to take the commitment with you. Be sure that you and the other person are compatible and that you understand your individual needs and are willing to help each other meet those needs. Make sure you also agree on a mutual need or goal. Remember, neither of you is in charge.

Agree on a time limit. Come up with a one-line statement that expresses your mutual goal. Maybe the group or mutual goal is to connect with your guides on a level where communication occurs. Or perhaps your goal is broader—to not only communicate with your guides, but to request help with some issue or project in your life.

If you don't mind spending some money, take a workshop that deals with spiritual communication. Or attend a conference that covers a gamut of metaphysical topics so that you can pick and choose the areas that appeal to you. The idea here is to engage in some type of group activity where you aren't in charge and have to interact with other people. Learn how to go with the flow. Take cues from your intuition. Follow your impulses.

MEETING YOUR GUIDES

The techniques in this section are general, intended for the average Aries. During your journey, you'll discover what works best and fine-tune the methods for yourself.

The Physical Body. As one of the most physically oriented signs, you actually relax when you're walking, hiking, biking, swimming, even rock climbing. Pam, an Aries producer, hikes three miles every weekend into the hills around her Malibu home. This is the time when she connects with her deeper self. It's what keeps her sane during the hectic week ahead.

If you have some type of physical activity that you do in solitude, then continue doing it alone. If your dog is your companion on these excursions, fine, keep bringing the dog. If you have a human companion, then continue the excursions with him or her. The point is to open yourself to inner dimensions during these physical excursions, to go deeper into yourself than you usually do, to relax into your body as much as possible. You might even give yourself a suggestion before you start out that some type of communication with your guides will occur.

Signs & Symbols. The language used by spirits and guides is often symbolic. Medium John Edward, writing in *One Last Time,* relates a fascinating story about symbolism. Shortly after his mother died, he went into his room and spoke quietly to her, asking that she send him some sort of sign that her soul had survived death. The symbol he requested was a white bird.

Days went by. He never saw a white bird. On the third and last day of his mother's wake, one of his cousins remarked on the many flowers that had been sent, but said that John's stood out the most. "It's not just the flowers," his cousin remarked. "It's those beautiful white birds."

Edward went over to the flowers to see what his cousin was talking about. "There were two white birds that I had completely overlooked for three days . . . ," he writes. "Suddenly, I realized the significance of my cousin's exact words. He said, 'White birds on *your* flowers.' "

The next day, Edward called the florist and asked about the white birds on that particular bouquet. They were, after all, for a wake. The florist was embarrassed and admitted he'd made a mistake. He'd been busy that day, he explained, and usually put the white birds only on bouquets intended for celebrations.

Signs, then, are often disguised or camouflaged. Don't overlook the obvious. If your deceased Uncle George was an expert on Monarch butterflies and one flits past you as you're thinking about him, realize you have experienced a communication. Pay attention to your dreams, which are often thick with signs and symbols that may be communication from guides or loved ones who have passed on.

If you're really ambitious, keep a record of these signs and symbols. Yes, it consumes time. Yes, it's just one more thing on an endless list of things to do. Yet, if you can do this over a period of time, the personal dictionary of signs and symbols that you compile will help you immeasurably in your communication with your own guides.

The Senses. During periods when you're consciously trying to develop psychically, the senses seem to become more finely attuned. Sights, sounds, touch, smells, and taste are heightened and may, with practice, lead you into the realm of inner senses.

John Edward lists these psychic senses as: clairaudience (clear hearing), clairvoyance (clear seeing), clairsentience (clear sensing), clairalience (clear smelling), and clairambience (clear tasting).

Hearing an inner voice that imparts wisdom or guidance is how *clairaudience* often manifests. This voice can be heard in dreams, during periods of deep relaxation, during meditation or any other altered state. With practice, it can be heard at virtually any time of the day or night. This sense is common among mediums.

Clairvoyance is the ability to see what is happening now or what will happen in the future in your life or the life of someone else. Many psychics use this sense. Although it's related to "seeing," it isn't confined to sight. It can be experienced as "gut feelings," mental images, sensory impressions, and strong emotions. Psychics tend to have a well-developed clairvoyance.

Clairsentience is the ability to sense details about a person, event, or situation through touch. One type of clairsentience is psychometry, the ability to "read" an object. The idea here is that personal items like jewelry and clothing retain the vibration of the individual who has worn them, and a psychometrist can pick up details about the individual by tuning in to that vibration. Psychics who work with police often use this method. This method has been used successfully in psychic archaeology, too, where psychics are invited to an archaeological site and provide information on what they pick up about the site and the artifacts found.

Clairalience and *clairambience* are less common than the first three inner senses. Clear smelling is the ability to glean details about an individual or situation through the sense of smell. An example of this would be when the scent of your grandmother's cologne suddenly permeates the air around you.

Clear tasting involves picking up details about an individual or situation through the sense of taste. Perhaps your deceased father loved key lime pie. If he's trying to communicate with you, the taste of key lime may fill your mouth.

Jane Roberts, in *The Seth Material*, quotes Seth about what he terms the Inner Senses: ". . . they reveal to us our independence from physical matter, and let us recognize our unique, individual multidimensional identity. Properly utilized, they also show us the miracle of physical existence and our place in it." According to Seth, there are nine of these Inner Senses. It isn't enough to list them; the explanations are necessary. If you're interested, read Chapter 19 of *The Seth Material*.

Aries individuals, due to the action orientation of the sign, usually have a strongly developed clairvoyance. There are numerous books on how to develop psychically, but here are a few pointers about developing clairvoyance:

- Trust your impressions. This is a big one for Aries, who is often too quick to dismiss his intuitive impressions as wishful thinking or fantasy or simply invalid.

- Give yourself a few minutes each day to relax fully into yourself. Put on music, burn incense, stare into the flame of a candle, get outside. Find some method that allows you to connect with your inner self. While in this heightened state of relaxation, give yourself the suggestion that your intuition is sharpening, growing, expanding.

- Pose a question and tell yourself that the next thing you see or hear will answer that question. It may be a voice on the TV, a song on the radio, or something you read.

- Develop techniques with your partner or your group that encourages the use of clairvoyance.

Stay Grounded. Years ago, there was a movie (and later a TV show) called *The Ghost and Mrs. Muir*. The premise was simple. A widow, Mrs. Muir, had moved into a grand old house on the sea somewhere in New England. She was grieving over her husband's death, and the move into the house seemed to be the best thing for her to do at the time.

A ghost lived in this house, the ghost of an old sea captain. He had been lonely, too, during his years as a ghost, and he fell in love with Mrs. Muir. Eventually, she fell in love with him, too. As interesting as the show was, the tragedy of it was that Mrs. Muir's primary relationship was with a man who had been dead for decades.

While it's unlikely that a forward-moving, action-oriented Aries will ever substitute a relationship with spirits for a relationship in the physical world, it's something to be cautious about. Our souls choose to be born into the physical world to *experience* it—the triumphs and love, the pain and the confusion. We're here to learn and assimilate what we learn.

So what grounds an Aries? That's like asking what dreams are specific to a particular sign. But there are broad areas that might apply: something physical, a project Aries has initiated, a passion he feels, a child, a particular animal, a certain kind of weather. Find what grounds you, Aries, and use it in your spiritual communication work.

Trust. This can be a challenge. You tend to trust only what comes from your own efforts, so that your inner world often gets the short end of things. Sharon, a thirty-four-year-old Aries who was widowed several years ago, initially denied "all that New Age stuff" after her husband died. She lost faith in any continuity of the soul.

Then one day while she was swimming laps in her pool, she glanced up and saw her husband and a young boy standing at the far end of the pool. It shocked her so deeply that several weeks later she went to a medium who told her that her husband was with a young boy, the child she had lost to a miscarriage earlier in her marriage. He wanted her to know that he was going to raise the boy on the other side while she raised their two kids in the physical world.

For you, the ability to trust in the continuity of the soul may come through an experience like Sharon's. Or it may come through some other experience. The bottom line is the same, however. Learn to trust what you can't see, hear, feel, taste, or touch. Learn to trust your gut.

The Flow. Mediums refer to "the flow" by various names, but the bottom line is the same—go with what's happening. If you, like Sharon, see a loved one who has passed on, don't freak. Don't slam your intuitive door. Instead, remain receptive to the experience. Notice details. How is the person dressed? How does he or she look? If the person speaks to you, what is he or she saying? If nothing is spoken, what do you feel the message is supposed to be?

If you get a strong impression of someone around you who is dead, question the presence. Who is it? What does it want? Any experience regarding one of the inner senses should be approached openly, without resistance.

In fact, if you get a psychic message, evaluate it. Test it against your common sense, your logic, your rational self. Do this when you get psychic information from other people, too. Always ask if the information *resonates for you.*

Protection. Many mediums and psychics "protect" themselves against lower energy by visualizing a white light around themselves. Or they say a prayer. John Edward, a Catholic, says the rosary before he does any readings. Millie Gemondo centers herself with some deep breathing and trusts that the energy that comes in will be of the highest quality.

If you have a particular room or area where you do this sort of work, smudge it first by burning some sage and letting the smoke permeate the air. Sage is one of the best ways to rid a place of any negative energy.

Aries isn't crazy about ritual, so you might just light a stick of incense or a candle and be done with it. Again, trust your instincts.

THE MAP

For your journey, the map is nothing more than a record of what you experience during the time frame you've set. Aries may find a written journal too tedious, so a tape recorder might be in order. Whatever type of record you select, it's important to include the date, time, and a brief description about the experience. The temptation for an Aries is to entrust it all to memory, but life is crowded and important details can easily slip through the memory cracks.

If you continue this record over an extended period of time, you'll be able to identify patterns in your spiritual communication. Perhaps weather and temperature are factors in the clarity of the communication. Or maybe communication is clearer at certain times of the day or night. If you have more than one guide, you may find that guide A comes through best at night, when the temperature is moderate and the weather is clear, while guide B comes through best when you're outdoors, hiking or biking. So note details like these.

If your dreams during this time are especially vivid and you have good recall, record your dreams as well.

The following questions are intended as guidelines to help you identify some of those patterns.

- What kinds of impressions do you receive? Are they visual? Auditory? Do they involve any of the other inner senses?
- Which of your senses seems to be the most heightened?
- Is there any apparent pattern in why one sense seems stronger with certain types of experiences?
- If one sense seems stronger than the others, what types of impressions do you receive through that sense?
- If you're recording your dreams, are there recurring dreams about someone you loved who has died? What is the content of those dreams? Mediums seem

to agree that spirits often communicate to us clearly in dreams.

- How does your body feel physically during these experiences?
- How do your feel emotionally?
- How do your experiences compare with those of your partner or group? Does working with other people enrich your experiences?
- Do the weather, time of day, temperature, and other external factors have any bearing on your experiences?
- What other details seem pertinent to these experiences?
- What insight does your partner or group provide about these experiences?
- How do you feel about your exploration? Does it seem to be changing your life in visible, tangible ways?

In the table below, list five areas you would like to explore and possible ways of doing it. Then use the records section at the end of this chapter to get started. The more details you include in your record, the clearer your experience will become for you.

Areas to Explore   How to Go About It

1._____ _____

2._____ _____

3._____ _____

4._____ _____

5._____ _____

THE GRAIL

For you, Aries, the end point, the grail, is as simple as the quest: *You learn to trust what you receive and then act on it.*

YOUR RECORDS

Date: _____

Time: _____

Weather: _____

Other Factors: _____

_____

Your experience: _____

_____

_____

_____

_____

_____

_____

_____

_____

_____

6. Taurus the Bull ♉

Everyone has different ways of using their intuition to
tune in.

—CHAR MARGOLIS

April 20–May 20
Fixed Earth
Ruled by Venus

THE SYMBOL

Remember Ferdinand the Bull? In this classic children's
story, Ferdinand is different from the other bulls, a
fact that worries his mother. He doesn't want to fight and
snort like the other bulls his age. He has absolutely no
desire to head for the ring in Madrid. Ferdinand's favorite
pursuit is grazing in the pasture, beneath the warm sun,
and snoozing in the shade of his favorite tree.

Then one day he sits on a bumblebee, and its sting
sends Ferdinand ballistic. He rips around the field, snort-
ing and bucking, as enraged as any bull in a ring. Unfortunately for Ferdinand, bullfighting officials from Madrid
witness this display and they're overjoyed. They think
they've found the next winning bull, and Ferdinand is
hauled off to Madrid.

The story fits the nature of Taurus. She's gentle, loving, earthy. She enjoys peace and solitude, although not necessarily in that order, and is happiest when she can go about her business, unimpeded by anyone or anything. She enjoys beauty in all its forms—music, art, nature. Many Taureans, in fact, are more physical than Aries, but for different reasons. Where Aries hikes and bikes and rock climbs as a competition with himself, always testing his own abilities, Taurus does these things because they provide her with peace, silence, and a sense of stability—the very things Taurus covets most. At the heart of her physicality lies a simple joy in the motion of her own body.

Not every Taurus is a nature lover, of course. And for those who aren't, the need for peace and silence is found in the arts, music, and within their own creativity. Musical talent among Taurus individuals isn't uncommon. But even among those who don't play an instrument or sing worth a hoot, music provides an anodyne for the stress in life.

The Taurean's strong need for security and stability often finds expression through what she owns, whether it's land, art, antique books, or her own home. Whatever it is, this becomes her cocoon, her little nest, the place where the world's madness can't touch her, where its cacophony bleeds away into a soft, summer stillness. This cocoon grounds her. Taurus has an innate distrust of drama and fads, the hoopla of the human condition.

As a fixed sign, she's slow to change her opinions. Taurus, in fact, is the most stubborn sign in the zodiac, so stubborn at times that she risks becoming entrenched in her opinions and beliefs, which ultimately leads to stagnation. The fixed earth nature of the sign, however, also endows Taurus with incredible persistence. She endures.

STRENGTH IN OPPOSITES: TAURUS/SCORPIO POLARITY

Taurus is perfectly content with the status quo, whatever that is for her. She isn't fond of change, particularly when it's sudden and unexpected. That kind of change disturbs her equilibrium. She keeps her own counsel and doesn't talk much about what she feels, even when those feelings run very deep. In one sense, she's uncomfortable with intense emotions—passion, hatred, obsession, rage. She isn't easily angered, but when she is, the bull's rush is rather like Ferdinand's display when he was stung by the bee.

Although she has a mystical side, it's tempered by her need for pragmatism, for concrete, tangible results. When she becomes stuck in this need, when a part of her keeps screaming, *"Prove it,"* her intuition shuts down, her left brain takes over, and she stumbles blindly through an existential dilemma. The dilemma is this: Some things can't be proven, they must be taken on faith.

That leap is difficult for a Taurus to make. Some deep and fundamental part of her balks at taking anything inexplicable and mysterious on pure faith. But for her spiritual journey to get off the ground, this is precisely what she must do. And the best way to do it is to draw on the strength of her polarity, Scorpio. Like all polarities, the two opposing signs form an axis of energy, so that the energy of one is always available to the other.

Where Taurus needs proof, Scorpio needs only the whispering of her intuition for confirmation. Taurus seeks peace, Scorpio seeks transformation at the deepest levels even if that shatters her peace. Taurus is sensual, Scorpio is seductive. Where Taurus is uncomfortable with her deeper emotions, Scorpio is the most intensely emotional sign.

As Taurus embarks on her spiritual journey, she must understand that it will transform her. It will change how she perceives herself and the rest of the world. It will alter her at the most fundamental levels. Throughout this journey, she must rely on her emotions, the very thing that makes her uncomfortable. When the hairs on the back of her neck stand up, when her palms sweat, when she responds viscerally to a person, event, or situation, she must pay attention. She must investigate, penetrate, get to the root of it.

Okay, so it's a tall order. But Taurus rises to any challenge.

In 1963, Jane Roberts, a double Taurus (Sun and Moon), and her husband experimented with a Ouija board. The responses that were spelled out were so compelling they took notes and continued with their experiments. Roberts, with her prove-it-to-me attitude, took the entity who responded through the paces. Questions like *"Who are you? Where were you born?"* quickly became more piercing, more serious, more demanding.

Within a month, Roberts could hear the responses in her mind before the planchette spelled them out. One night, she simply stood up and began speaking as Seth. Her first book about the experience was *The Coming of Seth,* a combination of Roberts's thoughts on metaphysical phenomena and Seth's own take on the nature of reality. The next book, *Seth Speaks,* was entirely channeled, except for notes by Roberts's husband, Robert Butts, that put the information into the context of their daily lives.

Seth and Jane produced a number of Seth books, but there are also nine books of material, called "the early sessions," in which the qualities of the Taurus Sun are painfully evident. In these books, Roberts and Butts concoct endless experiments and tests for Seth that are intended to prove his validity. This is the prove-it-to-me syndrome of the Taurus Sun.

Prove that you're telepathic. *Prove* that you can perceive what we don't. *Prove to me that you are what you say you are, that reality is as you say it is.*

These experiments consisted of sketches or photographs in sealed envelopes that Seth had to describe or "tests" in which he had to describe the activities of certain people at other locations, and other similar situations that could be verified. For a reader, these tests become tedious. For an astrologer, they are testimony to the Taurus psyche in action and to how that psyche can change when the proof becomes beside the point because the information penetrates to a visceral level.

True to the Taurus archetype, it took Roberts several years to become convinced, *to relinquish her need for proof.* Once she pierced the mystery of who Seth was (the Scorpio part of the polarity equation), she moved forward in true Scorpion fashion, digging deeper with every session, every book, until twenty years later and crippled with rheumatoid arthritis, Roberts understood just how stubborn she was despite the extent to which her life had been transformed by the Seth phenomenon.

THE QUEST

Distilled to its essence, the Taurus quest is: *To allow your deepest emotions to lead you into the mystery of spirit communication.*

This doesn't mean you should accept everything you experience on this journey as "The Truth" or that you should park your doubt at the door. You're simply going to be using different tools on this journey, emotional tools. Your feelings and intuitions will act as a kind of barometer to "test" the validity of an experience.

Imagine that you're awakened in the middle of the night by a voice. You bolt upright in bed, your heart hammering, your eyes darting through the darkness, looking for the person who spoke to you. When you realize no one is there, you stretch out again and shut your eyes. You hear the voice again and this time realize its source is internal. Instead of doubting the experience, you embrace it. Afterward, you use your emotions to gauge the voice. Does the message *feel* right? Does it resonate for you?

This example illustrates one way in which emotions can be used to probe and investigate any of the experiences you have with spirit communication.

THE JOURNEY

Your packing list for this journey is simple: a notebook or tape recorder, a willingness to explore whatever happens, and an awareness of your particular belief system. This last item is especially important because your belief system is sure to expand and change during this journey.

The notebook or journal is entirely optional, of course, but it helps to have a record of some kind for your experiences. A record provides a way to scrutinize your experiences for recurring themes or patterns, and it offers a continuity. The tape recorder is best used when you don't have your journal handy, but isn't recommended as the primary record for your experiences. Taurus likes what she can hold and touch, so a recorder won't provide it. A computer file is fine, as long as you print it every couple of days so that you have a hard copy.

Taurus can be as much of a loner as Aries, and you

may prefer to keep it that way during this journey. If you and someone you trust share a common interest in expanding your intuitive abilities and spiritual experiences, then undertake this exploration together. It's helpful to be able to brainstorm and share experiences with someone else. Quite often, your partner will have insights that you don't and vice-versa. If your partner is a different Sun sign, he or she should read the section for their sign and follow those guidelines. You'll each be following the same general path, but in a way that best fits your individual temperaments.

Whether you work with a partner or by yourself, you should have some general idea of what you hope to accomplish. It's best not to define a specific goal; it may limit you. Instead, think of the *big picture*. What is the ultimate purpose for this journey? What do you hope to learn from it? Are you emotionally committed to the exploration?

Quite often, our purposes for metaphysical explorations aren't apparent immediately. They unfold, over time, or they transmute as the exploration deepens. When Roberts, for instance, first began speaking for Seth, her purpose and that of her husband seemed to be one of intense curiosity due to the clarity and power of the material. But over the more than twenty years that Roberts spoke for Seth, the tone of the books she wrote under her own name changed considerably. What began as intense curiosity had become her life's work.

She personified the essence of Taurus exploration. She kept at the work, speaking twice a week for Seth while her husband transcribed what was said, and didn't let up even at the end, when she was so crippled that she could move only her mouth and her fingers to type. The final Seth book, in fact, *The Way Toward Health,* was channeled during the last year of Roberts's life, when she was bedridden and hospitalized, her legs frozen up against her chest. She finished the book six days before she died. She *endured*.

Here are some guidelines to help you clarify and define your present belief system. This is merely to provide you with a frame of reference. Check the statements that pertain to you.

I believe:

- In life after death.
- In heaven and hell.
- In good and evil.
- That spiritual guidance is possible.
- That reality is far more than what we can perceive with our five senses.
- That energy can't be destroyed.
- In the continuity of the soul.
- That each of us creates the reality we experience through our deepest beliefs.

MEETING YOUR GUIDES

The procedure outlined here is general, intended for the average Taurus. Tailor it to *your* needs.

The Physical Body. Your body is so finely tuned to the earth and earth cycles that any type of physical exercise you do only enhances this connection. Certain physical disciplines can also be used to open yourself intuitively to communication with guides. Yoga and tai chi are two possibilities.

One of the benefits of yoga is flexibility. As your physical flexibility increases, you become more flexible in other areas of your life as well. Rob, a Taurus writer, started taking yoga when he was in his late forties. Within months, he was teaching it. Not only did his physical flexibility increase, but so did his mental, emotional, and spiritual flexibility. He became more intuitive, more willing to embrace new ideas and beliefs.

In tai chi, certain body movements, done in a kind of slow motion, allow you to shift around your energy. In shifting the energy, you remove blockages and increase your ability to concentrate and focus, both of which are necessary in spiritual communication.

Signs & Symbols. Taurus is unusually adept at interpreting symbols, a language often used by spirits and guides. James Van Praagh relates an interesting story about symbols in his book *Reaching to Heaven.* He was doing a reading for a young woman whose mother had died. "Suddenly, I felt a very strange sensation and didn't understand what was happening to me. I closed my eyes, and as if being taken over, I began to feel as though I was enclosed in a box."

He broke off communication by opening his eyes, and asked his spirit guides to explain what had happened. They replied that the sensation was necessary because it described how the young woman's mother had felt most of her life. He asked the young woman if her mother had been confined in some way. The woman admitted that her mother had been agoraphobic and had spent most of her life in the house.

For Van Praagh, this symbol was expressed as a physical sensation. But symbols come through each of our senses and through events, people, animals, and dreams. We can stumble into them virtually anywhere. Even the most obvious things can be symbolic of spirit communication.

Remember the story about the straight pins earlier in this book? Linda, from that story, had a begonia in the windowsill of her apartment in college. Her grandmother, who loved begonias, had given it to her. On the day her grandmother died, the begonia plant suddenly wilted and died—before she had heard about her grandmother's death.

It's important that you include all signs and symbols in your records. Over time, you'll amass a dictionary of signs and symbols that are unique to you and your situation.

The Senses. Our senses are exquisitely designed for life in the physical world. Every moment of every day, these senses transmit information that allows us to live more fully. When you're developing psychically, however, your senses become more finely honed, heightened, and with a little practice, lead you into the realm of inner senses.

John Edward lists these psychic senses as: clairaudience (clear hearing), clairvoyance (clear seeing), clairsentience (clear sensing), clairalience (clear smelling), and clairambience (clear tasting).

Hearing an inner voice that imparts wisdom or guidance is how *clairaudience* often manifests. This voice can be heard in dreams, during periods of deep relaxation, during meditation or any other altered state. With practice, it can be heard at virtually any time of the day or night. This sense is common among mediums.

Clairvoyance is the ability to see what is happening now or what will happen in the future in your life or the life of someone else. Many psychics use this sense. Although it's related to "seeing," it isn't confined to sight. It can be experienced as "gut feelings" or mental images and impressions. Psychics tend to have strongly developed clairvoyance.

Clairsentience is the ability to sense details about a person, event, or situation through touch. One type of clairsentience is psychometry, the ability to "read" an object. The idea here is that personal items like jewelry and clothing retain the vibration of the individual who has worn them, and a psychometrist can pick up details about the individual by tuning in to that vibration. Psychics who work with police, like Renie Wiley and Noreen Renier, often use this method.

Clairalience and *clairambience* are less common than the first three inner senses. Clear smelling is the ability to glean details about an individual or situation through the sense of smell. An example of this would be when the scent of your grandmother's cologne suddenly permeates the air around you.

Clear tasting involves picking up details about an individual or situation through the sense of taste. Perhaps your deceased father loved key lime pie. If he's trying to communicate with you, the taste of key lime may fill your mouth.

Jane Roberts, in *The Seth Material,* quotes Seth about what he terms the Inner Senses: ". . . they reveal to us our independence from physical matter, and let us recognize our unique, individual multidimensional identity. Properly utilized, they also show us the miracle of physical existence and our place in it." According to Seth, there are nine of these Inner Senses. It isn't enough to list them; the explanations are necessary. If you're interested, read Chapter 19 of *The Seth Material.*

Taurus individuals have such a developed sense of touch that they often excel at clairsentience.

The easiest way to develop this sense is to work with

objects that hold emotional significance to another person. Ask your partner to bring you a piece of jewelry or some other object about which you know nothing. In the beginning, it's best if the object is metal, preferably gold, which seems to retain strong emotional imprints from whoever owned it. Hold the object in both of your hands and shut your eyes. Focus on the object. Does it feel hot? Cold? What's its texture?

As you're exploring the object with your normal senses, give yourself the suggestion that your sense of touch is going to expand and allow you to tune in the person who owned the object. You may get mental images, feelings that clearly aren't your own, or you may taste or hear things that don't originate in you. Go with your first impression, regardless of how silly or far-fetched it seems.

When clairsentience is highly developed, it can yield psychic information simply through touching another person. In Stephen King's classic *The Dead Zone,* the protagonist had to wear gloves most of the time because the mere act of shaking someone else's hand resulted in a deluge of information about that individual. In the TV version of that story, the character John Smith avoids touching people and is careful about touching objects as well.

Stay Grounded. This really shouldn't be a problem for Taurus; you are naturally grounded. But if you feel overwhelmed at any point by this exploration, go do whatever brings you pleasure and restores your connection to the earth. Go into a garden. Run. Do some yoga. Take your dog for a walk. Of all the signs, you are the least likely to get lost in some etheric wonderland.

Trust. For each sign, the type of trust that should be nurtured differs. Aries, for instance, has to learn to trust what he can't see, hear, touch, smell, or taste. And you, Taurus, have to learn to trust what you can't prove in a million years. Whether it's a message you receive in a dream or an impulse to do something radically different from what you're accustomed to, you need to *trust* what you can't explain.

The Flow. It's a state of mind, a type of awareness. You have a sense of being adrift in a river flowing inexorably toward . . . well, *something*. The *something* is actually less important than the *absence of resistance*.

The mystical part of you understands this process, has always understood it. The prove-it-to-me part of you insists it's the domain of yogis and Zen masters. But in your dreams you are part of this flow. When you're doing something that brings you immense pleasure, you're part of it. When you are fully in your body, you're a part of this flow. *You go with whatever is happening. You don't resist it.* If you resist, you slam the door of your intuition.

You can enter the flow while doing yoga or tai chi or when you meditate. Meditation, in fact, is something a Taurus takes to much more readily than, say, an Aries or a Gemini, both of whom are usually much too restless to sit still for long. Your meditation period can be as short as five or ten minutes a day; the length of time isn't as important as the state of awareness you attain—the flow. Once you know what the flow feels like, it's easier to conjure it when you need it. Don't worry too much about *what* it feels like. You'll recognize it when you feel it.

Protection. Many mediums and psychics "protect" themselves against lower energy by visualizing a white light around themselves. Or they say a prayer. Psychic Char Margolis has a special protection prayer she wrote herself and includes in her book *Questions from Earth,*

Answers from Heaven. She advises students to say this prayer or one of their own choosing.

As an earth sign, Taurus, you might consider smudging your area with sage, one of the best ways to get rid of negative energy.

THE MAP

When you travel, you select cities and landmarks to explore. On this exploration, you're going to do the same thing. But instead of selecting cities and landmarks, you'll choose ideas and topics, then formulate questions that relate to spirit communication.

If you're interested in what the great spiritual traditions say about the afterlife, then you may want to explore the cultures that have grown up around these traditions, either in the present or the past. Money and time permitting, this might entail trips to some of the magnificent ruins in Central America and South America, for example, the Mayan pyramids or Machu Picchu. Or you might sign up for a spiritual trip to Native American sites in the Southwest.

If deepening your intuition is one of your "destinations," then a workshop may be in order. If you want to explore the afterlife, then perhaps you should consider a program at the Monroe Institute, where participants are taught how travel out of body to the various levels of the afterlife that Monroe mapped.

Below is a table for areas you would like to explore. This isn't intended to be any sort of rigid *must-do* list. These are merely possibilities. If you want to list more areas of exploration, extend your list. Next to each idea, jot at least two ways in which you might accomplish the exploration of the respective area. If, for example, you want to explore afterlife concepts among the Hopi Indians, jot that on the left-hand side of the list, and on the right-hand side jot a possible way of doing this.

Areas to Explore   How to Go About It

1._____   _____
2._____   _____
3._____   _____
4._____   _____
5._____   _____

THE GRAIL

For you, Taurus, the grail is: *To pierce the camouflage of ordinary life.*

YOUR RECORDS

Date: _____
Time: _____
Weather: _____
Other factors: _____
_____

Your experience: _____
_____
_____
_____
_____
_____
_____
_____
_____
_____
_____

7. Gemini the Twins ♊

We are each responsible for all of our experiences.

—LOUISE HAY

May 21–June 21
Mutable Air
Ruled by Mercury

THE SYMBOL

The winged messenger is mythological Mercury. He was the ancient equivalent of e-mail, a networker, a transmitter of information. In fact, information and communication were his specialties. As the ruler of both Gemini and Virgo, information is what binds these two signs together.

Gemini is the first of the dual signs, and that duality is intrinsic to everything Gemini is—and isn't. Imagine identical twins. Who can tell them apart? A parent, perhaps. Or their respective spouses. But what distinguishes two people who are physically identical in every way? The very things that aren't physical. Personalities. Interests. Passions. Moods. The twins. One is optimistic and social, the other is a depressed loner. One loves baseball, the other hates sports. Now roll these twins together, into one body, one mind, one spirit, and you have Gemini. Never make the mistake of believing that what you see is what you get! You can never be entirely sure which twin is dominant on a given day. Or in a given moment.

The bookish twin soaks up information like the proverbial sponge and does it primarily through schooling (workshops, seminars, online courses) and through the media (books, movies, radio, TV, the Internet). The other twin also soaks up information, but he does it mostly through people. Friends and acquaintances form an intricate network. This twin can be a gossip at times, passing on information that may be injurious to someone else. He doesn't do it to be mean, just as he isn't intentionally tactless. Things just slip out and get away from him.

Gemini asks *why. Why are you wearing blue today? Why do you believe in those particular ideals? Why are you traveling to Russia on your summer vacation? Why do you think that book (or that movie, that experience, that individual) is so great?* He's in love with ideas, possibilities, concepts, and how everything fits together. It's all part of his need to gather and disperse information. Through this process, he crystallizes and hones his intellect and beliefs. Always, though, curiosity is what propels him, an insatiable hunger for experience.

STRENGTH IN OPPOSITES: GEMINI/SAGITTARIUS POLARITY

Gemini is a master of trivia, with superficial knowledge about a great many things. He excels at connecting the dots in areas that interest him, but gets into trouble when he wades into unfamiliar terrain and acts like an expert.

Regardless of how proficient he is at fitting one bit of information with another bit, he rarely sees the larger picture. It's the old adage about not being able to see the forest for the trees.

His challenge is to recognize how grand and mysterious this bigger picture may be and to realize that some things can't be explained regardless of the facts he accrues. Quite often there's a triggering event that forces Gemini into a state of mind where facts fail to explain what's going on: the loss of a job, the end of a relationship, the death of a loved one. It's usually at this point that Gemini is forced to draw on the strength of his sign's polarity, Sagittarius, and then his spiritual exploration begins in earnest.

Two signs that are opposed to each other form an axis of energy. Either sign can draw on the energy of the other. When it's done with conscious intent, the effects can be powerful. Where Gemini collects and disseminates *information,* Sagittarius quests for *knowledge.* Gemini seeks *connections* among ideas, people, and events. Sagittarius seeks *expansion* and *integration* of those connections. Gemini says, "Give me the facts." Sagittarius says, "Forget facts. I *know* this is true." Gemini's approach to life is diverse and multidimensional, whereas the Sagittarius approach is holographic. The archetypal forces that shape each of these signs are complementary, yet very different.

For Gemini to take advantage of his Sagittarian polarity, he must allow his imaginative right brain to direct the show. This doesn't mean facts should be forgotten or shunted aside, only placed within their proper contexts, as adjuncts to what the imagination discovers.

Ray, a Gemini and an English teacher, had been brought up a Catholic, and for years believed in the

Catholic version of the afterlife: heaven, hell, limbo, purgatory. Then he lost a close friend in a car accident, and, suddenly, his Catholic beliefs no longer provided answers or comfort.

His friend Lou had never been baptized, so in the Catholic version of the afterlife, he was condemned to limbo. Lou hadn't been Catholic, had never gone to church, had never confessed or taken communion. Therefore, in the Catholic scheme of things, Lou had lived his entire life in a state of sin and was condemned to either purgatory or hell. Yet, Ray felt that Lou was one of the kindest, most compassionate people he ever had known. Didn't that count for anything?

Lou's death was the triggering event that launched Ray's spiritual exploration. Ray realized that the religious beliefs he'd held for all these years weren't really *his* beliefs, but those he had adopted without question. He recalled that even during catechism classes when he was younger, no one ever presented irrefutable facts that the Catholic version of the afterlife was *true*. In the absence of facts from Catholicism or anywhere else, he decided to find out what he believed by delving into various spiritual traditions.

Without realizing it, Ray took the Sagittarian route. In his spare time, he started reading books on many types of spiritual belief systems, from Native American to Buddhist to Wicca. During summer break, when he wasn't teaching, his travels were primarily spiritual explorations. He dabbled. He sampled. He expanded his spiritual foundations. He wasn't collecting facts or information—he was *experiencing*.

During his studies and travels, Ray's intuitive abilities expanded rapidly and deeply. He had no factual evidence for the things he experienced, but his dependence on facts and logic was no longer as important as it once was. He took the experiences at face value, and, gradually, his new belief system began to come together. By opening himself to a myriad of possibilities and refusing to recognize limitations, Ray's life changed dramatically. He no longer teaches; he's an intuitive counselor. Even more importantly, his firm convictions about the afterlife—which bear no resemblance to the Catholic beliefs he held for so many years—are part of his counseling practice.

THE QUEST

Look for the bigger picture. That's the simplest way to put it, Gemini. Facts will provide you with many necessary things, but they won't paint the big picture. Only your imagination will do that. You can connect as many dots as you want, but in the end you still have to step back so that you see the picture that the dots create.

Gemini Rita didn't really understand what her quest entailed until she woke suddenly one night and saw her ailing aunt standing at the foot of her bed. She looked like "one of those holographs in the haunted house at Disney World," she explained. "I could see right through her, could see the door behind her, the wall. To say that it scared me is hardly the point. It completely overturned my concept of what is possible, that's how real it was."

Rita called her parents the next morning to find out if her aunt, who lived halfway across the country, had died. It turned out she had broken her hip, which sometime later led to her death.

With your quest in mind, Gemini, now it's time to plan for the journey itself.

THE JOURNEY

For each Sun sign in this book, the packing list for the journey includes a notebook and/or tape recorder. Gemini is no exception. But unlike the recommendation for the previous two signs, your notebook isn't intended to be a record of your spirit communication. Use it, instead, to record your thoughts about how your belief system and worldview are expanding as a result of this journey. What you're looking for in this journey is *direct personal experience,* not vicarious experiences that you read about or hear through other people.

The notebook or recorder isn't intended to be a record of your attempts at spiritual communication, although it can be. Initially, use it to talk about how your belief system and worldview are expanding and the impact this expansion is having on your life.

Since Gemini is such a people-oriented sign, you may want to undertake this journey with another person. A partnership, as long as it's conducive to the growth of both individuals, is an exciting way to explore spirit communication. The drawback, at least for you, Gemini, is that you may become so fascinated by the other person's exploration that you neglect your own!

By working with a partner, you gain additional insight into your experiences. Keep the exploration to a twosome. This maintains a streamlined simplicity and allows sufficient space for give-and-take between you and your partner. If your partner is a different Sun sign, then he or she should follow the general guidelines under the respective Sun sign.

If you prefer undertaking this exploration alone, then by all means do so. A partner isn't a prerequisite for success. In either case, you should decide on a few basics. Consider these guidelines:

- Is a time frame necessary? Aries probably needs one and Taurus probably doesn't, but what about you? If you think you'll get bored with this exploration, then you probably shouldn't be trying it to begin with. On the other hand, if you're approaching this as an adventure, then a time frame may not be necessary.
- If you decide on a time frame, make it realistic, longer than five minutes, Gemini. A month or six weeks should be long enough to determine if this adventure suits you.
- What's your ultimate goal? For Ray, the ultimate goal was to discover what *he* believed.
- At this moment in time, what are your beliefs about the afterlife? It's important to know this so that you have some means of comparison later on. Did you grow up in a household where a conventional religion was followed? If so, how have these religious beliefs colored your life?
- Are you open to the kind of change that transforms your life?
- Can you commit to this exploration?

MEETING YOUR GUIDES

The techniques and suggestions in this section are intended for the average Gemini. During this exploration, you'll expand these techniques, create your own, and find what works best for you.

The Physical Body. Nervous energy. Think about that a moment. Are you always on the move? Do you feel so restless at times that stillness seems anathema to your normal state? On the one hand, all that nervous energy probably keeps you slender. But on the other hand, it may make it difficult for you to focus for prolonged periods. For you, Gemini, your body may simply be a vehicle that gets you from point A to point B as quickly as your mercurial feet will carry you. But consider this: Suppose you could use your body as a vehicle for your intuition?

Your nervous system is so finely tuned to your environment that you are constantly bombarded with information. You wake in the morning with an immediate sense of the weather, of how hungry you are, and how heavy and comforting your cat feels as she snoozes on your chest. Your busy little mind immediately slams into hyperdrive, puzzling over the vestiges of a dream that already is fading, fretting about the five thousands things you have to do by noon. By the time you actually get out of bed, your energy level may be flagging, and you're tempted to just roll back under the covers and pull them up over your head.

If you can bleed off some of this kinetic energy through physical activity, your nervous system is more likely to respond to *your* will, rather than the other way around. The big question is the kind of activity. It should be something fast and energetic to suit your temperament. Running. A trampoline. Dancing. Swimming. An aerobics class. Even walking fast would do the trick. The point is to do *something* and to do it regularly.

Once you find some sort of physical release for your nervous energy, your nervous system acts like a giant antenna, allowing you to transmit and receive psychic energy. You can more clearly "transmit" your desire to communicate with your guides and will be better equipped to "receive" input from your guides.

Right about now, your left-brain self is balking. *What? Ridiculous. Impossible. Silly.* Maybe. But you won't know until you try it, Gemini.

Signs & Symbols. Remember the story about Thomas Edison earlier in this book? The invention he was working on was a kind of telephone between this world and the next. Unfortunately, communication between us and people who have died usually isn't that straightforward. There's static on the line.

James Van Praagh, in *Talking to Heaven,* has an insightful take on this aspect of spirit communication. "In order to attune to the thoughts and feelings of a spirit, I have to raise my vibrations higher and, in turn, a spirit has to lower its vibrations somewhat. Sometimes, this can be very difficult . . . When a spirit says, 'Hello, how are you today?' I may hear, 'lo, are yo day.' "

Not everyone hears voices. It's more likely that in the beginning the signs and symbols will be more tangible. If your grandmother, for instance, loved hummingbirds and you spot one as you're thinking of her, then the hummingbird is probably a sign of communication from her. Don't overlook the obvious.

The Senses. As you develop psychically, your inner senses become more attuned to the unseen. Medium and author John Edward lists these psychic senses as: clairaudience (clear hearing), clairvoyance (clear seeing), clairsentience (clear sensing), clairalience (clear smelling), and clairambience (clear tasting).

Hearing an inner voice that imparts wisdom or guidance is how *clairaudience* often manifests. This voice can be heard in dreams, during periods of deep relaxation, during meditation or any other altered state. With practice, it can be heard at virtually any time of the day or night. This sense is common among mediums.

Clairvoyance is the ability to see what is happening now or what will happen in the future in your life or the life of someone else. Many psychics use this sense. Although it's related to "seeing," it isn't confined to sight. It can be experienced as "gut feelings" or mental images and impressions. Psychics tend to have strongly developed clairvoyance.

Clairsentience is the ability to sense details about a person, event, or situation through touch. One type of clairsentience is psychometry, the ability to "read" an object. The idea here is that personal items like jewelry and clothing retain the vibration of the individual who has worn them, and a psychometrist can pick up details about the individual by tuning in to that vibration. Psychics who work with police often use this method.

Clairalience and *clairambience* are less common than the first three inner senses. Clear smelling is the ability to glean details about an individual or situation through the sense of smell. An example of this would be when the scent of your grandmother's cologne suddenly permeates the air around you.

Clear tasting involves picking up details about an individual or situation through the sense of taste. Perhaps your deceased father loved key lime pie. If he's trying to communicate with you, the taste of key lime may fill your mouth.

To these senses, James Van Praagh adds "inspirational thought." He defines this as receiving "thoughts, impressions, knowledge—all without forethought." In this type of sensing, a spirit or group of spirits "melds their thoughts together and impresses the person to write a certain piece of music or paint a particular picture." In other words, the vehicle is creativity.

Jane Roberts, in *The Seth Material,* quotes Seth about what he terms the Inner Senses: ". . . they reveal to us our independence from physical matter, and let us recognize our unique, individual multidimensional identity. Properly utilized, they also show us the miracle of physical existence and our place in it." According to Seth, there are nine of these Inner Senses. It isn't enough to list them; the explanations are necessary. If you're interested, read Chapter 19 of *The Seth Material*.

Geminis generally don't have much difficulty developing clairvoyantly. Intuitive Laura Day has some excellent suggestions in her books *Practical Intuition* and *Practical Intuition for Success* on how to develop and enhance intuition. You may want to glance through those books for ideas, then you and your partner can design experiments for each other.

As you develop intuitively and clairvoyantly, you may begin to do some automatic writing. In this type of communication, spirit guides communicate through the writing itself. Some of the best books that illustrate how automatic writing works were written by Ruth Montgomery, who claims that a group of guides worked through her in this way. If you find that your talent develops in this way, then your journal becomes central to your exploration.

Stay Grounded. This can be a challenge for any of the air signs, but particularly for you, Gemini, because you live so much of your life in your head, through your intellect. To stay grounded, it's important to become more aware of your body—how it moves, what it needs, how it feels at any given moment in a day. This entails nothing more than turning your focus inward for a few minutes.

When you feel you need more than that, put on music and dance. Or go swimming. Either one of these activities will make you acutely aware of your body and its movements.

Trust. How do you know that the impressions you're receiving are actually spirit communication and not your own imagination? In the beginning, you may not be able to distinguish one from the other. So the old trap will tempt you: *Where are the facts? What does my left brain have to say about this?* The trick is to trust what you receive. Don't question it, don't analyze it as it's happening, just allow yourself to be open and receptive.

As you gain experience with spirit communication, however it comes to you, it will become easier to distinguish between your imagination and genuine communication with spirits. Van Praagh defines the difference in *Talking to Heaven.* "In mediumship all thoughts, feelings, and sights are transmitted through a medium's superconscious or spirit mind. We are all picking up spirit impressions in this way, but it is the medium who is able to interpret them. The message then moves into the conscious mind and is revealed."

Once you are able to trust the impressions you receive, then run it past your left brain, your logical self, for confirmation. But the trust has to come first.

The Flow. Think of this state of awareness as nonresistance. You simply move with whatever you're experiencing instead of throwing up mental blocks or questions. When you're in the flow of things, experiences of all kinds seem to unfold naturally, without glitches and detours. *You go with whatever is happening.*

As a Gemini, you'll enter the flow most easily when you're dreaming, immersed in creative work, or engaged in something that occupies your logic and reason, which allows your right brain to function without being censored. When you're in the flow, synchronicities tend to happen more frequently. You experience more impulses, urges, and hunches. Once you know what the flow feels like, it becomes easier to put yourself in that state of mind at will.

Protection. Many people involved in psychic work "protect" themselves from lower energies through visualization, prayer, and smudging the area where they work. Visualization involves nothing more than imagining a cocoon of white light around yourself as you work. The prayer you use for protection is less important than the act of praying. It's especially powerful when you create your own prayer.

You're not into ritual any more than Aries is, so create something short and sweet. As an individual who values language, perhaps you might consider composing a short prayer for protection.

THE MAP

Your map for this exploration, Gemini, consists of two parts. The first part entails learning about the "country" you're going to visit, just as you might buy travel books before taking your vacation. The second part involves the "doing."

Here are some of the best books on mediumship and psychic development. You'll find others in Appendix 2.

- *The Nature of Personal Reality* by Jane Roberts. This is the most practical of the books Roberts channeled for Seth, the entity for whom she spoke for twenty years.
- *Talking to Heaven* by James Van Praagh. Contains practical information on mediumship and psychic de-

velopment, and also provides insight into how mediums and spirits work together.

- *One Last Time* by John Edward. The author's story of his own development as a psychic medium is fascinating. He also provides practical information at the end of the book for anyone seeking to develop these abilities.
- *Lessons from the Light* by George Anderson. The author covers many facets of his working relationships with spirits, and provides examples of "discernments" (readings) that cover everything from suicides to pets in the hereafter.
- *Questions from Earth, Answers from Heaven* by Char Margolis. Practical insights into the development and use of psychic ability and spirit communication.
- *A Seer Out of Season: The Life of Edgar Cayce* by Harmon Hartzell Bro. What makes this book fascinating is that the author knew Cayce and worked with him.

If you're not a reader, then check out these movies to get a sense of what it's like to communicate with spirits: *Ghost; The Haunted; The Sixth Sense; The Haunting of Hill House* (the original with Julie Harris); *The Gift; The Shining; The Dead Zone; What Dreams May Come.*

Once you have a clear sense of what this "country" may be like, decide what types of experiences you would like to have. Maybe you would like to communicate with spirits and guides through your dreams. This might require that you work on your dream recall. You could also start a dream group online or with a small group of friends.

In the table below, list five areas you would like to explore and possible ways of doing it.

Areas to Explore	How to Go About It
1._____	_____
2._____	_____
3._____	_____
4._____	_____
5._____	_____

THE GRAIL

Gemini's grail: *In finding the bigger picture, you're able to integrate what you learn into who you are.*

YOUR RECORDS

Date: _____

Time: _____

Weather: _____

Other factors: _____

_____

Your experience: _____

_____

_____

_____

_____

_____

_____

_____

_____

8. Cancer the Crab ♋

After-death communications—ADCs—are spiritual gifts,
intended to reignite our spiritual awareness of who we
are and why we're here, and our awareness that there is
no death . . .

—JUDY GUGGENHEIM

June 22–July 22
Cardinal Water
Ruled by the Moon

THE SYMBOL

Watch how the crab moves, darting sideways, evading pursuers, leaving traces in the wet sand. She's an elusive creature, but who can blame her? Only a shell lies between her and oblivion. Yet, when she's backed into a corner, her life on the line, watch how she takes her stance, claws clacking like castanets, her body feinting one way then another, seeking an escape route.

Now glance up at the Moon, Cancer's ruler. That softly lit disk is just camouflage. What you see is definitely not all there is. And that's how it is with Cancer, ninety percent of who she is hidden beneath the surface. Although all water signs perceive the world primarily through their emotions, Cancer is superbly equipped to

108

feel her way through life. Her senses precede her like tentacles, testing the emotional environment in which she finds herself, and they read that environment at lightning speed.

This sign is the most subjective of the three water signs and the most nurturing. Show her a bleeding heart and she attempts to fix it, to mother it, to kiss and make it well. Adults, children, animals, it makes no difference to her. If they hurt, she embraces them. And yes, she's a sucker for a sob story. But whoever tries to break through the durable shell that surrounds her quickly realizes the shell is made of steel. No one enters her world uninvited.

Return, again, to the crab's movement. Sideways, evasive. This is how Cancer moves when confronted with unpleasant or explosive emotions. Ironic, really, that she's so unerringly comfortable within her own feeling world, yet so terrified when emotions—hers or those of someone she loves—veer out of control. The passionate eruptions in the life of a fiery Aries would exhaust her, scorch her to the depths of her soul.

She takes everything personally, even when the remarks or actions aren't intended that way. She's like that with herself, too, constantly mulling over a situation she might have handled differently even when it's apparent to other people that she did the best she could given the circumstances.

More than any other sign, perhaps, Cancer needs to feel that she belongs *somewhere*—a family, among a group of coworkers who are like family, among a circle of friends, in a particular house, town, or area. Roots. That's what Cancer craves. And when she finds those roots, she sinks so deeply into them that stagnation may result.

STRENGTH IN OPPOSITES:
CANCER/CAPRICORN POLARITY

Most of us need roots, someplace we call home. For
Cancer, this is often her actual home, a house on a plot
of land that is all hers. Here she gardens, beautifies,
paints, writes, takes care of her family and her pets, im-
merses herself in her inner world with quiet abandon.
This is where her genuine life unfolds. Everything else
is real, of course, but not real in the same way.

Cancer could go along like this indefinitely, with the
waters of her own being flowing around her, through her,
everything perceived through the lens of her subjectivity.
In this state, she is swept along through her inner world,
like a leaf riding the currents of a river, the past more
real to her than the present. Her challenge is to place
all of this sensitivity and subjective awareness into a practical context. To do that, she must leave her shell and
enter the world.

This is where Capricorn proves to be useful. Cancer
perceives, Capricorn *constructs*. Cancer *nurtures* and
mothers, Capricorn *lays down a strategy*. Cancer's perceptions are primarily *subjective*, Capricorn's perceptions are
primarily *objective*. Cancer's inner life, despite its rich-
ness, can become a trap, a prison where she hides from
the outer world. Capricorn seeks recognition in that
outer world, then follows her strategy and plans to attain it.

In terms of spirit communication, this combination of
signs is close to ideal. Cancer senses spirits everywhere.
They hover around her while she tends to her family, her
pets, her plants. Spirits speak to her in dreams. They are
simply *there*, an intimate part of her daily life. But she
lacks the skills to use spiritual guidance in a practical way.

She balks at the very idea of putting spiritual matters into a pragmatic context. Yet, if she could do this, it would help to ground her, to make her more conscious and aware.

THE QUEST

You may be hearing the theme song for *Mission: Impossible* as you read this, but the quest for Cancer really isn't impossible; it simply requires an attitude adjustment. The quest is this: *To create a concrete strategy for your spiritual exploration and implement it in a practical way.*

This doesn't mean you have to figure out how spiritual guidance is going to pay off your credit cards. All you're doing here is altering your *approach.* Remember the children's story, *Little Engine That Could?* To get over that hill, he uses the sheer force of his will. *I think I can, I think I can . . .* He thinks he can get over that hill and see what lies on the other side. That's going to be your approach, Cancer, to use your *will* to bring about positive change in your life.

THE JOURNEY

For any trip you take, you pack what is appropriate for the area you're going to visit. The same is true for this trip.

Two absolute necessities for this exploration are a notebook and a tape recorder. The notebook provides you with an ongoing record of your experiences and also will contain your overall strategy. The recorder is primarily for those times when it isn't convenient to write. It shouldn't be used as the permanent record. A computer file is fine, too, as long as you print out what you write every few days so that you have a hard copy.

Unlike the previous three signs, you should begin this exploration on your own rather than with a partner. You work from such depth that a partner, at least in the early stages, might slow down your progress. Also, you might be tempted to nurture that person's exploration rather than your own. Remember, this journey is about *you*.

In creating your strategy, it's important to define your goals and some sort of structure within which you can conduct your exploration. Here are some guidelines that may help you do that:

- What do I hope to learn/gain through spirit communication?
- Can I direct my intuition in a practical way to facilitate this communication?
- How deep is my commitment to this exploration?
- What are my expectations about spirit communication?
- Do workshops and seminars on intuition and related topics interest me?
- Is there a specific spirit with whom I would like to communicate?
- Where might this exploration take me? What impact might it have on my daily life?
- Do I really believe this stuff is even *possible?*

Ellen, a forty-two-year-old nurse, became interested in spirit communication after the death of one of her patients, an elderly woman with whom she became quite close in the weeks under Ellen's care. In many ways, this woman reminded Ellen of her own grandmother, who had died many years before and of whom she had many fond childhood memories.

"I've always been intuitive," says Ellen. "I get feelings

about things and usually those feelings are right. One afternoon shortly after June Lumasco died, I was in the staff room on break and suddenly I smelled a cologne that Mrs. L loved. The scent was so strong I actually whipped around to see who was wearing it. But I was alone in there.

"My arms were covered in goose bumps, the back of my neck prickled. I knew she was there. I was so sure of it I even whispered her name. After a few minutes, the scent just faded away."

This experience launched Ellen's exploration of the unseen world. She signed up for a workshop on the practical use of intuition and discovered that she was particularly adept at sensing health problems in people. She began to develop this ability and, pretty soon, was able to do it with astonishing accuracy.

Through a friend, she learned of a reputable medium and attended a group gathering at which the medium did random readings. The medium claimed to see a female spirit next to Ellen and gave the spirit's initials—J. L.— and said she simply wanted to thank Ellen for caring for her in the final days of her life. The medium also said he saw other spirits around Ellen, two of whom were doctors she had known in other lives, who were here to help her develop into a medical intuitive.

Not long afterward, Ellen found a book about Jose Arigo, a humble Brazilian man who was hailed as the country's greatest psychic healer. Arigo, who had no medical knowledge and only an elementary school education, operated on thousands of people during his short lifetime. While he was in a trance, the spirit of a German physician, Dr. Fritz, supposedly worked through Arigo, often using nothing more than a rusted knife. Yet, the patients never suffered from post-op infections or from any of the other complications found in Western medicine.

Ellen's discovery of the Arigo material led to the next phase of her journey. Through contacts at her hospital, she found a physician in private practice who was willing to oversee her work as a medical intuitive. This phase of her exploration taught her how to hone her intuitive ability. During this period, she also began to communicate with her guides—first in dreams and later during brief meditation periods.

A single experience—the scent of a dead woman's perfume in an empty room—opened up an entirely new life for Ellen. But if she had not been willing to ask questions and to lay out a strategy that would allow her to explore within certain given parameters, she might have simply dismissed that scent as wishful thinking.

Before you continue reading this chapter, map out your strategy and, if possible, the structure of your search. It doesn't have to be anything complex, but it should provide the broad strokes. The broad strokes of Ellen's strategy might look like this:

- Intuitive development workshop: Sharpen intuitive skills so I can use them more effectively in my work and in my life.
- Find reputable medium for a reading: Did Mrs. L really visit me?
- Books on spirit communication: Find out how communication occurs.
- Explore medical intuition: Maybe I have a talent for it.
- Spirit communication in dreams: Suggestions for this happening, how it happens, how to tell when it happens.

The strategy is simple, but clear. Use the records section at the end of this chapter to get started. The more details you include in your record, the clearer the experience will become for you. You probably are going to resist doing it, Cancer, but it's important to see it written out. Once you embark on the exploration, the strategy and structure may change, but that's fine. It's part of the process.

Meeting Your Guides

The techniques and suggestions in this section are intended for the average Cancer. Tailor and alter them to fit *your* needs.

The Physical Body. During this exploration, some type of regular physical exercise will keep you grounded. Swimming, dancing, tai chi, or yoga usually appeal to Cancer because all involve fluid movement. But any kind of exercise will do.

James Van Praagh, in his bestseller *Talking to Heaven*, notes that diet is also an important component in spirit communication. "The purer the diet, consisting mostly of vegetarian cuisine, with very little or no refined sugars and caffeine, the better the body can channel spirit." He contends that the endocrine system—and the adrenal glands in particular—are important in spirit communication and that sugar and caffeine speed up the adrenals, putting additional stress on them. Alcohol, drugs, and red meat should be avoided because they lower the body's vibratory rate and make it more difficult to communicate with spirits.

Signs & Symbols. We live in a world of symbolism, and you, Cancer, are fluent in this language. Signs and symbols run through your dreams when you sleep, bubble up from your unconscious as you move through each day. The challenge for you is to learn how to differentiate signs and symbols that relate to your ordinary life from those that emanate from your spiritual guides.

George Anderson, writing in *Lessons from the Light,* notes that spirits "use my brain as a big toolbox, pulling out any information that I have read or seen and using it to illustrate what they want to say."

Quite often, that information is couched in signs and symbols that may not make any sense to Anderson, but which make sense to the person for whom he is reading. He relates a story that is particularly striking. During one reading for a family who had lost a daughter named Stephanie, the daughter's spirit showed him a character from an old movie. Anderson remembered the character as a 1930s black comedian named Step'n Fetchit. He asked the family if the name meant anything to them. ". . . her very surprised mother told me, 'It was her nickname!' Although it was the most bizarre nickname I have ever heard for a young girl, it showed me once again that the souls in the hereafter are resourceful when it comes to communicating information . . ."

You can expect the same kind of resourcefulness from your own guides. If your Aunt Ruthie's favorite book was *Gone With the Wind,* and that book literally falls at your feet while you're browsing in a bookstore, then you've just experienced communication.

"Some images are easy to interpret," writes John Edward in *One Last Time.* "I have been shown Mickey Mouse to indicate there was a trip to Disney World. A badge might symbolize something to do with law enforcement . . . Because errors in interpretation are the most common problem in readings, I sometimes try too hard to get it right and wind up overinterpreting. As the saying goes, sometimes a cigar is just a cigar."

This last part is important to remember. When you receive information, think of the simplest interpretation first. If that doesn't resonate, then look at the message as a symbol.

The Senses. This is one area where you won't have any problems, Cancer. Your senses are already attuned to the unseen. As you embark on your exploration, however, your inner senses may become much sharper.

Medium and author John Edward lists these psychic senses as: clairaudience (clear hearing), clairvoyance (clear seeing), clairsentience (clear sensing), clairalience (clear smelling), and clairambience (clear tasting).

Hearing an inner voice that imparts wisdom or guidance is how *clairaudience* often manifests. This voice can be heard in dreams, during periods of deep relaxation, during meditation or any other altered state. With practice, it can be heard at virtually any time of the day or night. This sense is common among mediums.

Clairvoyance is the ability to see what is happening now or what will happen in the future in your life or the life of someone else. Many psychics use this sense. Although it's related to "seeing," it isn't confined to sight. It can be experienced as "gut feelings" or mental images and impressions. Psychics tend to have strongly developed clairvoyance.

Clairsentience is the ability to sense details about a person, event, or situation through touch. One type of clairsentience is psychometry, the ability to "read" an object. The idea here is that personal items like jewelry and clothing retain the vibration of the individual who has worn them, and a psychometrist can pick up details about the individual by tuning in to that vibration. Psychics who work with police often use this method.

Clairalience and *clairambience* are less common than the first three inner senses. Clear smelling is the ability to glean details about an individual or situation through the sense of smell. An example of this would be when the scent of your grandmother's cologne suddenly permeates the air around you.

Clear tasting involves picking up details about an individual or situation through the sense of taste. Perhaps your deceased father loved key lime pie. If he's trying to communicate with you, the taste of key lime may fill your mouth.

To these senses, James Van Praagh adds "inspirational thought." He defines this as receiving "thoughts, impressions, knowledge—all without forethought." In this type of sensing, a spirit or group of spirits "melds their thoughts together and impresses the person to write a certain piece of music or paint a particular picture." In other words, the vehicle is creativity.

Jane Roberts, in *The Seth Material,* quotes Seth about what he terms the Inner Senses: ". . . they reveal to us our independence from physical matter, and let us recognize our unique, individual multidimensional identity. Properly utilized, they also show us the miracle of physical existence and our place in it." According to Seth, there are nine of these Inner Senses. It isn't enough to list them; the explanations are necessary. If you're interested, read Chapter 19 of *The Seth Material.*

You're likely to experience all of these psychic senses during your exploration. Through practice, you'll find which senses work the best for you. If you're in a healing profession, you may find, as Ellen did, that your inner senses expand around the health area. Or you may find that your inner senses take you in new but allied directions. Vivian, a psychiatric nurse, is especially attuned to animals—how and where they hurt, what they need, what they want. In other words, with very little effort, she could become an accomplished animal communicator.

The most important detail to remember about these inner senses is that you don't have to move in a direction that you don't want to go. *You* are in charge.

Stay Grounded. One of the best means you have of staying grounded is a regular physical exercise routine. It should be something you enjoy. Don't sign up at the gym just because you feel you *should;* do it because you want to. Set goals that keep you interested. If, for instance, you decide that you're going to swim four times a week, then each week extend the distance—two more laps, a dozen more laps, a half mile.

You can also ground yourself with deep breathing, something you can do anywhere, any time. If, at any point in your exploration, you begin to feel panicky, stop what you're doing and place your right hand just under your breastbone. Inhale and feel the air moving deeply into your lungs. As you exhale, feel it against the palm of your hand. Do this for five inhalations and exhalations, then pinch your right nostril shut, breathe in through the left nostril, hold to the count of ten, and exhale through the right nostril. Repeat this several times and switch nostrils.

This is a yoga breathing exercise that should make you feel centered and grounded.

Another method for staying grounded is to have a particular area—a room, a place outdoors—where you do your spiritual work. If it's inside the house, surround yourself with items that remind you of the here and now, of physical existence. These items can be anything from posters and photographs to rocks and crystals. Use colors in your work area that are tranquil, conducive to meditative work. You may want to have a small fountain of some kind in this area; the sound of running water is soothing and conducive to this kind of work.

Trust. You shouldn't have any problem in this area, either. You probably have lived with feelings and hunches most of your life and know by now to trust and act upon any impressions you receive. But just in case you've mislaid your trust, give yourself a suggestion as you're falling asleep and before you attempt spirit communication that your intuitive impressions will be accurate and clear.

The Flow. Again, this is your domain, Cancer. As a water sign, you don't have a problem with the concept of "flow"—nonresistance to whatever is happening. For you, though, the challenge is to continue this nonresistance even when you're attempting to make spiritual guidance practical.

Ellen, the Cancer nurse mentioned earlier, was spooked by her experience in the staff room. But her curiosity to explore what had happened and what it really meant was greater than her resistance to stepping out of her safety zone to take a workshop. Remember, it's an adventure and it's intended to stretch your intuitive muscles.

Protection. A prayer, a mantra, a visualization—any one of these techniques works to protect you against lower energies during spiritual communication. Char Margolis, author of *Questions from Earth, Answers from*

Heaven, wrote her own prayer for protection. John Edward meditates before he begins to work. Since he's a Catholic, he also says the rosary.

You may want to conjure a memory of a time or an event in which you felt protected and safe. You have such an extraordinary memory that it shouldn't be a problem to "pull" the emotions of that time around yourself and use those emotions as your protection.

THE MAP

You land in Los Angeles, a city you've never visited, and pick up a rental car at the airport. As you leave the lot, you open the glove compartment, looking for a map. There isn't one. In fact, you can't find a map anywhere in the car. Do you just keep on driving or do you return to the rental agency?

The obvious thing to do is to return for a map. Without one, the Los Angeles freeways are an exercise in futility. In much the same way, you also need a map for your exploration of spirit communication. For you, Cancer, that map consists of whatever area you select to explore, then your strategy for going about it. Use the spaces in the table below to get started.

Areas to Explore	How to Go About It
1._____	_____
2._____	_____
3._____	_____
4._____	_____
5._____	_____

THE GRAIL

Your grail, Cancer, is: *Using what you learn in this exploration in a practical way that enriches your life.*

YOUR RECORDS

Date: _____

Time: _____

Weather: _____

Other factors: _____

_____

Your experience: _____

_____

_____

_____

_____

_____

_____

_____

_____

_____

9. Leo the Lion ♌

Death is the ornament of life.

—JOSEPH CAMPBELL

July 23–August 22
Fixed Fire
Ruled by the Sun

THE SYMBOL

I *am king,* the lion roars, *and don't any of you ever forget it!* Beneath that roar and bravado beats the heart of a gentle, loving kitten.

Welcome to the world of Leo, a dichotomy even to himself. He roars, he purrs, he defends his turf, and through it all, the exuberance of his personality never wanes, never dims. He's the consummate performer. Like the Sun that rules the sign, the brilliance of his personality is perpetual, infinite. As a performer, though, he needs applause and craves appreciation. *Notice me,* a part of him pleads. *Tell me how grand I am.*

And that's fine; we all need to be appreciated. But it's fine only as long as it doesn't run to extremes.

Leo is passionate, consumed with the glorious intensity of his emotions. When he loves, he does so completely, with his entire being. But first, the loved one must prove herself. She must agree wholeheartedly with everything Leo says—with his opinions, his beliefs, his interests. To differ sends a message to Leo that love has conditions, even if the message isn't intended that way. The source of this need for proof lies in a fundamental insecurity of the sign.

Where Cancer often clings to the past and her memories of the past, Leo is firmly rooted in the present. *Now* is what matters to Leo, *today* not yesterday. This focus on the present can lead to a certain extravagance. Leo walks into a store and sees something he wants but can't afford. *Got to have it now,* he thinks, and plunks down his credit card. Part of his challenge in this regard is to express himself creatively in a way that satisfies him in the moment but which doesn't put him at risk in the future.

Leo is honest. No reason to ever question his integrity. But when he feels insecure or unappreciated or he's trying to impress someone, he can be a braggart. It's as if he has to make himself sound smarter or more talented, richer or more experienced than who he is with, so the other person will appreciate the full magnitude of his personality. When this boastfulness becomes pride, it only turns other people off.

STRENGTH IN OPPOSITES: LEO/AQUARIUS POLARITY

Most of the time, Leo's emphasis is on himself. *His* creativity, *his* joy and exuberance, *his* triumphs and loves. There's nothing inherently wrong with this because Leo's heart is big enough to accommodate the creativity, joy, and challenges of the people he loves. He even extends this generosity to strangers in need. The problems arise at the ego and pride end of things, when Leo's need for appreciation and applause descends into *me me me* stripped of the compensating generosity.

So how does Aquarius help? Where Leo is concerned about himself, Aquarius is concerned about the group, the tribe, humanity. Leo *expresses,* Aquarius *reforms.* Leo acts and then thinks about it; Aquarius thinks and then acts. Leo is *dramatic* and *bold* in his actions, Aquarius is *eccentric* in his beliefs and interests. Leo is *present-oriented,* Aquarius is *future-oriented.* Leo demands *freedom in his creative expression,* Aquarius demands *freedom from the status quo.*

In terms of spirit communication, Leo probably knows more than he's telling about his contact with the deceased. He may be keeping it to himself because he's afraid of ridicule. But then something happens—a life event of some kind, a marriage or birth or divorce, the loss of a job, a death in the family. Then suddenly Leo's life is turned roughly in another direction. *Ridicule?* he asks. *So what?* And suddenly he doesn't hold back any longer. He talks about what he knows, senses, and feels concerning spirits and spiritual communication. He becomes more like an Aquarian.

Psychologist Carl Jung, mystic in the mist, is an ideal example of the Leo/Aquarius polarity. Despite his interest in psychic phenomena, Jung didn't share that interest until he split with Sigmund Freud. A part of him feared ridicule from the man he admired. But once their split occurred, Freud's opinion about his interests no longer mattered to him.

In his autobiography, *Memories, Dreams and Reflections,* Jung relates a curious story about a "haunting" that he and his family experienced in 1916. It began, Jung said, with "a restlessness" whose meaning eluded him. "There was an ominous atmosphere all around me. I had the strange feeling that the air was filled with ghostly entities. Then it was as if my house began to be haunted."

His oldest daughter saw "a white figure pass through a room." His second daughter told the family that the blanket on her bed had been snatched away in the middle of the night—not once, but twice. And his young son had a nightmare, which he drew for Jung in great detail the next day. The same day, the doorbell rang frantically. Jung was sitting close to the door and actually saw the bell moving. But no one was at the door. "The atmosphere was thick . . . The whole house was filled as if there were a crowd present, crammed full of spirits," he wrote. "They were packed deep right up to the door, and the air was so thick it was scarcely possible to breathe . . ."

Over the course of three nights, he wrote the *Septem Sermones* ("The Seven Sermons of the Dead"), which was later privately printed and is included in the appendix of his autobiography. It's a strange piece of writing, with awkward syntax. Jung allegedly regretted writing it, yet the sermons hold clues about ideas that Jung later included in his scientific writings. The sermons have the feel of channeled material. Reading them, you wonder if perhaps the spirits crammed in that room were responsible.

Jung connected the experience with his emotional state at the time, ". . . which was favorable to parapsychological phenomena." When confronted with an experience like this, he notes that the intellect would like to "write the whole thing off as a violation of the rules. *But what a dreary world it would be if the rules were not violated sometimes!"*

This late statement is pure Aquarius. Jung the Leo had made an astrological leap. By the end of his life, he hadn't just broken the rules sometimes; he had broken many of psychology's most dearly held tenets, and a good number of them had come from Freud.

Even his conclusions about life after death are more Aquarius than Leo, more intellect than heart. "It seems probable to me that in the hereafter . . . there exist certain limitations, but that the souls of the dead only gradually find out where the limits of the liberated state lie." But in the next breath, he added, "We lack concrete proof that anything of us is preserved for eternity. At most we can say that there is some probability that something of our psyche continues beyond physical death."

Let the visionary part of you, Leo, lead the way in this exploration.

THE QUEST

Be who you are and proud of it. Live genuinely.

That last statement may annoy you. Even as you read it, you'll be thinking that you already live genuinely. Yes, in some respects you do. But at the heart of it, Leo is a performer, and how genuine are performers? They zip themselves in the skins of the characters they are portraying. They become the speech they are giving, the book they are writing, the mythology they are creating. They become their performance.

This doesn't mean you should stop performing, merely that you should be aware of how and where you stir up melodrama in your life. Learn to recognize it when it's happening, cut it loose then and there. Melodrama, after all, isn't the same thing as performance.

What's the difference between the two? Here's one example. Your significant other doesn't like your closest friend and finally voices her opinion. You take umbrage. The two of you argue about your friend. You just can't believe she doesn't like this guy, that she can't stand him, in fact. Deep down your anger stems from your belief that if your significant other doesn't like your closest friend, then what she's really saying is that she doesn't like *you*. The two aren't actually related, but in your mind they are and that's that.

Melodrama. These types of scenes are repeated in your life time and again, Leo, and Aquarius just won't stand for it. Aquarius just rolls his eyes and murmurs, "Oh, c'mon. Enough already."

Melodrama combined with communication won't make the exploration easy. If you seize on every image, every impression, every sign and signal as communication from someone in the afterlife, as origination from the afterlife, you risk confusion or, worse, lack of grounding and credibility. But if you can enter the exploration as an adventure, your senses alert, your logic and reason balanced with your imagination, then you will take to this terrain like a duck to water.

THE JOURNEY

Your packing list. There are two prerequisites for this trip: a journal and a tape recorder. Every sign gets this suggestion. It's part of the package for spirit communication, rather like a round-trip airfare when you travel on an oceangoing luxury liner. Even though the past holds nothing on you, you respect records as a frame of reference.

So this will be a record of your experiences with spirit communication. Maybe it will bolster your confidence about your innate abilities. Maybe you won't even look through it when all is said and done. But the mere act of recording what you feel as you feel it and detailing your experiences will be beneficial.

The other things you bring along on this journey are less tangible: an open mind and an eye on the journey itself, not on the results. You usually have an open mind. But as a fixed sign, you may have rigid beliefs or opinions about what's possible, which can be a hindrance. The last part should be easy for you because you usually live so centered in the moment.

If possible, start this exploration with a partner who shares your interests in this area. This type of sharing deepens each person's insight and understanding of spirit communication. But in working with a partner, remember that you are equals in every way. The partnership can't be used as a stage for performances for either of you.

You and your partner should agree on the basics: how often you're going to meet, what techniques you're going to use, your broad goals, a time frame (if either of you feels that you need one), and how you can work alone to further your common goals. In other words, if one of you is particularly good at experiencing communication through dreams, that person can give the other person tips that would help his or her dream communication and recall. It's a process of give-and-take.

When you're preparing for a trip, you usually familiarize yourself with the area before you go there. You read travel books, find the appropriate sites on the Internet, talk to other people, and gradually form a clear sense of the place and what you would like to see. It's a good idea to do the same thing with your exploration of spirit communication, even if you already have some familiarity with the territory. Glance through the book list in Appendix 2 and select two or three to read. Attend a workshop. Get a reading with a medium. Search for resources in your area.

MEETING YOUR GUIDES

This section is intended for the average Leo. Tailor it to fit *your* needs.

The Physical Body. Leo rules the heart and the fourth chakra. According to medical intuitive Carolyn Myss, the mental and emotional issues associated with this chakra are: "love and hatred, resentment and bitterness, grief and anger, self-centeredness, loneliness and commitment, forgiveness and compassion, hope and trust." All of this basically boils down to a single broad issue: love. How do we love? How do we receive love? How do we express love?

In undertaking this kind of exploration, your heart and the fourth chakra become focal points. If your heart is in good physical shape, then chances are the rest of you probably is, too. When you feel good, your body is a clearer channel for spiritual energy. Jogging, jumping on a trampoline, biking, even brisk walking are all excellent aerobic exercises. Also, certain types of exercise like yoga and tai chi are conducive to altered states of consciousness that make spirit communication easier.

Signs & Symbols. Think, for a moment, about the symbolism that runs through your dreams. The neglected basement of a dream house may represent some part of your unconscious that you have disowned or ignored. A newborn kitten may represent a new chapter in your life. Even if you aren't especially proficient at dream recall, some symbols surface with you when you wake. In much the same way, spirit communication often comes through in the symbolic language of the unconscious.

Patrick, a twenty-three-year-old graduate student, was cleaning out his grandparents' basement one afternoon shortly after his grandfather had passed away. The task depressed him. There was so much *stuff,* some thirty-plus years' worth, and it seemed that everything he touched had a memory attached to it. He was thinking about the good times he and his grandfather used to have fishing during the summer at a lake where his grandparents had a cottage. A few minutes later, he opened a carton of books and there, on top, was a poster he had made for his grandfather when he was a kid. It showed a boy and a man fishing and under it were the words *Remember the good times.*

A skeptic would write this off to coincidence. But Patrick realized his grandfather had just communicated with him.

Sometimes, the signs involve electricity, as in Jung's case with the doorbell and the room "crammed full of spirits." Lights may flicker, an appliance suddenly goes on the fritz, a TV comes on by itself, and the first words you hear relate to a dead relative you've been thinking about.

James Van Praagh, writing in *Talking to Heaven,* emphasizes the importance of cooperation between you and the spirit guides you're trying to contact. "You have to let them know *how* you want them to communicate. Tell them to impress you in a certain way. For instance, if you want to know if it is a female or male energy coming through, ask them to impress you with their gender."

In other words, let your needs be known. Van Praagh says he has established a system of communication with his guides and spirits that lets him know which side of the family a particular spirit comes from. For the father's side of the family, Van Praagh invites the spirit to stand on the left side of the individual. For the mother's side of the family, the spirit is to stand on the right side of the person. If the spirit is a child, he asks that it stand in front of the individual. A grandparent is asked to stand behind the person. "In this way, there is a clear system for the spirit to use."

If you don't see spirits, but receive impressions or mental images and symbols, then ask the spirits to be clear about the impressions and symbols, and then look for the simplest interpretation first. If that doesn't resonate, then use a combination of your reason and your intuition to decipher the symbol.

The Senses. Our five senses are exquisitely designed for physical existence. Every second of every hour, these senses convey information that allow us to navigate through our daily lives. In much the same way, our inner senses convey information about the unseen world.

Medium and author John Edward lists these inner senses as: clairaudience (clear hearing), clairvoyance (clear seeing), clairsentience (clear sensing), clairalience (clear smelling), and clairambience (clear tasting).

Hearing an inner voice that imparts wisdom or guidance is how *clairaudience* often manifests. This voice can be heard in dreams, during periods of deep relaxation, during meditation or any other altered state. With practice, it can be heard at virtually any time of the day or night. This sense is common among mediums.

Clairvoyance is the ability to see what is happening now or what will happen in the future in your life or the life of someone else. Many psychics use this sense. Although it's related to "seeing," it isn't confined to sight. It can be experienced as "gut feelings" or mental images and impressions. Psychics tend to have strongly developed clairvoyance.

Clairsentience is the ability to sense details about a person, event, or situation through touch. One type of clairsentience is psychometry, the ability to "read" an object. The idea here is that personal items like jewelry and clothing retain the vibration of the individual who has worn them, and a psychometrist can pick up details about the individual by tuning in to that vibration. Psychics who work with police often use this method.

Clairalience and *clairambience* are less common than the first three inner senses. Clear smelling is the ability to glean details about an individual or situation through the sense of smell. An example of this would be when the scent of your grandmother's cologne suddenly permeates the air around you.

Clear tasting involves picking up details about an individual or situation through the sense of taste. Perhaps your deceased father loved key lime pie. If he's trying to communicate with you, the taste of key lime may fill your mouth.

To these senses, James Van Praagh adds "inspirational thought." He defines this as receiving "thoughts, impressions, knowledge—all without forethought." In this type of sensing, a spirit or group of spirits "melds their thoughts together and impresses the person to write a certain piece of music or paint a particular picture." In other words, the vehicle is creativity.

Anything that involves creative expression should come easily to you. You might try automatic writing, another form of channeling. Spirits use your hand instead of your vocal chords to convey information. If you're artistically inclined, you might try giving yourself suggestions that your guides will communicate with you through your art.

We all have inner senses, and the best way to find which sense works best for you is through trial and error.

Jane Roberts, in *The Seth Material,* quotes Seth about what he terms the Inner Senses: ". . . they reveal to us our independence from physical matter, and let us recognize our unique, individual multidimensional identity. Properly utilized, they also show us the miracle of physical existence and our place in it." According to Seth, there are nine of these Inner Senses. It isn't enough to list them; the explanations are necessary. If you're interested, read Chapter 19 of *The Seth Material.*

Stay Grounded. Mediums and psychics have different ways of grounding themselves. Again, with practice, you'll find the best way for you to ground yourself. Here are some suggestions:

- Stay physically fit.
- Practice deep breathing before you attempt spirit communication.
- Use colors in your work area that remind you of the earth, physical reality, the here and now.
- Weather permitting, go outside barefoot and rub the soles of your feet against the ground. This establishes a connection with the earth.
- Have live plants in your work area.
- Let fresh air circulate through your work area.
- Have good lighting in your work area. Natural light is best.

You really shouldn't have too much trouble staying grounded because you're such a present-oriented person. The main thing you have to guard against, Leo, is pageantry—performing when there's no need to do so.

Trust. Trusting the impressions you receive won't be difficult. Without some detached Aquarius energy, though, you can easily go overboard and mistakenly believe that every impression you receive is a communication from a spirit. Be discerning. Weigh each impression against your intuition. Does the impression resonate? Does it *feel* correct?

The Flow. For you, as a fire sign, "flow" differs from "flow" for a water sign. For you and your fire sign brothers, flow is action, doing, expressing—and not resisting whatever is happening. Patrick, the young man mentioned earlier in this chapter, could have thrown up all kinds of emotional barricades and blocks concerning his experience with the poster he found in his grandparents' basement. Instead, he remained open to the experience. He *didn't resist* it.

Protection. Prayer, visualization, smudging—everyone has a different method for protection. The idea here is that spirits, like people, exist on different levels. When you're attempting spirit communication, you want to be sure you don't attract negative or lower energy.

Char Margolis, in her book *Questions from Earth, Answers from Heaven,* believes protection is necessary on three different levels: from lower energy or negative spirits; from our own negative thoughts; and from psychic debris—"the negative energy that others can release and then leave behind."

Medium John Edward, a Catholic, says a rosary before he works. Psychic intuitive Millie Gemondo often says the ninety-first psalm. Whatever you choose for your protection, Leo, it will probably be grand, bold, and dramatic. The bigger the better!

THE MAP

For you, Leo, the map for your journey is actually your journal. It not only tells you where you have been, but also points out the direction in which you're headed. Here, you also record any detours you take, landmarks you see, places you would like to revisit.

When author and researcher Robert Monroe began to experience spontaneous out-of-body travel, he was terrified that he was going crazy. Yet, he kept meticulous records. Throughout his forty years of research, as he mapped inner states of consciousness and then levels of the afterlife, these records became a valuable resource. And so will your records.

You may want to begin your records with a list of areas you would like to explore that relate to spirit communication and how you can best conduct your exploration of those areas. Let's say you would like to explore your inner senses. To do that, you might buy books on the subject and sign up for workshops or seminars on developing your intuition or working with your dreams. Maybe you would like to attend the Monroe Institute and learn how to do what Monroe did.

In the table below, list five areas you would like to explore and how you might undertake that exploration. Then use the record sheet that follows to get started.

Areas to Explore   How to Go About It

1. _____   _____
2. _____   _____
3. _____   _____
4. _____   _____
5. _____   _____

THE GRAIL

Simply put, Leo, your grail is: *The integration of your spiritual exploration into your creative expression.*

YOUR RECORDS

Date: _____

Time: _____

Weather: _____

Other factors: _____
_____

Your experience: _____
_____
_____
_____
_____
_____
_____
_____
_____
_____
_____

10. Virgo the Virgin ♍

Imagination opened up the entire nonphysical world to
my perception.

—BRUCE MOEN

August 23–September 22
Mutable Earth
Ruled by Mercury

THE SYMBOL

Imagine an endless beach: sand as far as the eye can
see, a virgin beach, struck with blinding sunlight. But
when Virgo looks at this beach, she immediately hones
in on details no one else can see: the way the beach
sparkles more to the east than to the west, a vague out-
line way off in the distance that might be a tree—or a
person. And there, off to her left, she spots footprints
that no one else has noticed, footprints she has spotted
because they spoil the *perfection* of all that brilliance.

Mercury rules both Virgo and Gemini, so the two signs
share a certain restlessness, a need to know, and an intellect as a sharp as razor. But Mercury finds a much different expression in the virgin. Gone is the maddening
Gemini duality, the constant probing to connect one fact
with another, the flitting about. With Virgo, there's anal-

ysis and attention to detail, a hunger for perfection, and a realism that is, at times, as stark as a minimalist painting.

Virgo is here to *discern*. Give her a job, and she'll do it better than anyone else. It isn't because she's necessarily smarter or faster or better trained for the job—although she may be all three of those things. It's simply that no other sign has such a grasp for details. To her, the perfection of anything lies in how well the details fit together. This is one of the reasons Virgos make good editors. They see what the writer misses.

The "service" part of Virgo isn't mere kindness. It's more of a byproduct of Virgo's need to do something for someone else because her skills allow her to do it. Say your novel has fallen apart. Your plot is unraveling, your characters are dying off, you're in a state of extreme panic. Who do you call? Your mother? Your editor? Not likely. You call your Virgo friend, the writer, who talks it out with you several hours long distance.

As a mutable earth sign, Virgo's vitality is usually good. But it can be undermined when her quest for perfection collapses into a picky pettiness that is aimed as often at herself as it is at other people. *I can't do it right . . . he's extravagant . . . she's careless . . .* When Virgo's shadow sneaks up on her like this, she begins to judge herself by everyone else's standards and to judge everyone else by impossible standards. She becomes her own worst enemy. Then she gets lost in details and can't see the forest for the trees. She loses sight of who she is. She can no longer envision the ideal.

STRENGTH IN OPPOSITES:
VIRGO/PISCES POLARITY

When Virgo can no longer envision her ideal, she's lost. She's like the mythological Diogenes, wandering in the dark with her candle, seeking the truth or redemption or her ideals. She may not consciously think about ideals, may not even be aware that her ideals are intrinsic to who she is. But when she can't envision the ideal—the utter perfection of something—she feels the lack deeply.

This may happen when details simply overwhelm her. It's like a child working on a puzzle with a thousand pieces. Find the corners, connect the colors, finish the dolphin's snout, put this piece with that piece . . . And suddenly none of it makes sense anymore. There are *so* many pieces, none of them fitting together, and the child shoves the whole thing away and that's that.

But Virgo doesn't trash her puzzles. She keeps at them with the same earthy persistence that characterizes her Taurus earth cousin. Sometimes she starts over or takes detours or rants and raves and criticizes herself *for not getting it,* but she rarely surrenders.

This is precisely when Pisces can help her. Two signs that are opposite each other form an axis of energy. The energy of one sign is always available to the other sign. Pisces knows that surrender is sometimes necessary. Not surrender in the sense of giving up, but surrender to greater forces, a greater power—surrender to the collective sea of the unconscious. Sounds vague? It really isn't. Virgo *discerns,* Pisces *dreams.* Virgo sees the trees, Pisces sees the forest. Virgo *analyzes,* Pisces *absorbs.* Virgo is left brain, Pisces is right brain. Virgo is fully immersed in the physical world, Pisces straddles worlds. Virgo *critiques,* Pisces *imagines.*

Medium James Van Praagh is a Virgo. Take a look at his chart in the Start Charts of the Appendices. Virgo is on the cusp of his 9th house at seven degrees and thirty-two minutes. The 9th house represents, among other things, the higher mind, philosophy and religion, and publishing. Because his Sun lies at zero degrees and eleven minutes of Virgo, it falls into the 8th house of shared resources and metaphysics. Pisces, the polarity of Virgo, lies on the cusp of his 3rd house of communication.

So, based just on the polarity, we know that Van Praagh must share his knowledge and resources (Sun in the 8th house) through some form of communication (3rd house). It isn't surprising that with Pisces on the 3rd house cusp, the way he communicates is through mediumship.

In astrological terms, Van Praagh certainly seems to be living out the potential of his birth chart. In *Talking to Heaven,* he discusses some of his early experiences with psychic phenomena—seeing spirits, *knowing things* before they happened. In fact, his first clairvoyant experience was seeing "the illumined hand of God," certainly an experience that fits into the 8th and 9th houses.

He attended Catholic schools, largely because his mother was a staunch Irish Catholic. He even attended the seminary, intending to become a priest, an idea that he admits was his mother's, not his. While he was in the seminary (9th house) he had an experience on a Good Friday when he realized that "God is unlimited." He understood that he "had to take this sense of God with me. From that day on, I never questioned the existence of God. I just had to look in my own heart to see God." After that experience, Van Praagh didn't feel obligated to finish the seminary. This seemed to be a clear demarcation between his experiences of the 9th house—and the 8th house, where he clearly lives today.

Van Praagh wanted to be a writer. During a stint in Hollywood that amounted to little more than stapling papers, he met a woman who proved to be instrumental to his profession as a medium today. She suggested that he accompany her to a reading with a medium. The medium told Van Praagh that he had natural ability for spirit communication and would one day be doing what he was doing.

Being a Virgo, Van Praagh attended to details. He read over a hundred books on mediums, mediumship, and psychic ability, including books written fifty or more years ago. "I spoke to as many psychics, mediums, and spiritual teachers as I could find." He designed experiments to test and expand his ability, and within a year was doing readings.

As spirits began to speak up and to materialize, Van Praagh developed a system for communicating with them, all very detailed and practical, true Virgo qualities. If he is communicating with a father or someone from that side of the family, he asks the spirit to stand on the left side of the person for whom he is speaking. The right is for spirits from the mother's side of the family; child spirits are supposed to stand in front, and grandparents in the back of the individual. His work is a service (Virgo) that stems from a Piscean source (speaking for the dead)—and the blend of the two is a practical system that works for him.

"Discipline," he writes, "plays a very intricate part in developing any spiritual gifts or spiritual communication." Discipline is Virgo territory. But to negotiate this exploration, you need to dive deeply into the mystical realms of Pisces.

THE QUEST

To grasp the deeper truths of your exploration by using your imagination and innate creativity: That's the heart of your quest into spiritual communication, Virgo.

You can do this fairly easily as long as you don't get mired in details. By being aware of the pitfalls and keeping your eye on the deeper truths right from the onset, you're less likely to get stuck in this exploration. Your imagination is one of your best resources in this regard. If you can *imagine* it, then you can experience it.

You'll know when you're stuck. You'll feel irritable, especially critical toward yourself and others, and it will seem that everything you do is slightly off. You'll be fussier about details, more nitpicky. You may drive yourself and everyone around half-crazy when you're in this mode. But as soon as you begin to look for the deeper truths, the bigger picture, you'll feel a palpable relief, almost as if some unbearable weight has fallen away from you.

To clarify your quest, think of a time when you had a sudden insight into an event, situation, or relationship. Think of that *aha!* moment when you understood the larger ramifications, when you *got* it. If you can keep that moment in mind, if you can conjure the emotions you felt in that moment, you won't lose your way.

THE JOURNEY

Before we take a vacation, we usually have some idea of what we want to take with us. There are the obvious things—certain kinds of clothes and shoes, shampoos, soaps, and other personal items, books, a laptop, an address book, maps and tour guides. On this trip, the primary items are a notebook and/or tape recorder.

The notebook is to be a record for your experiences with spirit communication, and should appeal to the part of you that is precise and orderly. The tape recorder is a backup for when you need to get down a thought and you are not in a situation that allows you to write—while driving, for instance.

Every sign so far, except for Cancer, is encouraged to start this exploration with a partner, if possible. A partner who shares your interests and is committed to this exploration can provide additional insight into your experiences, and vice versa. However, this isn't a prerequisite. If you prefer to undertake this exploration on your own, then do so. The point is that you should feel comfortable and excited about what you're doing.

Even if you already have knowledge of spirit communication or have had some experiences, you—like Gemini—benefit from researching the area. Glance through the suggested reading list in Appendix 2 and select a couple of books to read. Attend a workshop. Get a reading with a psychic or a medium. If you don't know who to go to, check out the resources in Appendix 2. Find Internet areas about mediumship and spirit communication. If you're honest about what you're doing and exploring, you're more likely to attract other people who have similar interests.

Thanks in large part to Neptune's transit through Aquarius, which began in late November 1998 and will end in early February 2012, there's an openness now about death, the afterlife, spirit communication, and everything else that astrologers refer to as "8th house and 12th house issues."

Thirty years ago, people who dabbled in spirit communication were considered a bit weird, eccentric, on the fringes. Attitudes have changed. Mediums and psychics have gone mainstream. They have their own TV shows, are regular guests on talk shows, and write bestselling books. So how can your exploration be out of step with the norm?

As you undertake your journey, Virgo, your capacity for delving into this area is impacted in important ways by the sign and house placement of your natal Neptune. So be sure to read Chapter 18 when you finish this chapter on your Sun sign.

MEETING YOUR GUIDES

The techniques and suggestions provided in this section are intended for the average Virgo. With practice, you'll modify and change these techniques to fit your own needs.

The Physical Body. What type of physical exercise do you enjoy? Do you play tennis? Are you a runner? Do you take an aerobics class? Do you dance regularly? Whatever it is, try to do it three or four times a week while you're involved in this exploration. Aside from the obvious health benefits, regular physical exercise of some kind is an ideal outlet for your nervous energy and also will provide grounding.

The sign of Virgo rules, among other things, the stomach. When you become upset or emotionally disturbed, it often hits you in the stomach first. So during your exploration, pay attention to what you eat, how often you eat, and how you feel when you eat. You may find that your diet changes during your exploration, that certain types of foods no longer agree with you. If so, make note of it in your journal.

Some mediums advocate a diet rich in fresh foods, as close to vegetarian as possible. Van Praagh, in particular, recommends little or no refined sugar, caffeine, or red meat. The latter, he says, slows down the body's vibratory system and makes spirit communication more difficult. Sugar and caffeine stress the adrenal glands, which are instrumental in spirit communication.

Include anything in your journal that relates to your physical body. After all, your exploration of spiritual communication isn't just a spiritual adventure. Because you are a physical being, this spiritual exploration will impact other areas of your life.

Signs & Symbols. We live in a world of symbols. If you ever doubt it, just get in your car and take a drive. Red octagonal signs mean stop, green lights mean go, and so on. Symbols aren't limited to road signs, of course. We have symbols for stocks, money, even for emotions. And our dreams are filled with symbols.

Quite often, though, symbols that hold personal meaning bubble up from our waking lives. Nancy, a Virgo, a writer, and a student of the I Ching, realized that the number eleven played a major role in the last year of her father's life. He was in a nursing home for eleven months and eleven days and died at eleven minutes past the eleventh hour. She knew the elevens were significant somehow, but the meaning eluded her until she read hexagram 11 of the I Ching. The name of the hexagram is "Peace." She understood that her father died "in peace."

Signs and symbols come in all shapes and sizes. "Sometimes when I'm doing a reading, an image pops into my head that makes absolutely no sense to me," says psychic Millie Gemondo. "I don't try to interpret it. I simply describe the image to the person for whom I'm reading, and usually the person immediately understands what it means."

When you're the one who receives the sign or symbol, however, and you don't understand what it means, you may have to mull it over awhile before you grasp the significance. Or you may have to wait for something to unfold in your life before the symbols becomes clear. Include it in your journal, date it, and add details concerning how you received the symbol. Did it come to you in a dream? Through something someone said? In a book? As a mental image? Were you meditating? Exercising? Driving?

Van Praagh, writing in *Talking to Heaven*, emphasizes the importance of cooperation between you and the spirit guides you're trying to contact. "You have to let them know *how* you want them to communicate. Tell them to impress you in a certain way. For instance, if you want to know if it is a female or male energy coming through, ask them to impress you with their gender."

Spirits aren't omniscient. If a spirit or guide presents you with a symbol you don't understand, ask for clarification. If you receive a sign or symbol in a dream, then request a dream that will clarify the symbol. *Ask for help.* The results may surprise you.

The Senses. Our five senses equip us for life in the physical world. Every moment of every hour, they convey information to use that help us to survive. In much the same way, our inner senses convey information about the inner landscapes of our psyches. They are the source of our psychic experiences.

Medium and author John Edward lists these inner senses as: clairaudience (clear hearing), clairvoyance (clear seeing), clairsentience (clear sensing), clairalience (clear smelling), and clairambience (clear tasting).

With *clairaudience,* you hear an inner voice that imparts wisdom or guidance. This voice can be heard in dreams, during periods of deep relaxation, during meditation or any other altered state. With practice, it can be heard at virtually any time of the day or night. This sense is common among mediums.

Clairvoyance is the ability to see what is happening now or what will happen in the future in your life or the life of someone else. Many psychics use this sense. Although it's related to "seeing," it isn't confined to sight. It can be experienced as "gut feelings" or mental images and impressions. Psychics tend to have strongly developed clairvoyance.

Clairsentience is the ability to sense details about a person, event, or situation through touch. One type of clairsentience is psychometry, the ability to "read" an object. Items like jewelry and clothing retain the vibration of the individual who has worn them, and a psychometrist can pick up details about the individual by tuning in to that vibration. Psychics who work with police often use this method.

Clairalience and *clairambience* are less common than the first three inner senses. Clear smelling is the ability to glean details about an individual or situation through the sense of smell. If you suddenly catch a whiff of your dead grandfather's pipe tobacco, and there's no apparent source for that smoke, then you may be experiencing a communication from him.

Clear tasting involves picking up details about an individual or situation through the sense of taste. Perhaps your deceased father loved key lime pie. If he's trying to communicate with you, the taste of key lime may fill your mouth.

To these senses, James Van Praagh adds "inspirational thought." He defines this as receiving "thoughts, impressions, knowledge—all without forethought." In this type of sensing, a spirit or group of spirits "melds their thoughts together and impresses the person to write a certain piece of music or paint a particular picture." In other words, the vehicle is creativity.

As a mutable earth sign, you may find that, like your mutable air cousin, Gemini, your sense of clairvoyance is well-developed. Or, like cousin earth sign, Taurus, you can pick up information through clairsentience and psychometry. There are many excellent books available on developing intuition. You'll find some suggestions in Appendix 2. Read them, try the experiments and exercises, and discover which of the inner senses are strongest for you.

Stay Grounded. With practice, you'll find the method that keeps you the most grounded while you're on this exploration. Maybe you'll meditate for a few minutes before you attempt communicating with your guides. Maybe you'll play eighteen holes of golf. Use whatever connects you most deeply to the here and now. Here are some suggestions:

- Stay physically fit.
- Practice deep breathing before you attempt communicating with your guides.
- Keep live plants in your work area.
- Use colors in your work area that remind you of the earth, physical reality, the here and now.

- Set up an area that is used specifically for spirit communication. Here, you can place objects that hold personal meaning or which help you focus—stones, photos, candles, incense, an aromatic oil burner— whatever suits you. Some people call this place an altar, but if that word bothers you, use some other word. The name you give the place isn't as important as the intent you bring to that area.
- Set aside a particular time to attempt communication.
- Do some yoga stretches or tai chi movements before attempting to contact your guides.
- Visualize your communication happening effortlessly, easily, smoothly.

Trust. When you receive impressions, Virgo, don't analyze them and pick them apart as you receive them. Don't question what you're getting. Trust that the impressions are genuine. Just allow them to flow until they dry up on their own. Jot them in your notebook or record the experience while it's still fresh. Then you can analyze them all you want.

In the beginning, it's especially important not to block your impressions. All this does is signal your intuition to shut up and disappear. Then next time you try to communicate with your guides, it'll be that much more difficult. Your *intent* is vital to your success in contacting your guides, so if you're sending out crossed signals, then all you'll get is confusion.

The Flow. We refer to "being in the flow," or "going with the flow." But what does it really mean? For our purposes, it refers to nonresistance. When you're "in the flow," Virgo, you're allowing yourself to move *with* an experience rather than against it. But if you're successful at *trust*, then entering the flow of the experience shouldn't be a problem.

Protection. Like trust and the flow, protection is an individual thing. But many mediums and psychics use some type of protective ritual before they attempt to contact their guides. Some use prayer, some visualize a white cocoon of light around themselves, some simply request that they attract only the highest spiritual energy. Psychic Char Margolis wrote her own prayer for protection. Medium John Edward, a Catholic, says a rosary before he works. Psychic intuitive Millie Gemondo focuses on drawing in higher energy before she reads for someone. For you, Virgo, the protective ritual or device must be *perfect*. A perfect rose. A perfect stick of incense. The perfect prayer. You must create it to fit your needs and specifications.

THE MAP

Your records are your map for this journey. Make them as detailed as possible, including anything at all that is pertinent to your experiences with spirit communication. If you're adept at dream recall, you may want to have a separate section of your journal just for dreams that seem to relate to communication with your guides.

Even though Virgo usually doesn't mind keeping records of this sort, just in case you balk at some point and think it's a waste of time, consider this. Ten years ago, Bruce Moen was an engineering consultant with an interest in metaphysics. His specific interest at the time was out-of-body travel, which led him to enroll in the Gateway Program at the Monroe Institute. He kept good records of his experiences before, during, and after the program, never realizing that the records would become the basis for his "Afterlife Series" of books.

Moen's interest in out-of-body travel grew into a fascination and talent for travel into the afterlife. Today, he writes about his experiences and gives workshops in which he teaches other people to travel into the afterlife and "retrieve souls." His records have proven to be invaluable.

And so will yours. Use the table below to get started. You don't know where your exploration might lead, Virgo, into what uncharted seas, and you don't know how your life might change because of this exploration. It's an adventure. Enjoy it!

In the table below, list five areas you would like to explore and possible ways of doing it.

Areas to Explore	How to Go About It
1. _____	_____
2. _____	_____
3. _____	_____
4. _____	_____
5. _____	_____

THE GRAIL

Your grail, Virgo, is: *You'll be able to use the deeper truths you discover in a practical way that benefits you and other people.*

YOUR RECORDS

Date: _____

Time: _____

Weather: _____

Other factors: _____

_____

Your experience: _____

_____

_____

_____

_____

_____

_____

_____

_____

_____

_____

11. *Libra the Scales* ♎

> Be alert, be self-aware, so that when opportunity presents itself, you can actually rise to it.
>
> —DAVID BOHM

September 23–October 22
Cardinal Air
Ruled by Venus

THE SYMBOL

Scales. Just imagine it: a simple tool as old as Aladdin's lamp. An instrument of balance. On one side, Libra places his needs. On the other side, he places the needs of others. They have to *balance*. Life, of course, is rarely balanced in that sense, and Libra knows this instinctively. But still, he struggles to attain that *balance*, that intricate harmony, that elusive peace.

Libra is a paradox. He is the tightrope walker suspended on a narrow cable a hundred feet above the earth, moving slowly and precisely along the cable, holding a staff that he dips or raises to keep himself from plunging to his death. His focus has to be so intense that he blocks out every distraction, every nuance in the audience below him. If he falters, it will cost him. It's the same way in his relationships. Equilibrium, that slippery little devil, must be maintained.

Libra, like Taurus, is ruled by Venus, which provides him with the outlet he needs to find and maintain his balance—art, music, beauty in all of its many and varied forms. When a stressed-out Libra enters a museum, tensions melt away like ice. When he listens to or plays music, when he paints, when he walks outside into a gorgeous sunrise, he finds peace.

More than any other sign, Libra sees both sides of an issue. It's his gift and his curse. Perhaps Libra witnesses his wife and daughter arguing about the daughter's messy room. Libra understands his wife's side perfectly well; the room looks like a disaster site. But he also understands his daughter's side, that she's in school until four, has three hours of homework, and who wants to clean a room at nine o'clock at night? Instead of taking one side or the other, he becomes the mediator. "How can we resolve this?" he asks. "How can we put this behind us?" And get on with the business of living.

When he's negotiating with himself, the bargaining goes something like this: *If I take an hour walk in the morning, then I'll devote the afternoon to the kids.* Or to his spouse, his work, to whoever and whatever needs him. This remedy is fine until the next crisis or until Libra learns that it's okay to put himself first sometimes.

STRENGTH IN OPPOSITES: LIBRA/ARIES POLARITY

Libra came into the world to learn cooperation. The danger in this particular lesson is that he is too willing to bend over backward in order to accommodate everyone else. The word "selfish" is anathema to his personality, but a good dose of selfishness is exactly what Libra needs to undertake this exploration successfully.

That word, selfish, has a tarnished reputation. From the time we're very small, we're told that it's not nice to be selfish or that it's wrong or that it simply isn't tolerated. As we get older the word is equated with self-involvement, egocentrism, greed, possessiveness, and self-indulgence. These definitions describe only the extreme end of selfishness and aren't what we're talking about here. On this exploration, to be selfish simply means to think of your own needs first.

When Aries steps in, the picture changes. Where Libra is *dependent* and *cooperative,* Aries is *independent* and *self-oriented.* Libra is *social,* Aries is a *loner.* Libra may seek *peace at any cost,* Aries simply *walks away without regrets.* Libra can argue any side of an issue, Aries sees only his side. Libra takes his time to make decisions, Aries makes decisions instantly and impulsively. Libra shies away from arguments, Aries leaps at the opportunity to make his point. The dichotomy between the two signs is obvious. Adapting some of the Aries traits, however, may be tricky.

For starters, Libra needs to set up some parameters for himself—and the people with whom he lives. And that begins with defining his quest.

THE QUEST

Let's keep it simple and straightforward, Libra. Your quest is: *To explore spirit communication independently, putting your own needs first, and then to share what you learn with others.*

The toughest part of this equation falls at the beginning of the italicized words, specifically with the word "independently." Initially, do this exploration alone, within the parameters you've established. These parameters don't have to be rigid—*I'll attempt spirit communication one hour a day, seven days a week*—but should show commitment. Maybe fifteen minutes a day, three days a week is enough for you. Maybe half an hour a week is enough. Whatever you establish, stick to it as long as the exploration interests you.

The second parameter you should establish concerns the specific place where you'll conduct your exploration. Are you going to use a particular room in your house? A spot in your yard? At the beach? In the woods? Wherever it is, use this area each time, at least in the initial stages of your exploration. It will facilitate your ability to enter an altered state of awareness.

The third parameter concerns other people. Since this is *your* time, don't allow other people to intrude on it. Turn off the phones and beepers. Let your family and significant other know that you need some time alone. Be gentle, yet firm.

One Libra mother informed her family that she needed fifteen minutes every evening for her exploration. She would go into her den and shut the door, put on some soft music, and drift away. But one evening, her young daughter had a friend over at the house and when the friend started to go into the woman's den, the daughter said, "You can't go in there now. My mom's working."

"Working at what?"

"She's talking to spirits."

The daughter's friend turned around and walked in the opposite direction.

THE JOURNEY

When you go on a trip, you pack clothing that suits the weather of the place where you're going and that reflects the kind of trip it is. A business trip to Seattle probably won't require a bathing suit, but a pleasure trip to the Caribbean probably will. The same rules apply for this trip, but in a slightly different way.

For this exploration, the most important items are your frame of mind and your attitude. Do you want to do this or are you doing it to accommodate someone else? If it's the latter, keep in mind that it works best when *your* interest and curiosity are behind it.

You're going to need a notebook or recorder for taking notes on your exploration. This will provide you with a detailed record of your experiences. The recorder is just a backup for those times when you aren't able to write down your experiences. Even if you open a file on a computer, you should have a hard copy of your records, too. In the event that you question why you should waste time recording your experiences, think of the records as fodder for something in the future.

When author and researcher Robert Monroe began his out-of-body explorations in the 1950s, he kept meticulous notes. Years later, those early notes became the basis for his first book, *Journeys Out of the Body,* and formed the foundation of research that ultimately led him to establish the Monroe Institute. Shortly before he died, he started the Lifeline program, which taught others how to reach what Monroe called Focus 27, a kind of afterlife reception area intended to ease the trauma of people who have died.

So keep notes. You never know where they may lead you, Libra.

Every sign except for Cancer and you, Libra, is encouraged to initially undertake this exploration with a partner. For Cancer, another cardinal sign, solitude is recommended so that there won't be a temptation to *nurture* someone else's exploration. For you, solitude is recommended so that you aren't tempted to help anyone else *balance* his or her experiences.

Once you're into your exploration and feel comfortable with what you're doing, then you may want to bring in a partner. But make it clear that what you're doing in your partnership is sharing insights about your individual experiences, nothing more, nothing less.

If you're the type of Libra who enjoys meditation, then by all means incorporate your spirit communication into your meditation period. But meditation isn't for everyone and isn't always the most direct route to communicating with your guides. Your dreams are the most reliable source for your initial attempts.

Many mediums and psychics have active dream lives and receive messages through their dreams from their guides. Kevin, a Libra and a photographer, first met one of his guides in a "dream lobby," where he was waiting for a recently deceased friend "to be processed." He became aware that the African-American woman sitting next to him wore what looked like tribal clothes—swaths of boldly colored fabric that gave her a regal look. She was reading the palm of another person in the lobby and Kevin, curious about it all, leaned closer to listen. To eavesdrop. The woman suddenly glanced up.

"For a couple of seconds, neither of us spoke. I was embarrassed because I knew she knew I'd been eavesdropping. Then she said, 'You need to remember me, Kevin. We can help each other along the path.' She said some other things I don't remember, and I woke up, startled and disturbed by the dream. A few days later, I was getting ready for a photo shoot—a wedding—and I saw this woman dressed exactly as she had been, through the lens of my camera. When I glanced up, she wasn't there.

"It spooked me. But I wrote it off to lack of sleep.

About a week later, I had another dream about her. She was imparting information, that's the only way I can put it. I didn't write the dream down, but the information seemed to be rolling through me somehow for the next few days."

Not long after this second dream, Kevin was on the phone with a potential client and, very clearly, heard the woman's voice in his head, warning him not to take the job. He ignored the advice because he thought he was imagining it, and the job was a disaster from beginning to end. The next time he heard her voice, he took her advice. "And she's been with me ever since, a character in my dreams when I sleep, a voice in my head when I'm awake. She and I have been connected for a number of lives and this time around, she chose to help me from the other side."

Medium and author George Anderson says that dreams are one of the most common ways for spirits to communicate with us. In *Lessons from the Light,* he relates many stories about spirits who visit their loved ones in dreams. He mentions that some individuals have nightmares in which they see their loved ones struggling in the afterlife, and assures readers that these types of nightmares aren't genuine communication. "A dream that puts souls in a negative situation is usually a manifestation or projection of our own fear. These should be considered nightmares and not visitations. After a true visitation from a loved one in the hereafter, the difference will become quite clear."

Van Praagh contends that the master teachers most of us have are with us from life to life. "These beings are tuned in to our spiritual selves and will help us to grow spiritually throughout our time on the physical plane, as well as assist us in between lives. In addition, we will have individual master guides during a particular lifetime."

Van Praagh notes that many people ask him whether guides are with us all the time or whether we have to ask them to communicate with us. "We are never alone," he says. "Our guides are with us always. Their spiritual task is to watch over us and assist us."

Our guides may differ according to whatever we're involved in at the time, but Van Praagh says they "know our needs."

According to Anderson, you don't have to be a medium to experience communication with guides and souls in the afterlife. "The souls in the hereafter have told me many times that they communicate somehow with their loved ones, just to let them know they are near."

Meeting Your Guides

The suggestions provided in this section are intended for the average Libra. As you progress through this exploration, you'll add to these techniques, create your own, and find the ones that work best for you.

The Physical Body. During your exploration of spirit communication, some type of regular physical routine will help keep you grounded. Thanks to Libra's refined sense of aesthetics, one of the best physical routines for you is regular walks in nature. A nearby park with a jogging trail is ideal. A path through a woods is even better.

The locale you select should appeal to your senses, so that you're aware of the soft rustling of leaves, the sweet taste of the air, the fragrant scents of the earth—the sheer beauty of it all. As you walk, develop an awareness

of how easily your body moves, the swiftness with which
it carries you forward, the perfect symmetry of bones
and muscles, joints and limbs. Be fully in your body, in
the here and now. Over time, you'll find that your mind
relaxes into the walking itself, that mind and body become one. At this point, you may begin to receive images
and impressions of your spirit guides. It helps, too, if
you request contact with your guides while you're on
your walk.

Signs & Symbols. Guides and guardian angels often
communicate to us through signs and symbols. Lights
may flicker off and on in a room, a particular scent may
fill the air, a certain song comes on the radio. We tend
to dismiss these events as coincidence. But they generally
happen when we're thinking of a person who has died.
The scent that seems to waft through the room as you're
thinking of your mother *just happens to be* the smell of
her perfume. The flickering of lights happens as you're
thinking of your grandfather. Coincidence? Think again.

One of the most common instances of communication
seems to happen through electricity. In Hollywood's version of ghosts and hauntings, these electrical events are
portrayed in negative and frightening terms. In reality,
the incidents may be startling, but they are rarely negative or frightening.

"I had just gotten off the phone with the nurse who
had informed me my mother had died when there was a
tremendous clap of thunder outside my window. Seconds
later, the lights went out," says Beth, a teacher. "Then
the lights came back on, flickered several times, and outside, it started to pour. At the time, I thought how fitting
it was that my mother went out with thunder echoing
through air. But later when I thought about the lights

flickering off, I asked my neighbor if her electricity had gone off that afternoon. When she said it hadn't, I knew the flickering of the lights was my mother's doing."

Sometimes, especially in the early stages of your exploration, a symbol may come to mind that makes no sense to you. Jot it in your notebook, with the date and a few notes about how you received the symbol. Its significance may become apparent when you make your notes. If not, you may have to mull it over awhile before you understand the symbol, or certain events may have to transpire in your life before the meaning is clear.

Toni, a writer, woke up one morning with the word "chattel" in mind. She knew she'd been dreaming, but the only thing from the dream she could recall was the word and she didn't have any idea what it meant in the context of her life. A couple of days later, she began working on a fiction proposal that involved a voodoo priestess in New Orleans in the nineteenth century and realized she already had the title: Chattel. Although this symbol didn't come through spirit communication, it illustrates how symbols may come to us through creative projects and endeavors.

In other words, signs and symbols can appear virtually anywhere, at any time. But it's up to you to recognize them.

The Senses. Without our senses, we probably wouldn't live very long. Every moment of every hour, our senses convey thousands of bits of information to us that allow us to negotiate the physical world successfully. In much the same way, our inner senses—usually lumped under the catchall of "intuition"—also convey information, but of a different kind.

Medium and author John Edward lists these inner

senses as: clairaudience (clear hearing), clairvoyance (clear seeing), clairsentience (clear sensing), clairalience (clear smelling), and clairambience (clear tasting).

Clairaudience occurs when you hear an inner voice that imparts wisdom or guidance. This voice can be heard in dreams, during periods of deep relaxation, during meditation or any other altered state. With practice, it can be heard at virtually any time of the day or night. This sense is common among mediums.

Clairvoyance is the ability to see what is happening now or what will happen in the future in your life or the life of someone else. Many psychics use this sense. Although it's related to "seeing," it isn't confined to sight. It can be experienced as "gut feelings" or mental images and impressions. Psychics tend to have strongly developed clairvoyance.

Clairsentience is the ability to sense details about a person, event, or situation through touch. One type of clairsentience is psychometry, the ability to "read" an object. Items like jewelry and clothing retain the vibration of the individual who has worn them, and a psychometrist can pick up details about the individual by tuning in to that vibration. Psychics who work with police often use this method.

Clairalience and *clairambience* are less common than the first three inner senses. Clear smelling is the ability to glean details about an individual or situation through the sense of smell. If you suddenly catch a whiff of the pipe tobacco that your dead grandfather smoked and there's no apparent source for that smoke, then you may be experiencing a communication from him.

Clear tasting involves picking up details about an individual or situation through the sense of taste. Perhaps your deceased father loved key lime pie. If he's trying to communicate with you, the taste of key lime may fill your mouth.

To these senses, James Van Praagh adds "inspirational thought." He defines this as receiving "thoughts, impressions, knowledge—all without forethought." In this type of sensing, a spirit or group of spirits "melds their thoughts together and impresses the person to write a certain piece of music or paint a particular picture." In other words, the vehicle is creativity.

These inner senses can be developed just as easily as our ordinary five senses. It merely takes practice and commitment. For Libra, as the cardinal air sign, clairvoyance should be the easiest of the inner senses to develop. You may also want to try automatic writing and, if you have artistic talent, psychic art. Both entail spiritual communication flowing *through* you—specifically through your hands.

Author Ruth Montgomery was one of the better known "automatic writing" mediums. All of her books are the product of automatic writing, in which Montgomery's group of guides—medium Arthur Ford among them—discuss metaphysical topics and provide predictions on any number of world events. Her most recent book, *The World to Come: The Guides' Long-Awaited Predictions for the Dawning Age,* provides predictions about the Aquarian Age.

Stay Grounded. Some type of regular physical activity is the best way to ground yourself. Like your fellow air sign, Gemini, you live much of your life in your mind, so any kind of physical movement forces you to be in the here and now. If you feel you need grounding and it isn't convenient to take a jog or walk, then simply turn your focus inward for a few minutes and concentrate on your body.

How do you feel? Are you aware of any aches or discomforts? Is your pulse rhythmic, steady? Notice how you breathe. Concentrate on deepening your breathing, pulling air down into your diaphragm, holding it for a few seconds, then releasing it. Two or three minutes of focused attention on your body can root you completely in the here and now.

As your exploration progresses, you'll discover other ways to ground yourself. Use what works.

Trust. This area usually isn't a problem for you, Libra. You are able to trust whatever impressions you receive and know how to act on them. You instinctively know how to distinguish between wishful thinking and genuine impressions.

For you, the challenge where trust is concerned may happen when you're dealing with other people. Perhaps you've received a spirit communication about a close friend and the message is disturbing. A part of you wants to interpret the message in a more favorable light, so you put a positive spin on it. Resist the temptation to do so. Simply tell your friend what the impression or communication is, and let him or her interpret it.

The Flow. Nonresistance—that's what the flow is. When you begin to receive spirit communications, a part of you may throw up emotional blocks. Perhaps the process makes you uneasy. Maybe you're getting flak from your significant other about "dabbling in weirdness." Whatever the pressure, try not to block what you receive, otherwise your intuition shuts down.

Protection. When you set out on this exploration, the type of energy you attract is an important issue. Most mediums and psychics have some type of protective ritual that they do before attempting spirit communication. For some, it's as simple as a request that they contact only the highest spiritual energy. For others, it may be a prayer or a visualization.

You enjoy rituals that are aesthetically pleasing and that appeal to your senses. Create a protective ritual that does both.

THE MAP

For every sign, the map to be used for this journey is the same and yet intrinsically different because each sign brings its own unique imprint. While the journal notes comprise the heart of any map, it's the energy you bring to this exploration that makes the map come alive. The map ceases being just words on paper and becomes a kind of hologram that lights your way through the dark.

Like your cardinal cousins, Aries and Cancer, you tend to move along a single, focused track. As long as that track isn't blocked or doesn't dead-end, you're okay. But if you reach a point on that track where you can't go any farther, panic begins to set in. You don't know where to go, where to turn, or how to find your way around the obstacle. You leave yourself only one choice—to retrace the steps you've taken.

On this particular journey, though, nothing moves in a straight, linear fashion. There's no hotline to the spirit world, no 800 number to dial. You're going to get sidetracked, take detours, and sometimes you'll take the long way around to wherever you're going. When it happens, just go with it. There are no hard-and-fast rules for this exploration. Besides, some of those detours may hold knowledge that you need. Flow with whatever works.

Just remember to include those detours in your notes! Now use the explore table below to get you started.

In the table below, list five areas you would like to explore and possible ways of doing it.

Areas to Explore	How to Go About It
1._____	_____
2._____	_____
3._____	_____
4._____	_____
5._____	_____

THE GRAIL

Your grail, Libra, is: *By applying what you learn through an independent exploration of spiritual exploration, you illumine the way for other people.*

YOUR RECORDS

Date: _____

Time: _____

Weather: _____

Other factors: _____

_____

Your experience: _____

_____

_____

_____

_____

12. Scorpio the Scorpion ♏

The galaxies exist in you . . .

—GEORGE LEONARD

October 23–November 21
Fixed Water
Ruled by Pluto, Mars

THE SYMBOL

Her eyes smolder like hot coals. Her movements are fluid but calculated. Her smile is warm, but doesn't touch those eyes. Nothing touches those eyes. They are masked, disguised, camouflaged, hidden behind layers of carefully constructed defenses. If it's true that the eyes are the windows of the soul, then a Scorpio's eyes say it all. *Keep your distance,* they warn. *Prove your loyalty.* And upon closer scrutiny, everything else becomes apparent: passion, intensity, power, secrecy, magnetism, vengeance, jealousy, sexuality. But even this list doesn't capture the depths of Scorpio.

This sign, like no other, craves intense experiences. This doesn't mean the high-risk thrills that an Aries seeks or the sensual pleasures that Taurus enjoys. Scorpio is after the emotional depths, the stuff in the deepest part

170

of the human ocean. So where might Scorpio find such intensity? An emergency room in a city would fit the ticket—sirens shrieking, gurneys rattling, every moment a life-or-death crisis, her own emotions on a roller coaster that never quits. Or she might find it on the streets as a private investigator, ferreting out the secrets of other people. Or she might find it as a nun or priest, a counselor to terminal patients, a past-life therapist, a medium. Regardless of where she finds this intensity, the emotional experience is the goal.

We all have emotional experiences, of course. But for Scorpio, emotions aren't simply a byproduct of life. They *are* life. At the most profound levels, Scorpio is transformed through her emotions. Her consciousness isn't a thought process; it's feeling. She must *feel* her way through life, much like Cancer does, but more intensely and deeply. She often does this by delving into areas that the mainstream considers taboo. Scorpio and Pluto rule the affairs of the dead. Inheritances. Wills and trusts. Probate. Shared resources. Reincarnation. Rebirth. Recycling. The only other sign as well equipped as Scorpio for communication with the dead is Pisces. Although both are water signs, their experiences are vastly different.

Scorpio seeks emotional intensity so that she can renew and transform herself and her world. Perhaps her spouse dies suddenly and unexpectedly. What are her choices? She can mope and dig herself into a depression, her perceptions turning constantly to the past to what she might have done differently. Or she can renew herself by choosing life.

STRENGTH IN OPPOSITES:
SCORPIO/TAURUS POLARITY

Back to Pluto. In mythology, Pluto was guardian of the underworld and of the dead. He wasn't especially pleased with the kingdom that his brother, Jupiter, had given to him. But Jupiter pointed out that all the wealth hidden in the earth was also part of his kingdom, so that Pluto also would be known as the god of wealth.

In time, Pluto got used to the gloom of the underworld. But he was lonely and wished for a wife. Jupiter promised him Persephone (also known as Prosperina), the daughter of Ceres, goddess of the harvest. Jupiter couldn't bring himself to tell Ceres that her daughter was going to Pluto. Pluto got tired of waiting and took matters in his own hands. He abducted Persephone to the underworld.

Her mother, frantic and worried, wandered the earth in search of her daughter, ignoring the harvest. Crops died, the threat of famine loomed. Jupiter realized he had to do something and told Ceres that if Persephone hadn't eaten any food in the underworld, which would bind her to the place, she would be returned to the surface of the world. As it turned out, Persephone had eaten six seeds from a pomegranate, so she had to return to the underworld six months out of every year. And whenever Persephone returns to the underworld, Ceres ignores her crops and there is winter.

The myth is a fitting metaphor for Scorpio. The "underworld" is the unconscious, all that is unseen, repressed, hidden—the kingdom that Scorpio rules. These matters represent Scorpio's "wealth."

Where Scorpio *embraces* emotional intensity, Taurus *shies away from* it. Scorpio doesn't need validation of anything she senses intuitively, but Taurus demands proof. Scorpio seeks *renewal and transformation,* Taurus simply craves *peace.* Through transformative experiences, Scorpio *destroys so that she can renew,* Taurus *builds.* Scorpio plumbs the depths and sometimes can't find the way out. Taurus rarely loses her way—she's too grounded and practical.

Before Scorpio even embarks on this journey, she should realize that the tools she usually uses won't work as well as they have in the past, if at all. Instead of diving into this exploration with an obsession that excludes everyone and everything else in her life, she is going to have to pace herself. Instead of pursuing emotional experience with the intensity of a force of nature, she must try to temper her intensity and detach emotionally.

As fixed signs, both Scorpio and Taurus are persistent in what they pursue. But only Scorpio is utterly relentless about it. The remedy? Chill, Scorpio. Sit back. Take a couple of deep breaths. You can get to where you're going, you merely have to change your tactics somewhat.

THE QUEST

Your quest is this: *To approach this exploration in a practical, measured way, without emotional attachment to the results.*

If you want to explore this area to prove conclusively that there's life after death, that the soul is reborn again and again, then stop now. There won't be any definitive conclusions, Scorpio. You may not even prove that you are actually communicating with spirits. But if this exploration enriches your life in a pragmatic way, then it deserves, at the very least, a commitment of time.

How much time? Whatever suits your lifestyle and curiosity. A week, three weeks, six. The length of time isn't as important as the depth of your commitment. Set a realistic time parameter. If your life is already jammed to the hilt with other commitments, then reserve your spiritual work for weekends. Once you decide on a schedule, stick to it for whatever length of time you've set.

David, a Scorpio and financial consultant, became interested in spirit communication when one of his business associates died suddenly. Although his life was busy and hectic with his family and clients, David set aside fifteen minutes every evening around ten o'clock to conduct his exploration. This time worked well for him. The kids were in bed, the phones weren't ringing, and his wife, a teacher, was grading papers.

His technique was simple—to just sit quietly in his den, his eyes shut, his senses open. For several weeks, nothing happened during the time he'd set aside. He started to resent the time he was in his den, eyes shut, waiting for an image, an impression, anything. He finally decided to cut back to every other night, and, suddenly, *things* began to happen. One night, he thought he smelled pipe tobacco—his associate had smoked a pipe. Another night, the lights in the den flickered.

About three weeks into his exploration, he had a dream one weekend afternoon while he was napping. It was about his friend and was so vivid and real that he woke with a start, certain the man was in the room. At this point, he realized he was definitely experiencing communication.

There are no rules and limitations in this exploration, except for the ones you create and impose. Sometimes communication happens quickly, other times it takes awhile. But when a sincere request is made, it's usually answered.

THE JOURNEY

Every sign has a packing list for this exploration, and at the top of the list are a journal and a recorder. For you, the journal is vital. It will become not only a record of your experiences, but will ground you as well.

The recorder is meant to be a backup, a way to record your thoughts or feelings when it isn't convenient to write things down. Your permanent record should be in hard copy. It's fine if you use a computer file for your journal, but make sure you print out the file every few days.

You tend to be something of a loner when it comes to spiritual explorations. It's part of your secrecy, your defense system. So on this exploration, find a partner who shares your interests. It's best if the partner is someone you trust and consider an equal. An employer/ employee relationship probably won't work because the hierarchy of power in that relationship is already established and may be difficult to change. In fact, power struggles don't belong in this partnership, on this exploration. That should be one of the ground rules. No one controls, no one is boss. There's no right or wrong about the way things are done or about what you experience.

Right from the start, you and your partner should agree on some basics. Here are questions to consider:

- How often are you going to meet?
- When you meet, are you meeting to discuss your experiences and offer each other insight or are you meeting for the exploration itself?
- What motivates each of you to explore this area?
- What is your time commitment?
- What do each of you hope to gain from this exploration?

- Can you work cooperatively together?
- Are your basic beliefs about guides and the afterlife the same?

David, the financial consultant mentioned earlier, began his exploration alone. Once he'd gotten into it, though, his wife became his partner. Even though they had worked on joint ventures before, primarily in business, they encountered rough spots in this particular partnership, and these had to be dealt with. But overall, during the course of their partnership in *this* venture, their relationship deepened.

The biggest challenge for you in working with a partner will be to resist the impulse to control things or to be the one in power. *Equal partners* means exactly that. The idea is to approach this as an adventure in the exploration of consciousness.

Meeting Your Guides

Techniques and suggestions provided in this section are merely guidelines. You'll add to them, expand them, create new ones.

The Physical Body. In this exploration, your body grounds you and is your most intimate connection to the here and now. It's important, then, that you have some type of regular physical exercise routine, if you don't already. Like your fellow water signs, Cancer and Pisces, you benefit from swimming or dancing, where your body's movements are fluid, graceful. Tai chi or yoga might also appeal to you.

One of the benefits of yoga is physical flexibility. For you, Scorpio, a fixed sign, yoga often makes you more flexible mentally, emotionally, and spiritually. As you become more flexible, you may find that you're more willing to try out new ideas, explore new belief systems, and strike up friendships with people who might not have interested you before. Another benefit of yoga is less visible—your body may become a vehicle for spiritual awareness.

Most mediums agree that diet is also an important component of spiritual communication. James Van Praagh advocates a diet that is as close as possible to vegetarian. Refined sugars, caffeine, alcohol, and drugs should be avoided. All of these foods and liquids either depress the body's vibrational rate or speed up the adrenal glands, which are instrumental to this work.

Signs & Symbols. You're a natural when it comes to recognizing signs and symbols. A dragonfly darts past your windshield as you're driving, and you are suddenly certain there's a positive and uplifting message waiting for you at home. The plumbing in your house backs up, and you realize immediately that there's something blocking communication in your family.

But the signs and symbols you encounter in communication with your guides are likely to be somewhat different. In *Reaching to Heaven,* James Van Praagh relates an interesting story about symbols. He was doing a reading for a young woman whose mother had died. "Suddenly, I felt a very strange sensation and didn't understand what was happening to me. I closed my eyes, and as if being taken over, I began to feel as though I was enclosed in a box."

He broke off communication by opening his eyes and asked his spirit guides to explain what had happened. They replied that the sensation was necessary because it

described how the young woman's mother had felt most
of her life. He asked the young woman if her mother
had been confined in some way. The woman admitted
that her mother had been agoraphobic and had spent
most of her life in the house. For Van Praagh, this symbol was expressed as a physical sensation. But symbols
can come through in many ways, through all of our
senses.

Your dreams are likely to yield symbols that relate to
spirit communication. Mediums and authors James Van
Praagh and George Anderson agree that dreams are one
way that spirits and guides consistently attempt to contact us. The trick is to recall your dreams, record them
as soon as you wake, and then study them for recurring symbols.

Over time, you'll compile a personal dream dictionary
that will reveal a great deal about what's going on inside
of you, Scorpio. This dream dictionary will make it easier
for you to decipher symbols that you receive from your
spirit guides.

In much the same way, record the symbols that come
to you through your attempts at spirit communication.
Include details—how you felt while you were receiving
the symbols, how you felt afterward, where you were
working, the time of day, even the weather. All of these
details can be helpful in future communications.

The Senses. Our five senses are beautifully designed
for physical life. Every second of every hour, they convey
information that allows us to make decisions and move
through the world with ease. In much the same way, our
inner senses allow us to navigate the inner world.

Medium and author John Edward lists these inner
senses as: clairaudience (clear hearing), clairvoyance

(clear seeing), clairsentience (clear sensing), clairalience (clear smelling), and clairambience (clear tasting).

Clairaudience occurs when you hear an inner voice that imparts wisdom or guidance. This voice can be heard in dreams, during periods of deep relaxation, during meditation or any other altered state. With practice, it can be heard at virtually any time of the day or night. This sense is common among mediums.

Clairvoyance is the ability to see what is happening now or what will happen in the future in your life or the life of someone else. Many psychics use this sense. Although it's related to "seeing," it isn't confined to sight. It can be experienced as "gut feelings" or mental images and impressions. Clairvoyance also occurs in dream states, when the same types of images and impressions convey information about issues in our lives now or about issues and situations that may be coming up in the future. Psychics tend to have strongly developed clairvoyance.

Clairsentience is the ability to sense details about a person, event, or situation through touch. One type of clairsentience is psychometry, the ability to "read" an object. Items like jewelry and clothing retain the vibration of the individual who has worn them, and a psychometrist can pick up details about the individual by tuning in to that vibration. Psychics who work with police often use this method.

Clairalience and *clairambience* are less common than the first three inner senses. Clear smelling is the ability to glean details about an individual or situation through the sense of smell. If you suddenly catch a whiff of the pipe tobacco your dead grandfather used, and there's no apparent source for that smoke, then you may be experiencing a communication from him.

Clear tasting involves picking up details about an individual or situation through the sense of taste. Perhaps your deceased father loved key lime pie. If he's trying to communicate with you, the taste of key lime may fill your mouth.

To these senses, James Van Praagh adds "inspirational thought." He defines this as receiving "thoughts, impressions, knowledge—all without forethought." In this type of sensing, a spirit or group of spirits "melds their thoughts together and impresses the person to write a certain piece of music or paint a particular picture." In other words, the vehicle is creativity.

With practice and commitment, these inner senses can be developed just as easily as any of our ordinary five senses. For you, Scorpio, a fixed water sign, clairaudience and clairvoyance, especially through dreams, should be easy to develop. But because you are so naturally intuitive, you probably already use your inner senses, so to develop one or several requires nothing more than focus and practice.

Books on psychic development are listed in the resources of Appendix 2. Check them out. Read a couple of them. Experiment with your partner.

In the movie *The Gift,* the psychic played by Cate Blanchett uses cards to focus her clairvoyance. The cards are actually made up of the symbols that researcher J. D. Rhine used in his telepathy experiments at Duke University during the 1930s. The symbols are a square, a circle, a triangle, a pair of wavy lines. If you find it easy to work with symbols, then make your own deck of cards and practice with them, experimenting with what images and impressions come to mind with which card. If symbols aren't your thing, try a deck of tarot cards.

Ted Andrews created a deck called the Animal-Wise

Tarot. It's easy to use because the meanings are printed right on the cards. Some psychics, like Millie Gemondo, use a regular deck of playing cards to focus. Experiment. Find the method that works best for you.

Stay Grounded. Regular physical activity helps to keep you grounded. But so does a healthy skepticism. When you begin to receive images and impressions, let them flow through you without judging them. Write them down. Then go back over your notes and question everything you received. Test each image and impression against your powerful Scorpio emotions.

Perhaps one of the impressions you received was of a pasture with horses grazing in it. Does that image relate to anything familiar in your life now? Might it relate to anyone you know? What do you *feel* about this image? By using the skepticism of Taurus, your polar opposite, and your own intuition to test what you receive, you establish a *tangible process* for evaluating the information you receive.

Trust. When it comes to your interactions with people, trust isn't especially easy for you. People have to prove themselves to you first—prove their loyalty and that their friendship is free of any agenda. But in spiritual pursuits, your ability to trust is usually without impediments. You're accustomed to acting on your intuition.

But because you may have trouble staying grounded during this kind of exploration, apply a healthy skepticism first, as advised, and *then* decide whether you trust an image or impression you've received.

The Flow. With metaphysical and spiritual pursuits, you live in the flow. You usually *don't resist* or throw up emotional blocks. But if you're exploring this area in order to contact a loved one who has passed away, the experience of contact may overwhelm you at first and cause you to block it. In an instance like this, it's best to just back off and wait until you're not so emotionally involved.

Otherwise, though, the flow shouldn't be a problem for you.

Protection. The type of energy you attract during spirit communication is vital to your success. You want to be sure that you contact the highest spiritual energy. Most mediums and psychics have some sort of protective ritual that precedes their work. It can be a prayer, visualization, the lighting of candles or incense, or just a simple request.

John Edward, a Catholic, says the rosary before he works. Psychic intuitive Millie Gemondo centers herself with some deep breathing and requests that only the highest spiritual energy comes through. Char Margolis, intuitive and author, wrote her own prayer for protection and says it before she works. Among Native Americans, it's common to use burning sage to smudge an area and cleanse it of negative vibrations.

For you, Scorpio, the protective ritual must be something that appeals to you emotionally and intuitively. Only you know what that might be.

THE MAP

Your journal is the heart of your map. But think of it as a hologram, a living entity that is greater than the sum of its parts. It's not only a record of your exploration and experiences now, but can serve as a reference point in the future about which methods worked for you and which ones didn't.

Like fixed signs Taurus and Leo, your beliefs can become so rigid that you stagnate. Over time, your journal will reveal the areas where your beliefs have become rigid and your experiences stagnated. In a journal, you can't hide from yourself, not if you've been honest about what you've written.

One of the ways to uncover rigid areas in yourself is to look at what you fear. What fears have surfaced in your experiences? What is the source of those fears? Do they go back to your childhood or is their genesis more recent? When you explore your fears, they lose their power over you.

If you keep a journal of your dreams during this exploration, it can also serve as a source of insight into the machinations of your own psyche. Fears often surface in dreams—sometimes as nightmares and sometimes as situations, events, or people that leave us with a deep feeling of discomfort upon awakening. Note any such dreams in your journal and try to get to the source of the fear.

Some of your experiences in this exploration may prove to be precognitive: You receive information about the future. Always evaluate this type of information with healthy skepticism. If, for instance, you receive a symbol about death or dream that you or someone you love has died, test the accuracy of the experience against your own intuition. Never accept a symbol or image about death as the absolute truth. Explore it, try to understand it. Some precognitive information will be positive and uplifting. Apply the same tests to that information to be sure it isn't just wish fulfillment.

As you become accustomed to this exploration, you'll bring your own techniques and methods to it.

In the table below, list five areas of spirit communication that you would like to explore and how you might go about it. If, for instance, one area is to communicate with your dead grandmother, then one of the ways you might accomplish this is to attend a workshop on communication with guides.

Areas to Explore   How to Go About It
1. _____   _____
2. _____   _____
3. _____   _____
4. _____   _____
5. _____   _____

THE GRAIL

Your end point, Scorpio, your grail, is: *You now know how to apply what you've learned in this exploration in a practical, measured way.*

YOUR RECORDS

Date: _____

Time: _____

Weather: _____

Other factors: _____

_____

Your experience: _____

_____

_____

_____

_____

_____

13. Sagittarius the Archer ♐

The body is always in time; the spirit is always timeless.

—ALDOUS HUXLEY

November 22–December 21
Mutable Fire
Ruled by Jupiter

THE SYMBOL

In the movie *Braveheart,* Mel Gibson plays a Scotsman named Michael Wallace, who lived during the 1200s. In this bleak and brutal time, English nobles and royals took what they wanted from commoners. Land and spouses were high on their list of wants. During a raid on a Scottish village, an English soldier tries to rape Gibson's wife and he assaults the soldier. He and his wife flee, but she's caught and her throat is slit by one of the English commanders.

This event propels Gibson to galvanize clans throughout Scotland to fight against the English crown and to reclaim their country as their own. Because he sees *the bigger picture, the larger truth*—that Scotland deserves the right to govern itself—he tries to *right the wrongs* by fighting back. And ultimately, Gibson/Wallace finds his destiny, the meaning of his life, and his spot in history. The movie embodies many Sagittarius themes, and foremost among them is the need for freedom. It's his battle cry. Without it, Sagittarius shrivels up and dies. Freedom isn't just a concept for him. It's a state of being, as vital to him as the air he breathes.

Sagittarius is a traveler—not travel to the local hardware store, although he'll take that if nothing else is available—but travel across oceans, to the tops of mountain peaks, through space to other planets. He travels so that in embracing cultures other than his own, his awareness *expands*. And that's another Sagittarius theme. Expansion. Jupiter, which rules the sign, seeks to expand everything it touches. Even on those trips to the hardware store or on business jaunts, Jupiter expands the Sagittarius awareness.

Sagittarius has an unshakable faith in life that can take various forms, but some sort of religious or spiritual belief system is usually behind it. In his exuberance for *his* belief system, he may make the same mistake as his fire brother, Aries. He may decide that *his* way, *his* beliefs, *his* religious principles are the only right ones. At the extreme, this can result in Sagittarius on his soap box, Sagittarius as fanatic, Sagittarius as the guy everyone avoids.

STRENGTH IN OPPOSITES: SAGITTARIUS/GEMINI POLARITY

Your sign and the one opposite yours—Gemini—form an energy axis. At any time, you can call on Gemini's energy. When you do this with conscious intent, it's a particularly powerful way to achieve what you need or want.

The archer and the twins. Imagine them together, for a moment, this odd threesome, one of them a centaur—half horse, half human—the other two identical in appearance and yet as different as summer and winter. Both are mutable signs, so they adapt easily to change. And their elements—fire and air—are compatible.

So what does Gemini have to offer Sagittarius on this exploration? Details. Where Sagittarius *sees the big picture,* Gemini collects all the *facts and information that comprise the big picture.* Sagittarius is *philosophical and theoretical,* Gemini is *intensely curious.* Sagittarius's approach to living is *holographic,* Gemini's approach is *diverse and multidimensional.*

For Sagittarius to take advantage of his Gemini polarity, he must allow his left brain, his logic and reason, its say in this exploration. He should try to proceed logically every step of the way, never assuming that he already knows the answers. Once he begins to experience communication with his guides, he should then evaluate the messages intuitively. Logic, then intuition—that's where it starts.

Even though Sagittarius may think he already knows about the afterlife, spirits, and communicating with the dead, it's important that he acquaint himself with the terrain before he undertakes his exploration. He should read about spirits, the afterlife, mediumship, anything related to the topic. There are book suggestions listed in Appendix 2. If he's not a reader, then he might check out some of the movies mentioned in this book. In the last few years, Hollywood has produced a number of entertaining and insightful movies about the afterlife, spirits, and communicating with the dead.

Another way that Sagittarius can get to know the terrain is to have a reading with a good psychic. Not all psychics are mediums, but some of them are able to tune in on spirits, especially if the spirits have something to say to him. If he never has had a psychic reading before, it's best to get a referral from a friend or acquaintance. If this isn't possible, the psychics listed in Appendix 2 are reputable, and their fees are reasonable.

Before you get a reading, read the last chapter (Chapter 21) of this book. It provides some important guidelines.

THE QUEST

Pretend that you're Tom Cruise in *Mission: Impossible,* about to receive your assignment. Should you choose to accept it, an adjustment in your perceptions is necessary.

Here's your quest: *To collect the facts about spirit communication, to network with other people who share your interest in this area, and to explore this area in a reasonable, logical way.*

To you, this probably sounds like an oxymoron. How it is even *possible* to explore something so esoteric in a reasonable, logical way? The simplest way to explain it is through an analogy. Unless you're a scientist or an electrical engineer, can you explain why one of your appliances works when you plug it into an outlet? Can you explain how electricity is generated?

When you communicate with your guides or guardian angels, you "plug in" to a different kind of energy source. To a medium, it may be business as usual, but to everyone else it's as mysterious as electricity is to a child or a nonscientist. The difference is that with spirit communication we come up against belief systems that have been laid down in our lives since we were very young.

These belief systems say one of several things: When you're dead, you're dead; when you're dead, you go to heaven, hell, or someplace in between; it's not possible to talk to the dead; only bad people speak to the dead . . . The list is long. Yet, none of these belief systems explains what many people experience.

You bolt awake in the darkness and see your grandmother standing beside your bed. She looks utterly real, so real you can see the wrinkles in her brow, the crease in her chin. Four thousand miles away, your grandmother has just died, but you don't know that yet; no one has called to tell you. But when you finally hear it through official channels, you realize your grandmother came to say good-bye that night she appeared at the side of your bed. You realize, perhaps, that the world really is a lot stranger than any of us have imagined.

THE JOURNEY

Your packing list. You're good at this. Packing means travel. Travel means freedom. Freedom means life. But for this exploration, your packing list is rather simple. A journal and a tape recorder. The recorder isn't mandatory; it's just a tool that allows you to record what you're thinking when writing isn't convenient. The journal isn't mandatory, either, but it's a great tool to consider. It illustrates, in your own words, how you feel about what you're experiencing.

Where you usually seek direct personal experience when you travel, this time you're going to seek *experience,* that's all. It doesn't have to be personal, it doesn't even have to be mind blowing, although it may be both of those things. In this exploration, Sagittarius, it's to your benefit to take notes. Honest notes. Be a reporter. *Present just the facts.* Later, you and your readers can draw your own conclusions.

The other item that goes on your packing list is attitude. It really doesn't matter whether spirit communication gives you *the big picture.* The idea here is just to experience whatever happens.

Nearly every sign so far is urged to share this exploration with a partner. That goes for you, too. You not only gain additional insights into your exploration, but it also seems more of an adventure when you have someone else to talk to about it. The challenge for Sagittarius in this instance, however, is to understand that your partnership is *equal,* that neither of you is an expert.

When psychic intuitive and Sagittarius Millie Gemondo does readings, she is here but not here, listening but *listening to elsewhere.* She is plugged in to the bigger picture, just as you would expect a Sagittarius to be. Yet what she receives and relays are bits and pieces of information. Images. Scents. Names. Concepts. Possibilities.

Take a look at her chart in the Star Charts of the appendices. Sagittarius lies on the cusp of the 8th house, the house of metaphysics, at three minutes and six seconds. The 8th house symbolizes metaphysics, shared resources, transformation. In other words, this house, according to the energy of Sagittarius, is Millie's life theme. Like Van Praagh, whose Sun is also in the 8th house, *she is here to help other people through her particular gifts.*

Millie was born and raised in West Virginia, the youngest child in a family of five. Like Van Praagh, George Anderson, Char Margolis, and nearly every other medium or intuitive mentioned in this book, she was psychic as a child. But then, we all are. The difference here—and the difference is important—is that the ability for Millie and people like her don't diminish as they get older. For some reason, in spite of whatever feedback these people receive as children, good or bad, they remain psychic. Since Millie's mother was psychic, her ability wasn't discouraged. Also, the area where she grew up is rich with stories about ghosts and hauntings and things that go bump in the night, so the prevalent attitudes are conducive to psychic abilities.

Millie is primarily a clairvoyant—she picks up images and impressions about the person for whom she is reading. When she connects with guides and spirits, however, she says the energy is different. "There's a distinctive shift. It's something I feel, difficult to describe."

According to James Van Praagh, spirit guides are unique for each person. He divides guides into three distinct groups:

- Personal guides: People we have known in previous incarnations, in between lives, or even someone we have known in this life who has passed over. Seth, who spoke through Jane Roberts, was supposedly involved with her in previous incarnations.
- Mastery or specialized helpers: "These are spirits who are drawn to us based on certain activities or work in which we are engaged," writes Van Praagh. Quite often, these guides help us in creative work.
- Spirit or master teachers: "These individuals may be quite spiritually evolved or may have never lived in the physical world, or may have been involved in some aspect of spiritual work during many lifetimes upon this earth," says Van Praagh.

You and your partner will have very different experiences on this exploration, and that's as it should be. Just because your partner hears voices and you don't doesn't mean your partner is making it up or doing something wrong. Remember, Sagittarius, there are no experts on this exploration. It's an adventure!

MEETING YOUR GUIDES

These techniques and suggestions are intended just as guidelines for the average Sagittarius. Use them to get you started, then alter them to fit your needs, change them, create new ones. With practice, you'll find what works for you.

The Physical Body. What type of physical exercise do you enjoy? Is there something you do regularly? Choose some type of physical activity that you enjoy and do it three or four times a week while you're involved in your exploration of the afterlife. This will help keep you grounded in the physical world, the here and now. It will also help make your body a clearer channel for spirit communication.

James Van Praagh recommends that anyone involved in spiritual work of this sort should have a diet that is mostly vegetarian, with a minimum of refined sugars and caffeine. Red meat should be eliminated from the diet because it slows down the vibration of the body. "The number one glandular system used in this work is our endocrine glands, and specifically, the adrenals. Therefore, we must protect them and put as little stress upon them as possible." Caffeine and sugar, he notes, speed up the adrenal glands, making them less effective for this kind of work.

Sagittarius rules the hips, thighs, arteries, and the metabolism of fat. When you become emotionally upset, these are the areas where you're hit first. You may, for instance, reach for a chocolate-chip cookie to assuage anger or soothe frayed nerves. Instead, reach for a carrot!

Your diet may change during this exploration, and, if so, make note of it in your journal. In fact, make note of everything in your journal, even how often you exercise and what kind of exercise you do.

Signs & Symbols. This is one area where Sagittarius is a natural. You already are aware of the fact that we live in a world of signs and symbols, and you get a kick out of figuring out what they mean. Even the significance of symbols in dreams don't elude you for long.

The Senses. Just as we have five ordinary senses, so we have inner senses that can help during this particular exploration. Spirit communication calls on all of these inner senses. As you begin to work with spiritual communication, these inner senses are likely to develop.

Medium and author John Edward lists these inner senses as: clairaudience (clear hearing), clairvoyance (clear seeing), clairsentience (clear sensing), clairalience (clear smelling), and clairambience (clear tasting).

Clairaudience occurs when you hear an inner voice that imparts wisdom or guidance. This voice can be heard in dreams, during periods of deep relaxation, during meditation or any other altered state. With practice, it can be heard at virtually any time of the day or night. This sense is common among mediums.

Clairvoyance is the ability to see what is happening now or what will happen in the future in your life or the life of someone else. Many psychics use this sense. Although it's related to "seeing," it isn't confined to sight. It can be experienced as "gut feelings" or mental images and impressions. Clairvoyance also occurs in dream states, when the same types of images and impressions convey information about issues in our lives now or about issues and situations that may be coming up in the future. Psychics tend to have strongly developed clairvoyance.

Clairsentience is the ability to sense details about a person, event, or situation through touch. One type of clairsentience is psychometry, the ability to "read" an object. Items like jewelry and clothing retain the vibration of the individual who has worn them, and a psychometrist can pick up details about the individual by tuning in to that vibration. Psychics who work with police often use this method.

Clairalience and *clairambience* are less common than the first three inner senses. Clear smelling is the ability to glean details about an individual or situation through the sense of smell. If you suddenly catch a whiff of the pipe tobacco your dead grandfather used, and there's no apparent source for that smoke, then you may be experiencing a communication from him.

Clear tasting involves picking up details about an individual or situation through the sense of taste. Perhaps your deceased father loved key lime pie. If he's trying to communicate with you, the taste of key lime may fill your mouth.

To these senses, James Van Praagh adds "inspirational thought." He defines this as receiving "thoughts, impressions, knowledge—all without forethought." In this type of sensing, a spirit or group of spirits "melds their thoughts together and impresses the person to write a certain piece of music or paint a particular picture." In other words, the vehicle is creativity.

As a mutable fire sign, you may already be strongly clairvoyant. You may also have a talent for precognition—receiving information about the future. One of the ways you might develop and expand both abilities is through automatic writing. This is when spirits and guides work through the muscles in your hand to transmit messages.

One of the best known automatic writing authors was Ruth Montgomery, who published a number of bestselling books on topics ranging from aliens to messages about the millennium. She claimed she worked through a group of guides, including the famous medium Arthur Ford.

You may also have a talent for channeling. Psychic intuitive Renie Wiley has had the same group of guides since she was a child. She usually hears them (clairaudience) in her head, much the same way that James Van Praagh and George Anderson do. Her Sagittarius Sun falls in the 8th house, just like Van Praagh's Virgo Sun, Millie Gemondo's Sagittarius Sun, and Edgar Cayce's Pisces Sun. When supported by other elements in the chart, the 8th house placement of the Sun can be indicative of mediumistic or psychic ability.

In Appendix 2, you'll find a list of books about developing psychic and intuitive abilities. Glance through and choose a couple to read. Learn the lay of the land, Sagittarius.

Stay Grounded. Like your fellow fire signs Aries and Leo, your constant rush of activity can easily burn you out. By the time you're ready to sit down and attempt spirit communication, you're too exhausted to receive anything. Learn to pace yourself during this exploration. Part of pacing yourself is to stay grounded.

Grounding for you, Sagittarius, is apt to be quite different from grounding for the other fire signs. One way to ground yourself is through working with animals. If you have children and/or pets, then spend more time with them while you're involved in this exploration. Another good method of grounding yourself is to try to do your spiritual exploration in the same area, whether it's a room or a special spot outside. Surround yourself with items that remind you of your physical life and that hold personal significance.

Psychic Millie Gemondo often grounds herself by writing poetry. Psychic Renie Wiley walks her dog. Sometimes, the most ordinary pursuits are those that root us most deeply in the present. Mediums and psychics also use the following methods to stay grounded:

- Deep breathing. Before you attempt spirit communication, try some deep breathing. This entails nothing more than breathing in deeply through the nostrils, to bring the air down into your diaphragm, then exhaling slowly.
- Use colors in your work area that remind you of the earth, physical reality, the here and now.
- Weather permitting, go outside barefoot and rub the soles of your feet against the ground several times. This establishes a connection with the earth.
- Have live plants in your work area.
- Make sure your work area has at least one window so that it receives sufficient Sunlight. Weather permitting, again, leave the window open so that fresh air circulates in the room.
- With practice, you'll add other methods that keep you grounded.

Trust. You rarely doubt your impressions. In fact, you're more likely to trust everything you receive. By scrutinizing your impressions and experiences with some Gemini logic and reason, you'll be able to identify genuine communications more easily.

Despite your generally optimistic Sagittarius outlook, there are times when you may feel as if nothing is working in this exploration. It's then that your trust hits an all-time low—not because you don't trust your impressions, but because you're aren't receiving any impressions! Spirit communication happens at an individual pace. If your partner begins receiving impressions the first time he or she attempts to contact guides and by your sixth attempt you haven't experienced anything, don't worry about it. Don't give up. Simply state your request clearly with each attempt.

The Flow. For you, a fire sign, "flow" is different from "flow" for an air, water, or earth sign. For you, the flow lies in action, doing, expressing—and not resisting what is happening. Remain open to possibilities and simply go with the experience, wherever it leads you. Afterward, jot down everything you can remember in your journal.

Each experience you have in which you don't resist the information or communications that you receive will illustrate some facet of how spirit communication works. The more open and receptive you are, the clearer the communication will be.

"A few deep breaths and then I'm centered, ready to receive," says Millie. With practice, it can be that easy for you, too.

Protection. The idea here is that you want to attract the highest spiritual energy possible during your communication. Spirits, like people, exist on different levels. Some mediums say a prayer before they do their spiritual work. Others visualize a dome of white light around themselves. Medium John Edward, a Catholic, says the rosary before he attempts spirit communication. Millie may recite the 91st Psalm when she feels she needs protection.

For you, Sagittarius, it may be enough to simply request that you will contact only the highest energy. Do whatever you feel comfortable doing. Let your intuition guide you.

THE MAP

Your map is your journal. It not only tells you where you've been and where you are, but also points out the direction where you may be headed. Here, you'll record any detours you take, landmarks that you encounter, places you would like to visit.

In case you're doubting the wisdom of a journal, Sagittarius, think about this. When engineering consultant Bruce Moen decided to explore out-of-body travel by taking a workshop at the Monroe Institute, he kept a detailed journal on his experiences. This journal later became the basis of his first book in his Afterlife Series.

When author and researcher Robert Monroe started experiencing spontaneous out-of-body travel, he was terrified that he was going crazy. He began keeping meticulous notes about his experiences, and these notes later became the basis for *Journeys Out of the Body,* his classic book on out-of-body travel. So, Sagittarius, if you ever question the wisdom of keeping a journal about this spiritual exploration, remember that you don't know what it might lead to.

To use a map the way it's intended to be used, you have to know where you would like to go and then decide how you're going to get there. The same is true for the map of this journey. In the table below, list five areas related to spirit communication that you would like to explore and how you might undertake an exploration in each of those areas.

Areas to Explore	How to Go About It
1. _____	_____
2. _____	_____
3. _____	_____
4. _____	_____
5. _____	_____

THE GRAIL

Your grail, Sagittarius, is: *By exploring this area through logic and reason, you learn what the big picture really is.*

YOUR RECORDS

Date: _____

Time: _____

Weather: _____

Other factors: _____

_____

Your experience: _____

_____

_____

_____

_____

14. Capricorn the Goat ♑

Is it worth it?

—Anonymous

December 22–January 19
Cardinal Earth
Ruled by Saturn

THE SYMBOL

A goat. On the surface, it seems like a rather undignified symbol for a sign. But the goat has a particular talent that describes Capricorn: the ability to climb steadily upward, with a gait so certain that the goat rarely falters. It may take her a long time to get wherever she's going, but she does get there and usually arrives in one piece.

As a cardinal sign, she moves in a single, focused direction, following the established path even if it's narrow, rocky, and precipitous. She instinctively knows this path is the fastest route to the top regardless of whether it twists and turns and doubles back on itself. She doesn't see any merit in straying from that path. Who needs that sort of unknown, that kind of risk and hazard?

Capricorn, of course, does take detours, just like the

rest of us. But she probably enjoys them less, even resists them, digging in her heels, wanting desperately to turn back to the trail worn into the earth by other climbers. She isn't adventurous, not in the sense that an Aries is. She isn't a pioneer. But she'll climb higher and farther, as long as she can move at her own pace.

This isn't to say that Capricorn is a follower. She's not. She's simply *focused*. She knows what she wants—or thinks she does—and possesses the stamina and endurance to reach for and achieve it. Like other earth signs, notably Taurus, she has enormous patience. Give her a problem, ask her to find the solution, and she'll eventually do it, but only as long as she believes it will take her further along the path she is following. Taurus, on the other hand, will stick with it as long as it takes simply because she has committed to it.

Astrologers often refer to Capricorn as "the achiever." While it's true that achievement in her chosen area is important to her, the idea doesn't go far enough. Capricorn doesn't want to *just achieve*. She wants to be the best, at the very top, the crème de la crème. The CEO, the most highly touted movie director, the number-one bestselling novelist—this is the rarefied air she intends to inhabit. And all of that is fine, as long as it doesn't go to extremes.

In its most extreme form, Capricorn's energy can best be described in a sequence of phrases: the materialist, the money monger, the opportunist, an individual consumed by ambition. Life at these extreme latitudes is one of constant internal pressure, in which everything and everyone has its assigned spot in the hierarchy of importance. Here, life is serious business, an endless parade of regimentation, rules, and responsibility. Pretty grim.

Astrologers place the blame on Saturn, the ruler of

Capricorn and the planet that reminds us we are not alone in the universe, that we share our lives with friends and coworkers and family, and that we have some degree of responsibility for them. Saturn is also referred to as the "karmic" planet, in that it reminds us of the debts we have to repay from other lives. Structure, that's what Saturn is really about, and without it, we wouldn't have societies. We would lack the glue that keeps us earth-bound.

Since Capricorn is so other-oriented, out there in the world, caught up in the external trappings of money and power, structure and responsibility, her challenge is to remember she has an inner life, too. She is entitled to downtime, to periods of lofty spiritual thought or simply vegging out in front of the TV. It's okay to relax, to let her emotions flow, to seek and enjoy solitude. She forgets that all too often, and this is where Cancer, her polarity, can provide much-needed strength.

STRENGTH IN OPPOSITES: CAPRICORN/CANCER POLARITY

In her endless climb to the top, a schism can develop between Capricorn's personal and public values. She becomes so caught up in the self she presents to others that her inner self becomes isolated and orphaned. The wider the schism, the more extreme the isolation of her inner self. She must somehow find a public self whose values reflect those of her inner self. Only then does Capricorn achieve her full potential.

Enter Cancer, the most subjective of the twelve signs. Cancer is the sign opposite Capricorn in the zodiac. Like all polarities, the two form an axis of energy. Either sign can draw on the energy of the other. Capricorn tends to be *detached and objective,* Cancer is *subjective.* Capricorn may ignore her inner life, but Cancer lives for her inner life. Capricorn *constructs,* Cancer *perceives.* Capricorn *lays down a strategy,* Cancer *mothers and nurtures.*

In terms of spirit communication, Capricorn may be too caught up in the outer world to even think about such things until she loses someone she loves. Then she begins to question all of her most intimate and personal beliefs. The spiritual or religious beliefs she has held for most of her life may change as a result of her questioning. If she has followed a conventional religion, she may find it no longer serves her needs or she may be able to fits parts of it into a new, emerging belief system.

Medium James Van Praagh started life as a Catholic and even attended the seminary before his mediumistic abilities were fully developed. Eventually, he realized the psychic experiences he had didn't fit into the conventional Catholic worldview, and he expanded his spiritual beliefs. In *Talking to Heaven,* he discusses the evolution of his beliefs and what he believes now. "I do believe in God. In fact, I believe we are all God . . . that we are made in the likeness of God . . . We are all made of the *God spark.*"

As Capricorn begins to question her spiritual beliefs, she travels deeper within, into Cancer's territory. She focuses less and less attention on *constructing* and *attaining,* more attention on *nurturing* and *caring* for herself. Ultimately, Capricorn won't have a problem putting her discoveries about spiritual communication to practical use, but to do that she must go within first.

THE QUEST

Don't balk, don't resist—simply read on. Your quest is: *To go within to discover your personal spiritual beliefs and then apply what you learn in a practical way.*

To do this, you don't have to create a plan or a strategy. You don't even have to set a goal. Just allow your intuition to guide you—another area where Cancer excels. You often get gut feelings or hunches about facets of your professional life, so you're no stranger to intuition. But on this exploration, you're going to alter your approach somewhat. Your intuition is going to be directed into the esoteric area of spirit communication.

You usually avoid the weird and the strange. In fact, if your life is going along well, if you're happy in your professional and personal life, spirit communication is about as far from what interests you as Pluto is from the Sun. But the very areas we ignore, the very emotions we seek to sublimate, are precisely the areas and the emotions we may have to confront. Better to confront them by choice rather than to have situations and events thrust on us that force us to deal with what frightens or disturbs us. So if you find yourself gravitating toward communication with your guardian spirits, Capricorn, get out of the way and just let it happen.

THE JOURNEY

When you sign up for an adventure tour, you usually receive some sort of literature that suggests what to bring—certain clothing and other items intended to facilitate your trip. That's how it is for this journey.

Instead of mosquito repellent and suntan lotion, the prerequisites are a notebook and a tape recorder. The notebook serves as a record of your exploration—what you experience and when, the circumstances surrounding your spirit communications, how you feel when it happens, and how you feel afterward. Here you will record any changes in your diet, exercise routine, relationships with family and friends, the minutiae of your life during this period.

For you, like the majority of the signs, it's recommended that the exploration be shared with a partner. This person can be a spouse or significant other, a friend, a neighbor. Your individual approaches to this exploration may differ, but you should agree on a few basics. For instance: Will you conduct your explorations together every time? Will you conduct your explorations separately and agree to meet every so often to share notes and insights? Keep your agreement loose and flexible. This isn't a *strategy* or a *business plan;* it's an adventure in the exploration of consciousness.

The other thing to remember about working with a partner is that no one is in charge. No one is top dog. No one is the CEO, delegating duties and responsibilities to anyone else. You each are exploring spirit communication for different reasons. If you can abide by these parameters, Capricorn, then working with a partner should deepen your insight into these experiences.

Maria, a forty-eight-year-old wellness director at an assisted living facility, became interested in spirit communication as a sideline to her job. Most of the residents in her facility were elderly, and death, for them, seemed to be a looming presence. Their mortality influenced their daily lives in the most intimate ways. As a nurse, Maria understood the mechanics of death and dying. A part of her believed that when you died, you went to God. When her own mother died, though, she began to question her beliefs about the afterlife.

Her questioning started with reports about near-death

experiences. Were the experiences these people reported simply the result of neurons firing in a dying brain or was something else at work here? She began to wonder whether the whole question was far more complex than what organized religion propounded. She had been raised a Catholic and later became a Born Again Christian. Both of these belief systems have tight structures and definitive answers. And for a long time, Maria flourished within both systems.

About a year before her mother's death, her marriage of nearly two decades fell apart. Then her mother died. Her life was in transition and turmoil, and the answers from organized religions didn't really give her everything she needed.

As a Capricorn, she didn't *leap* into the unknown. But she began to take gradual and measured steps toward discovering what *she* believed about guardian spirits and the afterlife. Her exploration is ongoing. She hasn't imposed a time limit or created a strategy. She is trying to let the experience itself guide her. And that's what the Cancer polarity is all about.

MEETING YOUR GUIDES

The techniques and suggestions provided in this section are for the average Capricorn. Tailor them to fit *your* needs. After all, *your* needs are what this exploration is really about.

The Physical Body. Remember how you felt the last time you had a bad cold or the flu? You probably felt just like the woman in the TV ad for one of those over-the-counter flu remedies, your nose dripping, your head pounding, your body aching so bad it was all you could do to get into the kitchen to make chicken soup.

When your body feels like your vital organs are shutting down, the contemplation of spiritual issues is at the bottom of your list of concerns. But when you're healthy, when your diet is good and your sleep is sound, you feel as if you can take on anything—and you usually do. So how does a Capricorn keep her body fit?

As an earth sign, you probably already value your physical body and take care of it. You're naturally inclined toward athletics, and the more solitary it is, the better. Running. Biking. Yoga. Whatever your physical pleasure, it's a good idea if you do it regularly during this exploration. The better you feel, the deeper you can go into yourself. The better you feel, the clearer a channel your body becomes, and the easier it is for your guides and guardian angels to communicate with you.

James Van Praagh advocates a nutritious diet that consists mostly of vegetarian food. Avoid red meat, he says, because it "slows down the vibration of the body and in doing so slows down one's higher ranges of sensitivity." Seth, the entity that communicated through author Jane Roberts, also advocated a diet as close to vegetarianism as possible. But he wasn't didactic about it. Diet, for Seth, wasn't anywhere near as important as *beliefs* about what to eat.

Signs & Symbols. You recognize signs and symbols in your professional life. Your challenge is to recognize them in your personal life as well. Why are your kids sick all the time? Why did the plumbing in your bathroom back up? Why is your roof leaking, your car in the garage, your intimate relationships messed up? Are these things mainly the vagaries of life or is something else at work here? Is there a message you aren't hearing?

When you communicate with your guides, some of your answers will be symbolic. In many ways, the symbolism is similar to what is found in dreams. A house with deep shadows, several floors, and numerous dark and crooked passageways may represent the parts of yourself or of some other person that are hidden, camouflaged, invisible to your conscious mind. A car in a dream or in your waking life that runs out of gas may mean that you are running on empty.

With time and practice, you'll become proficient at interpreting the signs and symbols in both your waking life and your dreams. Even though this kind of interpretation isn't written into your business plan, Capricorn, you'll find that you *want* to investigate.

The Senses. Vine-ripe blueberries, their fragrance rich and warm from the sun, melt on your tongue. Symphonic sounds or the sight of a bird riding invisible currents of air sweep you away. The touch of your lover's hand is sweeter than all your other senses combined.

We are beautifully equipped for physical life. This is true even when what we sense isn't as pleasant as any of the descriptions in the previous paragraph. We taste sour watermelon. We smell garbage. We fall and injure ourselves. We *hurt.* But just as our physical senses can be sharpened, so can our inner senses.

Medium and psychic John Edward lists these inner senses as: clairaudience (clear hearing), clairvoyance (clear seeing), clairsentience (clear sensing), clairalience (clear smelling), and clairambience (clear tasting).

Clairaudience occurs when you hear an inner voice that imparts wisdom or guidance. This voice can be heard in dreams, during periods of deep relaxation, during meditation or any other altered state. With practice, it can be heard at virtually any time of the day or night. This sense is common among mediums.

Clairvoyance is the ability to see what is happening now or what will happen in the future in your life or the life of someone else. Many psychics use this sense. Although it's related to "seeing," it isn't confined to sight. It can be experienced as "gut feelings" or mental images and impressions. Clairvoyance also occurs in dream states, when the same types of images and impressions convey information about issues in our lives now or about issues and situations that may be coming up in the future. Psychics tend to have strongly developed clairvoyance.

Clairsentience is the ability to sense details about a person, event, or situation through touch. One type of clairsentience is psychometry, the ability to "read" an object. Items like jewelry and clothing retain the vibration of the individual who has worn them, and a psychometrist can pick up details about the individual by tuning in to that vibration. Psychics who work with police often use this method.

Clairalience and *clairambience* are less common than the first three inner senses. Clear smelling is the ability to glean details about an individual or situation through the sense of smell. If you suddenly catch a whiff of the pipe tobacco your dead grandfather smoked, and there's no apparent source for that smoke, then you may be experiencing a communication from him.

Clear tasting involves picking up details about an individual or situation through the sense of taste. Perhaps your deceased father loved key lime pie. If he's trying to communicate with you, the taste of key lime may fill your mouth.

To these senses, James Van Praagh adds "inspirational

thought." He defines this as receiving "thoughts, impressions, knowledge—all without forethought." In this type of sensing, a spirit or group of spirits "melds their thoughts together and impresses the person to write a certain piece of music or paint a particular picture." In other words, the vehicle is creativity.

As a cardinal earth sign, Capricorn, clairsentience is probably the inner sense that you can develop most easily. Psychic intuitive Noreen Renier, who has done some work with police, sometimes requests a lock of hair from a client. It isn't witchcraft, as some people believe. It's a way to connect with a person's inner vibration, the source and heart of who the client is. It's called psychometry.

Psychometrists read objects, specifically the emotional residue that remains on the object. Your grandmother Claire wore her wedding ring until the day she died, then that ring went to you. When you slipped it on your finger, what did you feel? When a psychometrist touches that ring, when he or she holds it tightly in the palm, images and impressions come to mind.

If you have a natural talent for psychometry, practice it by using objects that your partner selects. Metal objects are the easiest to work with—gold or silver jewelry, for instance. The objects your partner selects should belong to someone, as opposed to jewelry fresh from a jewelry store. As you hold the object in one hand and then the other, you'll feel either warmth or coolness. The sensations may differ depending on which hand you use. Center yourself with deep breathing, and request that information about the object flow into your awareness. It will take some practice, but eventually you'll receive images, impressions, or even sensations about the individual who owns the object.

Keep track of your progress in your journal.

Stay Grounded. This usually isn't a problem for most earth signs. Your best method of staying grounded, in fact, may be through regular physical exercise.

Deep breathing is also an excellent way to ground yourself. Better yet, you can do it anywhere, at any time, whenever you feel a bit panicky or overwhelmed. If, during this exploration, you feel disturbed at any point, simply place your right hand under your breast and inhale. Pull the air deeply into your lungs, hold to the count of five, then exhale slowly, feeling it against your hand. For other types of breathing exercises, glance through any of the yoga books currently on the market. Most should have breathing exercises included.

Trust. Usually when we talk about trust, it's within the context of relationships. In the area of spiritual communication, however, when we talk about trust, we're referring to your trusting the guidance you receive. This can be a challenging area for you because you tend to trust your instincts primarily in your decisions about your profession and career. The remedy? When you get what appears to be guidance from a spiritual source, weigh it intuitively in the same way that you would an impression about a career decision or choice. Then ask yourself the following questions:

- Does the guidance feel right to you?
- Is the guidance uplifting? Positive?
- Is it within your capacity to act upon?
- Are you able to distinguish genuine guidance from your own wishful thinking?

Once you've proven to your own satisfaction that intuition is your strongest ally in this exploration, trusting your impressions won't be an issue.

The Flow. For earth signs, "the flow" isn't about action and doing, as it is for fire signs. It's about the smooth continuation of stability and reliability. But in the course of this exploration, the flow refers to nonresistance.

Let's say you and your partner are experimenting with psychometry. She has just handed you a plain gold ring. You request guidance on receiving information about the ring's owner, hold it in your hand, and shut your eyes. Almost immediately, you're bombarded with disturbing images. Perhaps you even begin to feel physically uncomfortable. What do you do? You resist, your eyes fly open, your intuition shuts down—and the flow of images and the physical discomfort stop.

You have just stepped *out of the flow*.

Instead of resisting and shutting off the intuitive flow, a wiser course might be to set the ring down for a few moments and use one or more of the protective measures discussed in the next section. You might request that the information come to you in a less disturbing way, without any of the physical sensations.

When psychic intuitive Millie Gemondo receives disturbing information during a reading, she may feel physical sensations as well. She describes to her client what she is receiving, what she is feeling, and then allows the information and the sensations to flow out of her. "When you get information that is disturbing to you," says Gemondo, "then invoke protection for yourself. I say the ninety-first psalm. It's best not to hold these disturbing images or impressions in your mind. Let them go."

Protection. Most psychics and mediums have protective rituals that they do before attempting spirit communication. It's not that you're protecting yourself against guides, guardian angels, or spirits in general. You're protecting yourself against lower energies in the spirit world. As Van Praagh points out in *Talking to Heaven,* spirits exist on different levels in the afterlife, according to their spiritual evolution. The "higher" the spirit energy, the clearer the information you receive.

For you, Capricorn, the best protective ritual is to simply shut your eyes for a few moments and focus on drawing the highest possible energy. You may want to have a few objects around you that remind you of what you're trying to achieve.

Experiment. Find what works best for you.

THE MAP

Unless you're the sort of person who has a built-in compass, you usually need a map when you're in a strange city or country and have to find your way around. In this exploration, your map is your journal. Granted, it won't be much help during your first attempt at spirit communication. The suggestions given in this book are intended to do that. But for every attempt you make afterward to communicate with your guardians and guides, your journal will provide a means to do it.

The clearer and more detailed your notes, the easier it will be for you to communicate with and obtain information from your guides. Even if you begin this exploration with nothing more than a curiosity about the afterlife or a need to see your dead grandfather, your experiences will deepen your intuition and offer you another approach to living. Your fear of death may be eased. Maybe you'll even learn how to relax!

That alone should make this exploration worth at least a few weeks of your time.

To help get you started, use the table below. List five areas you would like to explore and possible ways of doing it.

Areas to Explore	How to Go About It
1. _____	_____
2. _____	_____
3. _____	_____
4. _____	_____
5. _____	_____

THE GRAIL

Your grail is: *By allowing your intuition to lead the way on this exploration, you are now prepared to let it lead you through the rest of your life.*

YOUR RECORDS

Date: _____

Time: _____

Weather: _____

Other factors: _____

_____

Your experience: _____

_____

_____

_____

_____

15. Aquarius the Water Bearer ≈

Identity is not dependent on physical existence.

—SETH

January 20–February 18
Fixed Air
Ruled by Uranus

THE SYMBOL

The water bearer. In the movie *The Gift*, actress Cate Blanchette played a psychic who used cards to focus her ability during readings she gave for clients. The deck of cards consisted of symbols that were used in J. D. Rhine's telepathy experiments at Duke University in the early part of the twentieth century. These cards are called Zener cards and consist of various geometric symbols: a circle, a square, a triangle, and a pair of wavy lines.

In one scene, Blanchett is reading for a client whose daughter is missing and several cards with wavy lines on them turn up, one after the other. The viewer immediately realizes the man's daughter may have drowned because the pair of wavy lines suggests water.

But in astrology this symbol of water and waves represents Aquarius, an air sign. So why is Aquarius called the water bearer?

The name and the symbol are so deceiving they have led the unsuspecting Aquarius to believe he is a water sign. Water signs feel their way through life. They are about raw perception. Aquarius, on the other hand, thinks his way through life. His perceptions are filtered through the mind.

Astrologers have various explanations for the Aquarius glyph that may or may not fit the sign. But that isn't the point. The qualities of Aquarius would be better served as a glyph for infinity, a figure eight. This symbol embraces all that the Aquarius mentality is about. The infinite in freedom. The infinite in individuality. The infinite paradigm for the twenty-first century.

The difference between Aquarius and Sagittarius is that Aquarius isn't just looking for "The Truth." He's looking for *his* truth. The big picture that Aquarius sees has large chunks missing—equality for all, food for the hungry, homes for the homeless. The individual is of prime importance in the Aquarius scheme of things because only through individuals can the collective reality be altered. What helps one, helps all. We are all interconnected: that's the Aquarius song.

The Aquarius perceptions are not like those of other people. The sign is ruled by Uranus, the planet that represents sudden and unexpected change, the development of individuality, and the ability to break through social and cultural paradigms. Uranus also symbolizes revolution and brilliance. With Aquarius, that brilliance is about thinking in ways that other people don't. Where many of us get trapped into believing that what we've been taught is the truth, Aquarius refuses to accept anyone else's truth as his own. *He* selects what is true and not true for him. *He* decides on his lifestyle, his creeds, his friendships.

As a fixed sign, Aquarius can be just as stubborn as Taurus. The risk is that he may become so stubborn that he gets stuck in certain patterns of behavior that are simply eccentric, not brilliant. Then, regardless of how sharp his intellect is, he ceases to integrate what he learns into who he is. He is no longer the paradigm buster, but the rebel who rebels simply for the sake of rebellion.

This is when the energy of his polar opposite, Leo, becomes a tremendous asset.

STRENGTH IN OPPOSITES: AQUARIUS/LEO POLARITY

Aquarius *reforms,* Leo *expresses.* Aquarius is concerned about individuality as applied to the larger world of humanity; Leo's concern is primarily himself. Where Aquarius thinks and then acts, Leo acts and worries about it later. Aquarius is *future-oriented,* Leo is *present-oriented.* Aquarius demands *freedom from the status quo,* Leo demands freedom in *creative expression.*

So how does all of this translate in terms of spirit communication? Intellectually, Aquarius already embraces the possibility that we can communicate with guides and guardian angels. Intellectually, he can believe that nearly anything is possible. But attempting communication is something else altogether.

If he's genuinely interested in attempting communication, then he needs to use Leo energy, which means approaching the exploration from the heart rather than with the mind. Be dramatic and bold in what you're seeking. Don't hold back just because this area may be one that is not familiar to you. Leap in, take the risk, embrace the experience.

Ann, an Aquarius and a lawyer, had a peripheral interest in the afterlife and spirit communication, but really didn't pursue the interest until her father passed away. His death suddenly opened up all the "Big Questions." What happens when we die? Where do our souls go? Is it possible to communicate with the dead? Her musings led to more questions, and her questions opened a deeper need for answers.

She always had excellent dream recall, but now her dreams and her recall took on even greater clarity. A number of her dreams about her father were so vivid that she awakened feeling as if she'd been with him. She started giving herself suggestions before she fell asleep at night that in her dreams she would meet up with her father, communicate with him. She didn't tell anyone, not even her spouse, about what she was doing. But she started keeping a journal of her dreams, and found she was able to recall three or four a night. Many were about her father, but just as many were about her grandparents, who had passed away years earlier. In most of the dreams of this kind, she felt that genuine communication was taking place.

Then, suddenly and inexplicably, the communication dreams stopped. Through a series of synchronicities, Ann ended up at a New Age conference where she heard author and psychiatrist Brian Weiss speak about reincarnation and his experiences with "the masters." According to Weiss, the masters are a group of evolved souls whose existence he first became aware of through a patient named Catherine. Her hypnotic regressions were what first led Weiss into his exploration of past lives and into the writing of his bestseller *Many Lives, Many Masters.*

She went home with a lot to think about, and that night had a dream in which her father seemed to be advising her to delve into spirit communication. Two days later, she enrolled in a workshop on intuitive development.

Ann's story is particularly interesting for several reasons. The conference and the workshop in which she enrolled are the kind of pursuits that Aquarius may follow. But her reasons for enrolling in the workshop came about specifically because of the dream in which her father advised her to pursue the exploration of spiritual communication. Her commitment, then, came from the heart.

THE QUEST

First and foremost, an exploration of spirit communication is an adventure that will broaden your intellectual scope. But it won't do that unless your exploration comes from the heart, from the deepest sea of your emotions. Already, you're resisting because you don't feel comfortable with emotions, with expressing them or feeling them or even thinking about them any more than you have to. On the other hand, it may consume more energy to resist than to simply embrace whatever happens and see where it leads.

Here's your quest: *Enter this exploration as though you're an actor playing a part.*

When good actors prepare for parts, they do research. *They learn the lay of the land.* When Dustin Hoffman prepared for a part as an autistic in *Rain Man,* he observed autistics—how they walk, talk, stand still. And in the movie, he played an autistic so convincingly that the audience was able to suspend their disbelief that he was Dustin Hoffman, famous actor. He became an autistic man who was able, at just a glance, to determine how many toothpicks were in a box when the box was knocked to the floor and the toothpicks came spilling out. He was able to discern patterns that no one else could perceive.

Pretend that you are talking to spirits. Let your imagination soar. If you pretend long enough, the pretense becomes real and things begin to happen.

The Journey

Aquarius often has a fixed agenda when he travels. He knows what he wants to see, do, eat, experience. So on this journey, you won't have an agenda. You won't even have a complicated packing list. The only tangible items you need for this exploration are a notebook and a tape recorder.

The tape recorder is optional and serves only as a backup for when it isn't convenient to write down your experiences. If you keep your notebook on a computer, print out your notes every few days so that you have a hard copy.

In this notebook, you should record whatever you experience, how you feel about your experience, the context, texture, and nature of what you experience, and how all of this contributes to your knowledge about *the lay of the land*. If, while you're lying in bed one night thinking about your deceased aunt, the bedside light comes on by itself, then jot it in your notebook. Write about how you felt when it happened, what the weather was like, about anything that may be remotely related to the experience. Even if the act of writing all this down strikes you as a waste of time or an exercise in futility, do it anyway. Be aware of how you feel as you're writing.

When Ann first began recording her dreams, she resented the fact that she woke in the middle of the night and felt compelled to write down her dreams. Sometimes, she would have to step into the bathroom or the hall to see what she was writing, and then it was more difficult for her to get back to sleep. She often woke tired the next morning.

Then she started using a tape recorder that she kept right next to her bed. This technique worked well because Ann didn't have to get up to record her dream and was able to fall back to sleep almost immediately. The next day, she transcribed her dream into her notebook.

Since she had a half-hour commute to work every morning, she started bringing the tape recorder with her and found herself speaking into it as she drove. Eventually, her thoughts on these early morning drives worked their way into her regular journal. Before each attempt that she made to contact her guides and spirits while she was awake, she read over her most recent notes. The information usually provided the necessary insight she needed at the time.

More than anything else, this exploration is about *you*. It's about *your* needs, *your* talents, *your* life. It's about *the part you're playing at this moment in time.*

For nearly every sign, it's been suggested that the exploration take place with a partner. If it's at all possible, you should do the same. It should be someone you know, but you don't have to know the person well. You should agree on the broad strokes of this exploration, yet retain spontaneity. No agenda, no lists, no goals other than the simple experience of it all.

Some of the broad strokes to discuss might be:

- How frequently will you meet to share insights and experiences?
- Do you need to meet at all? Will the phone or e-mail serve the same purpose? If so, then your partner can easily be someone in another state or country.
- Understand where your partner is coming from. Ask about their motives concerning this exploration.
- Should intuitive experiments be part of what you share?
- Do you need a time limit? Two weeks? A month? Six weeks? Or should you just play it by ear?

Regardless of whether you undertake this exploration alone or with a partner, stay rooted in the here and now. Be fully present. Allow yourself to feel.

MEETING YOUR GUIDES

The techniques and suggestions provided here are for the average Aquarius, if there is any such individual. Experiment with them, revise them, *re-form* them to fit your needs.

The Physical Body. Monday, you had a migraine that laid you up. Tuesday, you were too tired to try any experiments. Wednesday, your son and his family showed up unexpectedly and stayed until the weekend. Now it's Sunday evening and what you really want is a bowl of chicken soup and about fifteen hours of sleep.

Go for a walk instead.

It doesn't have to be a long walk. Two blocks are fine.

But make them count. Walk fast, swing your arms, breathe the air. Feel the movement of your legs, be aware of how the ground feels against the soles of your shoes. Let your body speak. What is it saying? How does it feel?

When you feel good, when you're healthy, you become a clearer channel for spirit communication. In fact, when you don't feel good, spirit communication is pretty low on your list of priorities and who can blame you? But a walk gets your blood moving, your mind working, your heart pumping. There are other benefits, too. A walk, whether it's with a partner or alone, takes you out into the world beyond your backyard. You meet other people who are walking. Perhaps you stop to converse, to trade stories. The point here is really twofold: the physical benefits and the everything-else benefits.

If a walk every evening doesn't suit you, find something that does. Something regular. Something you enjoy as you're doing it.

Signs & Symbols. Spirits and guides often convey information in symbols. Maybe one of the symbols you receive is that of a train. There doesn't appear to be anything unusual about the train; it looks like a standard version. You're not planning a trip anywhere, and neither is anyone else in your family. So how do you go about deciphering what the symbol means?

First, determine if the symbol is significant. This is mostly a feeling, a gut reaction. Some symbols simply *feel right.* They *resonate.* If the train is that sort of symbol, then request clarification about its significance. If you received the symbol in a dream, then before you fall asleep ask for clarification. If you received it during meditation, ask for clarification as you're meditating. If the symbol came to you through some other means—automatic writing, an image that simply popped into your head, clairvoyance, or as a repetitive image in your waking life—then brainstorm with the symbol.

The best way to brainstorm with a symbol or image is to write it in a journal and then quickly make a list of associations. With a train, for instance, the associations might be:

- A method of transportation.
- To "train" for something.
- A trip on a train.
- A series or progression of events.
- An entourage or convoy.
- Aftermath.

These words, in turn, may trigger other associations. Always look for the most obvious meaning first.

In his book *Talking to Heaven,* medium James Van Praagh notes, "You are not doing this work alone. You are in partnership with those in the spirit world." He encourages people to work cooperatively with their guides by requesting additional clarification or additional information when a message isn't clear. "You have to let them know *how* you want them to communicate. Tell them to impress you in a certain way. For instance, if you want to know if it is a female or male energy coming through, ask them to impress you with their gender."

Van Praagh, like many psychics and mediums, established a communication system with his guides and spirits that lets him know which side of the family a particular spirit comes from. For the father's side of the family, Van Praagh asks the spirit to stand on the left side of the individual. For the mother's side of the family, the spirit is to stand to the right of the person. If the spirit is a child, he asks that it stand in front of the individual. A grandparent is asked to stand behind the person. "In this way, there is a clear system for the spirit to use."

If you don't see spirits, but receive impressions or mental images and symbols, then ask the spirits to be clear about the impressions and symbols, and then look for the simplest interpretation first. If that doesn't resonate, use a combination of your reason and your intuition to decipher the symbol.

The Senses. Which of your five senses is the strongest? Are you able to identify the herbs and spices in food simply by the taste? Is your hearing or sight exceptionally good?

Our five senses enable us to successfully navigate through our daily lives by conveying information about our environment. As you read this book, your hearing is picking up sounds in your environment—a TV or radio, children's voices, music, birds singing. Your sense of touch conveys information about the weight of the book, the texture of the pages, the smoothness of the cover.

In much the same way, our inner senses convey information about our inner lives and the invisible world around us. Inner senses are used in all psychic work and in communicating with your guides.

Medium and author John Edward lists these psychic senses as: clairaudience (clear hearing), clairvoyance (clear seeing), clairsentience (clear sensing), clairalience (clear smelling), and clairambience (clear tasting).

Hearing an inner voice that imparts wisdom or guidance is how *clairaudience* often manifests. This voice can be heard in dreams, during periods of deep relaxation, during meditation or any other altered state. With practice, it can be heard at virtually any time of the day or night. This sense is common among mediums.

Clairvoyance is the ability to see what is happening now or what will happen in the future in your life or the life of someone else. Many psychics use this sense. Although it's related to "seeing," it isn't confined to sight. It can be experienced as "gut feelings" or mental images and impressions. Psychics tend to have strongly developed clairvoyance.

Clairsentience is the ability to sense details about a person, event, or situation through touch. One type of clairsentience is psychometry, the ability to "read" an object. The idea here is that personal items like jewelry and clothing retain the vibration of the individual who has worn them, and a psychometrist can pick up details about the individual by tuning in to that vibration. Psychics who work with police often use this method.

Clairalience and *clairambience* are less common than the first three inner senses. Clear smelling is the ability to glean details about an individual or situation through the sense of smell. An example of this would be when the scent of your grandmother's cologne suddenly permeates the air around you.

Clear tasting involves picking up details about an individual or situation through the sense of taste. Perhaps your deceased father loved key lime pie. If he's trying to communicate with you, the taste of key lime may fill your mouth.

To these senses, James Van Praagh adds "inspirational thought." He defines this as receiving "thoughts, impressions, knowledge—all without forethought." In this type of sensing, a spirit or group of spirits "melds their thoughts together and impresses the person to write a certain piece of music or paint a particular picture." In other words, the vehicle is creativity.

As a fixed air sign, Aquarius, clairvoyance and "tuning in" through creative expression should come fairly easily to you. Glance through the list of books in Appendix 2 for titles pertaining to the development of intuition and psychic abilities. You might also want to check out Julia Cameron's classic on creativity: *The Artist's Way*.

Stay Grounded. This area is especially important for air signs, who live so much in their minds. It simply means to stay rooted in the here and now, in the physical world—an important facet of exploring communication. Mediums and psychics have various techniques for staying grounded. Here are some suggestions:

- Stay physically fit.
- Before attempting spirit communication, center yourself with some deep breathing.
- Use colors in your work area that remind you of the earth, of physical reality, of people whom you care about.
- Weather permitting, rub your bare feet against the ground several times. According to intuitive Renie Wiley, this helps establish a connection with the earth.
- Put live plants in your work area.

Trust. Learning to trust the impressions and information you receive can be challenging, especially in the beginning, unless you're aware of and familiar with your intuitive impressions. As an Aquarius, your intuitive impressions may come to you in flashes of images or symbols. If you already have an intuitive tool that you use— the tarot, for instance—then take close notice of how your intuition manifests. Once you understand how the intuitive process manifests for you, you'll be much better able to judge the impressions you receive and to trust those that *feel right*.

The Flow. For an air sign, "the flow" happens when your thoughts and creativity move through you unimpeded. In much the same way, the flow in spirit communication occurs when you don't erect blocks or obstacles to whatever you're experiencing. *Nonresistance*—that's the key.

Experienced psychics are usually able to enter the flow as soon as they focus their inner senses. For psychic Millie Gemondo to enter the flow, it takes a few deep breaths, some deep concentration, and then images and impressions start moving through her. Once you familiarize yourself with the state of consciousness that characterizes the flow, it's easy to find your way to it.

The funny thing about the flow is that if you try too hard to attain it, it eludes you. For several nights in a row, give yourself the suggestion that you'll be able to attain the flow the next time you attempt to communicate with your guides. Then get out of the way and just let it happen.

Protection. Mediums and psychics seem to agree that spirits, like people, exist on different energy levels. When you attempt spirit communication, you want to be sure you attract the highest possible energy. Prayer and visualization are two popular ways to ensure that you do.

Medium John Edward, a Catholic, says the rosary before he attempts spirit communication. Psychic intuitive Char Margolis wrote her own prayer for this purpose, which is in her book *Questions from Earth, Answers from Heaven*. Another popular technique for protection is to imagine a cocoon of white light surrounding yourself.

You can also smudge your work area with the smoke from burning sage, an effective energy cleanser, or surround yourself with "power" objects like certain rocks and crystals. Your protective techniques, like everything else in spirit communication, become clarified with practice. If you're at a loss about what to try, psychic intuitive Millie Gemondo suggests the 91st Psalm.

As an Aquarius, the most visionary of signs, you'll come up with something that no one else is doing and whatever it is will work for you. Experiment!

THE MAP

Your journal is your map for this journey. Even though it initially won't tell you how to get where you're going, subsequent explorations of spirit communication will be easier because of it.

Think of your journal as a script that you're following for this great game of pretend. It will be filled with techniques, experiences, and all of the emotions you feel during this exploration. It's there to remind you that there's nothing to fear about what you feel, that your emotions are your most powerful resource for spirit communication.

Just to get you started, use the table below to list five areas you would like to explore and how you might undertake this exploration. If, for example, you would like to develop a particular inner sense, jot that down and a possible way that you might develop it.

Areas to Explore	How to Go About It
1. _____	_____
2. _____	_____
3. _____	_____
4. _____	_____
5. _____	_____

THE GRAIL

Your grail, Aquarius, is: *To use what you've learned on this exploration to expand your worldview.*

YOUR RECORDS

Date: _____

Time: _____

Weather: _____

Other factors: _____

_____

Your experience: _____

_____

_____

_____

_____

_____

_____

_____

_____

_____

_____

_____

_____

16. Pisces the Fish ♓

$$E=MC^2$$

—Einstein

February 19–March 20
Mutable Water
Ruled by Neptune

THE SYMBOL

The symbol for Pisces, like that for Gemini, comes in pairs. Instead of twins, though, there are two fish swimming in opposite directions. They represent the constant struggle Pisces has between her head and her heart. Her mind insists on one thing, her heart insists on something else. In this struggle, winners are rare. Usually, a compromise of some kind is in order, a bargaining between head and heart. *We'll do it your way this time and my way the next.*

Maybe it isn't always that obvious, but the general idea here is that Pisces isn't always at her best when it comes to making decisions. When she appears most indecisive and ambivalent to others, however, she is actually sinking deep into the waters of her own being, then deeper still into the vast ocean of the collective unconscious where she is most comfortable.

In the *Star Trek* scheme of things, the Borgs are an alien race that assimilates individuality into the collective mind. They are like bees so intimately connected to their hive that a distress call from the queen will automatically turn them homeward. They can't help it. It's how nature has programmed them. In much the same way, this is how nature programmed Pisces. This isn't to say that Pisces is devoid of individuality. But the pull of the collective unconscious is incredibly strong in these individuals.

What collective? What unconscious? Pisces asks.

In Carl Jung's worldview, the collective unconscious is the place where we are all connected. It's the Aquarius idea that what affects one, affects all. But for Pisces, it's not just an intellectual idea—it's home. It's really the deepest part of the ocean.

Here, life is about *feeling,* but feeling so profound, so powerful, that it extends well beyond family and third cousins four times removed. Here, the feeling is extended to the homeless woman on the street, to the stranger in room four whose bones are eaten up with cancer, to the hundreds of thousands of AIDS victims, to the animals at the local animal shelter. Here we find people with missions, with causes, people who are willing to make sacrifices that ultimately benefit everyone. Here we find dreamers, mystics, Mother Theresas, Einsteins. Here is the intuitive of the zodiac.

But here, too, are addictions. Booze, drugs, sex, gambling, abuse . . .

For Pisces, the veil between ego and *other* is thin, almost insubstantial at times. Blame Neptune, the ruler of the sign. Neptune dissolves the boundaries between worlds, between ego and imagination.

For Pisces, there usually isn't much doubt that the soul

survives death and that it's possible to speak to those who have passed on. Pisces knows there are always greater forces at work in our lives and that we can access these forces through dreams, mystical experiences, creative and spiritual work, and the imagination. More than any other sign, Pisces instinctively knows that what can be imagined can be made real.

The challenge for Pisces in any esoteric exploration, however, is transcendence without losing her objective self. This is where Virgo, the polarity for Pisces, comes into play.

STRENGTH IN OPPOSITES: PISCES/VIRGO POLARITY

Pisces and Virgo are polar opposites. They form an axis of energy that either sign can draw on when needed. This was discussed to some extent in relation to Edgar Cayce's chart in Chapter 4. But here, we're bringing it right up close and personal.

Where Pisces *dreams,* Virgo *discerns.* Pisces sees the forest, Virgo sees the trees. Pisces *absorbs,* Virgo *analyzes.* Pisces *imagines,* Virgo *critiques.* For Pisces, surrender to a greater power is no big deal. She does it daily without even thinking about it. But before Virgo surrenders, she must scrutinize this greater power, place it under the microscope of her sharp perception. Even then, she may not surrender herself completely.

"Discipline," writes James Van Praagh, "plays a very intricate part in developing any spiritual gifts or spiritual communication."

And Virgo is good at discipline, at following rules and guidelines, at tending to details. For Pisces to gain from spirit communication, she must gather details, then analyze and dissect them. She must connect the dots in her experiences so that a fuller, larger, and more perfect picture emerges. Instead of letting her imagination roam the universe, her journey as unstructured as her fascination for what she finds, Pisces has to apply some Virgo strategy to her exploration. She must study the details of her own consciousness, how it functions, how it reaches and stretches, how it recoils and rejoices, how it grasps and surrenders.

As a mutable sign like Virgo and Gemini, Pisces possesses a natural flexibility. She is able to adapt to changes. This adaptability is one of her greatest assets and, in this exploration, will help her to grasp the vagaries of her experiences with her own guides.

Pisces Edgar Cayce didn't seem to remember much of what he said while he was in trance, reading for himself or for others. But in his waking, conscious life, he struggled to fit the material into the context of his religious beliefs. The first time information about reincarnation was presented in the readings, Cayce and his wife went through the Bible, trying to find some reference to past lives so that he would feel comfortable bringing through past-life material. In other words, he sought details that would verify and support the psychic information he was receiving. This is how the Pisces/Virgo polarity works at its best.

To make the most efficient use of your Pisces/Virgo polarity, follow these guidelines:

- Note all *details* in your experiences with spirit communication. Note how you feel, note the time of day, note the weather. Note the impressions and images you receive.

- Allow the experience to flow while it's happening. Don't put up barriers. But afterward, scrutinize everything that happened or didn't happen.
- Try to use what you learn in a practical way. How can it help you to enrich your life? How can it help other people?
- If this exploration begins to interfere with the way you function in your daily life, then take some time off. Engage in activities that ground you in the here and now, in the physical world. Then resume the exploration, but in a more measured way.

The Quest

To scrutinize the details of your experiences with spirit communication so that you fully understand the process itself. This is your quest, Pisces.

Details are probably the last thing you want to deal with. But for the purpose of this exploration, your attention to details, to analysis, to logic, and to reason can spell the difference in the quality of your experience. This doesn't mean that everything you experience has to make sense. It simply has to fit a *pattern*. And the pattern is what evolves, over time, from one experience to the next.

If you're unsure what is meant by a pattern, look to your dreams. Pisces individuals tend to be vivid dreamers. Once they learn how to recall their dreams, their recall is excellent. If you're already proficient at recalling your dreams, then keep track of your dreams for a week. Write them down. Notice repetitive themes and symbols. Spirits and guides often communicate with us through our dreams. So if you're conversing with the dead in your dreams, it's likely this is spirit communication.

THE JOURNEY

Only two items are required for this trip: a notebook and a tape recorder. The notebook is to be a record of your experiences with spirit communication. In it, you'll record all of the details about your experiences. The more details, the better. You can include your dreams here, too. The recorder is optional, mainly a backup for when it isn't convenient to write in the journal.

Nearly every sign has been encouraged to undertake this exploration with a partner. This is especially important for you. A partner will help to keep you grounded in the real world, will provide insight into your experiences, and will make it more of an adventure. If at all possible, your partner should not be another Pisces, simply because your approaches to this type of exploration may be too similar. Your partner should be someone whose interests are compatible with your own yet whose beliefs are different enough so that you each have insights to offer the other.

Even if you and your partner already have knowledge and experience in this area, do some research before you get started. Read books on the topic, attend a workshop, search through the resources and related topics on the Web, have a reading with a psychic or medium. If you don't know who to go to, check out the resources in Appendix 2.

Astrologically, your experiences of spirit communication are strongly influenced by the sign and house placement of your natal Neptune. Check Appendix 1 to find your Neptune sign. Then be sure to read Chapter 18 on Neptune signs and houses.

MEETING YOUR GUIDES

The guidelines and suggestions in this section are general, intended for the average Pisces. You already may have guidelines that you follow, or you may alter these and create others during this exploration.

The Physical Body. Physical exercise grounds you. It makes you aware of your body—of the magnificent internal connections that create movement, that allow you to think, to breathe, to exist. In this exploration, Pisces, it's important that you are grounded. If you already have a physical exercise routine, continue it. If you don't, then create one. The exercise itself can be anything—walking, running, biking, swimming, yoga, workouts at the gym. As a water sign, you would especially benefit from swimming.

During this exploration, try to eat as little red meat as possible. According to James Van Praagh, "Red meat . . . slows down the vibration of the body and in doing so slows down one's higher ranges of sensitivity." In other words, if your diet is high in red meat, it may be more difficult for you to communicate with spiritual guides. Van Praagh points out that the endocrine glands, especially the adrenals, are of prime importance in spiritual communication. These glands are particularly stressed by caffeine, sugars, refined foods, alcohol, and drugs.

If your diet or exercise routine changes during this exploration, make note of it in your journal. In fact, make note of anything pertaining to the physical body that facilitates or impedes spirit communication. The more detail you include, the easier it will be to enter the state of consciousness where spirit communication is possible.

Signs & Symbols. Pisces is fluent in the language of symbols. It's where she lives and breathes. A hawk soars past her window, and for her it's a personal message. Her car runs out of gas or the battery dies, and she immediately draws the connection to some area of her life where she is "running on empty" or where her "energy has died." Whether the symbols appear in her waking life or in her dreams, this is an area that Pisces understands.

When symbols are involved in spirit communication, you generally can figure out what they mean. In this exploration, at least initially, record the symbols you receive, note how you received them (dream, waking life), and note anything else that's pertinent. Jot down what you think the symbol means or to what it refers. Over time, you'll develop a dictionary of personal symbols.

Most mediums and psychics work out some sort of communication system with their guides and spirits. Van Praagh, for instance, advises that you let your guides know *how* you want them to communicate. "Tell them to impress you in a certain way. For instance, if you want to know if it is a female or male energy coming through, ask them to impress you with their gender."

When psychic intuitive Millie Gemondo needs clarification on an impression she receives, she requests clarification, then sets the issue aside and returns to it later. By then, the impression is usually clearer. So when you're puzzled by something you've received, *ask for help*. As Van Praagh says, "You are not doing this work alone. You are in partnership with those in the spirit world . . . You do your part, and spirit does its part."

The Senses. Just as our five senses are vital to our ability to negotiate daily life, our inner senses are vital to our psychic functioning.

Medium John Edward lists these psychic senses as: clairaudience (clear hearing), clairvoyance (clear seeing), clairsentience (clear sensing), clairalience (clear smelling), and clairambience (clear tasting).

With *clairaudience,* you hear an inner voice that imparts wisdom or guidance. This voice can be heard in dreams, during periods of deep relaxation, during meditation or any other altered state. With practice, it can be heard at virtually any time of the day or night. This sense is common among mediums.

Clairvoyance is the ability to see what is happening now or what will happen in the future in your life or the life of someone else. Many psychics use this sense. Although it's related to "seeing," it isn't confined to sight. It can be experienced as "gut feelings" or mental images and impressions. Psychics tend to have strongly developed clairvoyance.

Clairsentience is the ability to sense details about a person, event, or situation through touch. One type of clairsentience is psychometry, the ability to "read" an object. Items like jewelry and clothing retain the vibration of the individual who has worn them, and a psychometrist can pick up details about the individual by tuning in to that vibration. Psychics who work with police often use this method.

Clairalience and *clairambience* are less common than the first three inner senses. Clear smelling is the ability to glean details about an individual or situation through the sense of smell. If you suddenly catch the scent of the cologne your dead grandmother used, and there's no apparent source for that scent, then you may be experiencing a communication from her.

Clear tasting involves picking up details about an individual or situation through the sense of taste. Perhaps your deceased father loved key lime pie. If he's trying to communicate with you, the taste of key lime may fill your mouth.

To these senses, James Van Praagh adds "inspirational thought." He defines this as receiving "thoughts, impressions, knowledge—all without forethought." In this type of sensing, a spirit or group of spirits "melds their thoughts together and impresses the person to write a certain piece of music or paint a particular picture." In other words, the vehicle is creativity.

As a mutable water sign, you're especially good at clairvoyance, precognition (picking up information about the future), and clairaudience. Any or all of these abilities can manifest through dreams or while you're conscious. Sometimes, however, your abilities may seem sporadic and random, so the challenge is to learn how to turn the abilities on when you need them.

This is an area where your partner can be a tremendous help. Each of you should select an inner sense that you would like to develop more fully. Then design experiments that test that sense. If, for instance, precognition is one of the senses you would like to develop fully, then you might try to come up with tomorrow's newspaper headlines. Or you might try predicting something for your partner.

Appendix 2 has a list of books on spirit communication, intuition, psychic ability, and related subjects. Select a couple of appropriate titles. Remember that tapping into your inner senses isn't difficult for you. The challenge is to learn how to tap into them on demand.

Stay Grounded. This area is important for you, Pisces, and may be one of the most challenging parts of your exploration. Because your natural inclination is often so mystical and otherworldly, the here and now sometimes feels alien to you, as if you don't really belong. Staying grounded will make your experience with spirit communication much richer and, in the end, more practical.

Here are some suggestions:

- On the days you're going to attempt communication with your guides, do something physically active for at least fifteen to thirty minutes. Walk, jump on a trampoline, swim, whatever you enjoy. Be acutely aware of your body, of how you feel physically, notice *details*.
- In your work area, include items that hold personal significance and that tie you to people and locations you care about. One Pisces woman created a kind of altar where she conducted her spiritual work. On it, she put a vase of freshly cut flowers, photos of her family and pets, and a selection of stones and crystals.
- Put live plants in your work area. Invite your pets to stick around when you're doing your spiritual work. Pets often detect the presence of spirits, and a pet's reactions will tell you quite a bit about the kinds of spirits you have attracted.
- Do some deep breathing before you begin your spiritual work.
- Let the process unfold.

Trust. This is easy for you. In the place where you live, hunches and intuition are business as usual. The business is so usual, in fact, that most of the time you don't even think about it. You have an urge, an impulse, a feeling—and you act on it. In this exploration, all you have to do is bring that same trust along with you.

The Flow. In your daily life, you may feel conflicted and torn between one thing and another. It may be difficult for you to make up your mind. You may resist certain experiences, situations, and people. But when it comes to spiritual concerns, you usually don't waffle. You enter the flow with astonishing ease—absorbing the experience, the process, the feelings, the whole nine yards. And you can do it anywhere—at home, in a car, asleep, while you're interacting socially, in the middle of your workday. You simply divert your attention elsewhere, and there you are, thick in the flow, in the rushing river of your own consciousness.

Protection. In the ordinary world, you're so naturally sensitive to other people's energy that it's vital for you to associate only with upbeat people. In spiritual work, the same holds true.

Mediums and psychics seem to agree that spirits exist on different levels. In the movie *What Dreams May Come,* there's a particularly disturbing scene when Robin Williams travels through an energy level where most of the spirits are embedded in what looks like black molasses. They are moaning, they are screaming, they are pleading for help and salvation. In the Catholic version of the afterlife, this would probably be purgatory. Williams has to pass through this area to reach his wife, a suicide, who exists on a bleak and isolated level where many suicides allegedly find themselves after death.

In death, as in life, we apparently exist on different spiritual levels. When you're exploring the area of spirit communication, you want to contact only the highest, clearest energy. To do this, most psychics and mediums have protective rituals they do before they work. The most common rituals are prayer, visualization, and a request that only the highest energy be attracted. Other effective techniques include smudging an area with burning sage, burning an aromatic oil, or defining your work area with a circle of salt. This last technique originated in pagan times, when evil spirits were as real as cantankerous next-door neighbors.

Don't limit yourself to just one protective ritual. As a Pisces, you'll be able to intuitively find a protective ritual or device that feels right for you.

THE MAP

A decade from now, you'll be cleaning out your attic and will run across your journal from this exploration. If you've followed the suggestions in this chapter, the details of that journey will astonish you. More important than this, though, is that the journal will provide you with a map that will enable you to return to the state of awareness needed for spirit communication. Your journal is your map.

To a great extent, your map's accuracy depends on the detail you provide. One of the things that makes the Seth material fascinating is the detail Seth provided on the ordinary and the sublime. From pets to love to Christ and UFOs, there wasn't much that Seth missed. Jane Roberts's husband, Robert Butts, also included notes on what was going on in their personal lives during most of the twenty years or so that Roberts spoke for Seth. His notes ground the material in ordinary, daily life, and they add a credibility that is often heartbreaking in its simplicity, particularly during the last year or so of Roberts's life. This is the kind of detail that will enable you to return to whatever you've forgotten, Pisces.

So what does this record look like? Nothing fancy, nothing too complicated.

To get you started, use the explore table below. List five or more areas you would like to explore and possible ways of doing it.

Areas to Explore	How to Go About It
1. _____	_____
2. _____	_____
3. _____	_____
4. _____	_____
5. _____	_____

THE GRAIL

Your grail, Pisces, is: *You can now see the trees in the forest.*

YOUR RECORDS

Date: _____

Time: _____

Weather: _____

Other factors: _____

_____

Your experience: _____

_____

_____

_____

_____

_____

_____

_____

_____

_____

_____

PART THREE

❀

Neptune & Spirits

17. The Planet Neptune ♆

Everyone may educate and regulate his imagination so as
to come thereby into contact with spirits, and be taught
by them.

—PARACELSUS

NEPTUNIAN ENERGY

A woman believes that people are stealing her clothes,
her jewelry, her money. She holds conversations
with her mother, dead now for thirty years, and sometimes thinks that her son is a distant cousin and that her
husband is her father. She hears voices and sees things
and people that aren't there.

Another woman also holds conversations with the
dead, hears voices, sees things that aren't there, and
knows that her son was her husband in a previous life.
People seek her out for precisely these reasons and pay
her handsomely for the messages she brings from the
dead.

The first woman is an Alzheimer's patient; the second
woman is a psychic medium. Both illustrate the elusive
nature of Neptune, its ethereal veil, the way it dissolves
the barriers between realities. Think of Neptune as a
tuning fork. Tap it. It hums. But no two people hear that
hum in exactly the same way. Neptune transported Edgar
Cayce into other realms and swept Einstein into the very

heart of scientific truth. It gave diarist Anaïs Nin penetrating insight into other people. But it can also lead into
the basest escapism through alcohol, drugs, sex, and the
darker side of the occult.

Neptune's energy is elusive, vague, unreal, nebulous.
Quite often, it is felt as a disturbance in the deeper layers
of the self, a sense that things aren't as they seem, that
something is amiss. Last night's dream clings to you
throughout the next day. Strange images dance across
your mind as you fall asleep. Poetry rises from your soul.
You see ghosts. You feel a psychic and spiritual connection to a larger universe.

As the natural ruler of mystical Pisces, planet Neptune
dwells in the hidden, the shadowy, the surreal, the etheric. It is numinous, connecting us to the divine. Yet it
often seems to be the psychic garbage pail of the zodiac.
This isn't a contradiction. It's simply Neptune's nature.
Nursing homes, hospitals, Alzheimer's units: these are
Neptunian. Environmental toxins, oil spills, mysterious
diseases that are difficult to diagnose, slippery viruses
that mutate and remain elusive—all are part of the Neptune contradiction. AIDS, Epstein-Barr or Chronic Fa-
tigue Syndrome, Lyme Disease, and the Ebola virus are
examples of Neptunian types of ailments.

The diseases that break down the human immune system bear disturbing parallels to the breakdown in the
planet's immune system through pollution, the depletion
of the ozone layer, and global warming. Yet, viewed in
terms of a "Sethian" universe, this parallel isn't strange
at all. It reflects our collective beliefs.

You're probably saying that *your* beliefs don't encom-
pass any of those things. You don't believe in global
warming or famine or human rights violations or animal
abuse. When the nightly news beams vivid scenes of star-

vation into your living room, your heart breaks. At work here are invisible beliefs, the core of who we are, beliefs that were formed in early childhood, the consensus beliefs that we share with everyone else in this reality, on this planet, at this point in history. These consensus beliefs create the paradigms that we live by.

At its highest and most evolved expression, Neptune reminds us that we have the innate power to create our own realities through what we believe. This awareness is intuitive, psychic, spiritual. Edgar Cayce embodied the highest expression of Neptune's energy.

At its basest expression, in addition to the escapist tendencies already mentioned, Neptune denotes problems and conflicts in dealing with reality in the physical world.

A FEW FACTS

Neptune's distance from the Sun staggers the imagination—nearly three billion miles. Even on a clear night, it's impossible to see Neptune with the naked eye. Even the most powerful telescopes record it as little more than a greenish swirl. Yet, its mass is seventeen times that of Earth, no small potato in terms of size. Due to its extended orbit, one year on Neptune is equal to about 165 of our years. Its day is about fifteen hours long. It takes Neptune about fourteen years to travel through a single sign of the zodiac.

Neptune was discovered because of Uranus's erratic orbit. When mathematicians calculated where Uranus was supposed to be at a given time, it sometimes arrived too early and other times arrived too late. Astronomers John Adams and Urbain Leverrier independently predicted that another planet, yet undiscovered, might be the cause of the disturbance.

On September 23, 1846, German astronomer Johanne Galle discovered the offender. Right from the start, Neptune was a trickster.

Some astrologers say that Neptune, like Uranus and Pluto, was discovered when humanity was psychologically ready for the discovery. In other words, Neptune's discovery wasn't just a physical event—it was also symbolic of man's readiness to embrace transcendence.

In that light, it's no coincidence that less than two years after Neptune's discovery, the Spiritualist movement was born in the Foxes' cottage, with those odd and terrifying rappings.

Neptune was in the sign of Aquarius when it was discovered. Humanitarian ideals were catching on, notably in the struggle against slavery. Romanticism had seized the collective imagination, Chopin and Liszt ruled the world of music, and then there were the Fox sisters.

In science, Howe patented the sewing machine, ether began to be used as anesthesia, and film was used to record images. This was also the time when Morse code started connecting people in the same way that the Internet connects people now. This was the year the Smithsonian was founded, protoplasm was identified, and John Deere constructed the first plow.

Howe's sewing machine was completed in a Neptunian way, through a dream that showed him the needle needed an eye at the end of it. The use of ether is also very Neptunian, since the planet rules drugs. Neptune governs the heights of imagination, so it's fitting that its discovery coincided with the publication of Hans Christian Andersen's autobiography, *Fairy Tale of My Life.*

NEPTUNE'S CYCLES: EVENTS

In Gemini: 1889–1902 The twentieth century began with Neptune in Gemini, so it isn't surprising that new ideas for trade, commerce, travel, and communication were born during this time. In Gemini, Neptune contributed to restlessness for change, interest in spiritual and philosophical writings, an escape into mental fantasy.

During this period:

- Max Planck formulated quantum theory.
- The Zeppelin had its first trial flight.
- R. A. Fessenden transmitted human speech through radio waves.
- Bertrand Russell wrote "A Critical Exposition of the Philosophy of Leibniz."
- Walt Disney was born.
- Paul Gauguin and Claude Monet were setting the art world on fire with such paintings as "Riders by the Sea" and "Waterloo Bridge."
- J. M. Bacon became the first man to cross the Irish Channel by balloon.

In Cancer: 1902–1915 Neptune here indicates idealization of the home and family. Although Neptune is exalted in Cancer, it's a difficult placement because Neptune's ideals don't fit easily in the practical world.

During this period:

- Albert Einstein formulated his Special Theory of Relativity.
- The Boy Scouts were founded.
- The first daily comic strip—*Mr. Mutt,* later called

Mutt and Jeff—began its run in the *San Francisco Chronicle*.
- Frank Lloyd Wright's star began to rise.
- In Europe, the fascist movements gained momentum.

In Leo: 1915–1928 Leo's emphasis is on creative self-expression. Neptune demands detachment. This isn't a particularly easy combination. Yet, during the period that Neptune was in Leo, the economy in the United States and Europe boomed, and much of that boom was based on illusion. It was like the emperor's new clothes.

During this time:

- Einstein's theory of relativity was borne out during observations of a total solar eclipse.
- The first experiments were conducted with short-wave radio.
- Babe Ruth hit a 587-foot home run in a Boston Red Sox versus New York Giants game.
- F. Scott Fitzgerald published *This Side of Paradise* and D. H. Lawrence published *Women in Love*.

In Virgo: 1928–1943 Reality check. It's no coincidence that shortly after Neptune went into Virgo, the stock market collapsed and a worldwide depression began. What had been the Roaring Twenties, the good times of flappers and wild speculation (Neptune in Leo), was now transmuted into despair and desolation.

During this period:

- Dashiell Hammett published *The Maltese Falcon*.
- A. S. Eddington attempted to unify general relativity and the quantum theory.
- Sinclair Lewis won the Nobel Prize for *Babbitt*.

- Al Capone was jailed for tax evasion.
- Amelia Earhart was the first woman to fly solo across the Atlantic. In 1937, she was lost in a flight over the Pacific.
- The U.S. Supreme Court ruled that the University of Missouri Law School had to admit African-Americans because of the lack of facilities in the area.
- Germany recalled her ambassador to the United States, and Adolf Hitler published *Mein Kampf.*

In Libra: 1943–1957 Three months before Neptune went into Libra, Allied troops landed in Normandy. Ironically, Neptune in Libra seems to bring more conflict and war than it does peace. There's an idealization of relationships with this placement. The first generation of Baby Boomers were born with Neptune in Libra. These people were at the forefront of social reform during the 1960s, redefining the context of relationships and marriage and spurring new interest in spiritual issues.

During this period:

- Ray Bradbury published *The Martian Chronicles,* Bertrand Russell won the Nobel Prize for literature, John Hersey published *The Wall.*
- President Harry Truman instructed the U.S. Atomic Energy Commission to develop the hydrogen bomb.
- Rachel Carson wrote *The Sea Around Us.*
- Martin Luther King, Jr., emerged as the leader of a campaign for desegregation.
- Jack Kerouac published *On The Road.*

In Scorpio: 1957–1970 With Neptune in Scorpio, ego boundaries dissolve through intense experiences and emotions. The emphasis during this period was on deep issues rising to the surface.

During this period:

- Cuba's President Fulgencio Batista fled the island and Fidel Castro seized power.
- The Postmaster General of the United States banned D. H. Lawrence's *Lady Chatterley's Lover* from the mails on grounds of obscenity. This was overruled a year later by a circuit court of appeals.
- Adolf Eichmann was hanged.
- Attempt on the life of Charles de Gaulle.
- John Steinbeck won the Nobel Prize for literature.
- James Meredith, an African-American applicant to the University of Mississippi, was denied admission, setting off racial riots.
- Martin Luther King, Jr., won the Nobel Peace Prize.
- Bay of Pigs invasion.
- Assassination of JFK.
- Publication of Truman Capote's *In Cold Blood*.
- Assassinations of Martin Luther King, Jr., and Robert Kennedy.
- Vietnam War, massive protests against war.
- Woodstock.
- Publication of Kurt Vonnegut, Jr.'s *Slaughterhouse-Five*.

In Sagittarius: 1970–1984 This Neptune placement had a major impact on idealism, a search for the larger truths, and a revival in religions and spirituality. True to Sagittarius, this placement brought spiritual influence from other countries.

During this period:

- Herman Wouk published *Winds of War*.
- President Richard Nixon was reelected.
- Gas shortages.
- Death of Agatha Christie.
- Five saints canonized by Pope Paul VI.
- Patricia Hearst kidnapped and later caught by FBI.
- Reverend Moon comes under scrutiny.
- Anglican Church in Canada approves ordaining women to priesthood.

In Capricorn: 1984–1998 This placement brought about structure, thrift, and practicality. This era witnessed the birth of the Internet as a vehicle of communication for everyone, the fall of the Berlin Wall, the end of Reaganomics, and the booming economy under President William Clinton.

A New Paradigm—
Neptune in Aquarius: 1998–2012

Neptune's placement in your chart indicates the area where you can transcend the parameters of consensus reality. It's the place where you can tune in to the hum of the tuning fork and experience inspiration, illumination, enlightenment. It's where you're most vulnerable to escapism and illusion and delusion. How its energy manifests itself in your life is, of course, entirely up to you.

In 1998, Neptune returned to the sign it occupied when it was discovered, and will remain there until 2012. In Aquarius, Neptune is the call of the spirit, the burgeoning of the psychic, the intuitive. Barriers between the conscious and the unconscious become progressively thinner, and in many cases dissolve altogether. As a result, much of the wisdom in our personal and collective unconscious becomes available to us. We tap the divine for our answers.

Medical breakthroughs are likely, but not in the ways we expect. Instead of finding a miracle drug for diseases like cancer and AIDS, we reach a deeper understanding of the intimate connection between body and mind, and how emotions and beliefs create health or *dis-ease.* The stage for these types of realizations already has been set by medical intuitives like Carolyn Myss (*Anatomy of the Spirit*) and Mona Lisa Schultz (*Awakening Intuition*). Deepak Chopra brought us the medical wisdom from the East. Andrew Weill's *Spontaneous Healing* bolstered the voice of alternative medicine in the 1990s, and in the new millennium the entire field is likely to flourish beyond even his wildest expectations. During Neptune in Aquarius, we'll witness the birth of a new medical paradigm.

The old paradigm, the medical establishment, won't slip quietly away. Already, they feel threatened by the fact that in the United States alone, more than a billion dollars a year is spent on alternative medical treatments. They debunk alternative medicine at every opportunity, calling for more government control over vitamins, herbs, and treatments like acupuncture.

The best outcome of this struggle between old and new would be a melding of the two. Medical intuitives would work alongside MDs. Doctors would treat the whole person, not just a set of symptoms. Patients would become educated partners in their treatments. Vitamins, herbs, acupuncture, yoga, massage therapy, and other types of body work would be used in conjunction with more conventional treatments. The emotional and spiritual causes of disease and illness would be addressed and studied, and patients would be educated in this area. It sounds like utopia. Yet, all of this is possible with Neptune in Aquarius.

The spiritual enlightenment that is possible with Neptune in Aquarius has been growing steadily since the early 1980s. Dr. Kübler Ross woke us up with her landmark work *On Death and Dying,* and Dr. Raymond Moody shook us up with his book *Life After Life.* These two individuals, both of them traditionally trained MDs, deepened our understanding of the continuity of life. Their works were followed by a spate of personal stories by people who died, then returned, only to find their lives irrevocably changed.

Check out these movies: *Jacob's Ladder; Brainstorm; Flatliners; What Dreams May Come; Siesta;* and *The Sixth Sense.* Their Neptunian themes about what may happen after death are perfect examples of the spiritual search that will characterize the millennium.

The idea of reincarnation will be more readily accepted in the Western world. Again, the stage for this acceptance has been set by luminaries like Dr. Ian Stevenson and physician Brian Weiss. Carol Bowman's books *Children's Past Lives* and *Return from Heaven: Reincarnation Within the Same Family* tap an area that has barely been explored. We're primed for this stuff. We desperately need a new paradigm for our evolving spiritual beliefs about the big cosmic questions. Who are we? Who or what is God? Where have we been? And, more to the point, just where are we going when we leave *here?*

Religious institutions are likely to go through the same type of radical change as the medical establishment. If our spiritual needs aren't being met by our churches, our synagogues, our Bible groups, then we'll go elsewhere for answers. The old religious paradigms won't succumb without a fight. They have too much to lose. But they *will* change. They have to. It's time.

The flip side, of course, may lead to more tragedies like Heaven's Gate. Our forays into the unseen, the unspoken, the barely imagined, can drive us off the deep end. In this scenario, we see conspiracies to rival those in the *X-Files*. We believe we are chosen or doomed. We forget that we have the power to change anything. We forget that one individual, infused with passion and intent, can literally change the world.

Keep in mind what has happened in the past with Neptune in Aquarius. Spiritualism took off—a wild, brilliant star that opened up the possibility that life really does continue after death. Mystical groups like the Theosophical Society were formed. Buddhism reached the West. Social awareness zoomed in on humanitarian ideals: the rights of women, the immorality of child labor and slavery, and the issue of poverty. In short, Neptune was discovered when we were ready, when we needed new patterns for growth.

Neptune in Aquarius can lend itself to millennial hysteria, as well. Widespread fear about the collapse of society, of the global economic structure, and of the Y2K scare is the kind of energy that feeds Neptune's darker side, where confusion is the modus operandi of the new society. This confusion and fear can run through such diverse areas as cloning, so-called miracle drugs, and mind control (as in remote viewing). But it doesn't have to be that way. If we pour our energy into the positive opportunities that Neptune in Aquarius offers us, then the *pattern* changes.

Remember: Neptune's placement in your chart indicates the area where you can transcend the parameters of consensus reality. It's the place where you can tune in to the hum of the tuning fork and experience inspiration, illumination, enlightenment. It's where you're most vulnerable to escapism and illusion and delusion.

In the next chapter, we'll take a look at how Neptune through the signs and houses impacts us personally.

18. Neptune in the Signs & Houses

There is a shadow world that exists all around us . . .

—BRAD STEIGER

THE BASICS

Neptune's sign describes how you transcend physical reality and connect with spiritual dimensions and your intuitive self. It also shows how you express your psychic abilities and your spiritual values. On the shadow side, it describes your blind spots, your illusions, and how you may express victimized behaviors. Since most people in your generation also share the same sign for Neptune, it describes how your generation experiences altered states of consciousness.

The house placement of Neptune is personally more important. It describes the area of your life where your ideals come into play. In this area, you may be subject to confusion because Neptune's nature is vague and mysterious. In this area, you express compassion and sympathy for others and must somehow face up to your psychic, intuitive, and spiritual nature.

If Pisces is prominent in your chart—Sun, Moon, or Ascendant—then Neptune's influence on you is likely to be much stronger.

Turn to Appendix 3 to determine your Rising sign, the Ascendant. Use the blank horoscope chart at the end of the book to set up your own birth chart. What you set up will be an approximation. An accurate birth chart can be obtained from an astrologer or a New Age bookstore that provides an astrological computer service. If you have access to the Internet, go to www.alabe.com or to www.astrology.com to obtain a copy of your birth chart. On both sites, you'll need an accurate time of birth.

NEPTUNE IN THE SIGNS

Aries. Even though people with this placement are long gone, it will come around again on January 27, 2026. This placement tends to fire up the imagination and allows you to act on impulses. You're up front about the expression of your psychic abilities. You are spontaneous and open about following your spiritual values. Spirit communication happens most easily through action that you take.

Shadow: Your blind spot is your own ego. You don't realize how your aggression and inconsiderate behaviors impact others.

Taurus. This sign for Neptune won't happen again until April 2039. This placement urges you to funnel your psychic abilities in a way that obtains practical results. Your spiritual values are important to you in your daily life, and you're faithful to these values. You idealize nature and practical reality. Spirit communication may sneak up when you least expect it. Your approach to it is practical and grounded.

Edgar Cayce had Neptune in Taurus. It gave him the

ability to embrace spirituality in a practical, focused way that also benefited others.

Shadow: Your point of illusion may be your own materialism, which sometimes manifests as stinginess with others.

Gemini. This placement will occur again in the latter half of the twenty-first century. You express your psychic abilities in diverse, imaginative ways. You are not shy about sharing your thoughts and beliefs with other people through various means of communication. Your spiritual values change with the wind until you find a spiritual system that fits you perfectly. You idealize the intellect. Spirit communication has to appeal to your imagination and curiosity.

Shadow: You are blind to how unreliable you can be at times.

Cancer. Your psychic abilities are expressed most consistently in matters involving your home and family, especially your mother or your role as a nurturing parent. Your spiritual values involve nurturing others and acting compassionately for strangers. You idealize emotions and the home. Spirit communication must appeal to your emotions.

Shadow: You're so impressionable at times that the line between illusion and reality blurs.

Leo. You are bold and dramatic in the expression of your psychic abilities. Your imagination finds outlets in the arts and in performance. Your spiritual values also hold an element of drama and creativity, and are large enough for genuine compassion. You idealize creativity.

Spirit communication must appeal to your goodhearted nature for it to work smoothly.

Shadow: *Your ego can get in the way of everything else in your life.*

Virgo. You are analytical and detailed about your psychic abilities, an apparent dichotomy that often puzzles you. You use your spiritual values and beliefs to solve problems in a concrete, practical way. You idealize work and duty. Spiritual communication must appeal to your sense of duty and service for the process to unfold.

Shadow: *Your tendency for analysis can blind you to the larger picture.*

Libra. You express your psychic abilities in relationships or with groups of people. You don't thrust your spiritual beliefs on others. You are, in fact, unerringly diplomatic about your spiritual values and psychic abilities. You idealize relationships. Spirit communication must appeal to your sense of fairness and your need for harmony for the process to unfold smoothly.

Shadow. *Misplaced idealism is your blind spot.*

Scorpio. You express your psychic abilities in a penetrating manner, through passion and intensity. Your spiritual values are intimately a part of you. You're most likely to undertake an exploration of spirit communication if there's a deep and penetrating reason for you to do so.

Shadow: *It makes perfect sense to you to get even with people who hurt you.*

Sagittarius. Your psychic abilities are part of your philosophical bent. You intuitively understand broad spiritual concepts and adapt the ones that appeal to you. You idealize truth, spiritual concepts, and the benefits of education. To explore spirit communication, you have to be convinced that it fits *your* larger picture.

Shadow: Your need to be right is your blind spot.

Capricorn. You express your psychic and intuitive abilities in a practical, responsible manner. Even your spiritual beliefs have a practical structure. You idealize work, practicality, and responsibility. For spiritual communication to be viable for you, you have to believe there will be practical benefits.

Shadow: You may become so practical that the voice of your imagination is stifled. All that pragmatism may result in depression.

Aquarius. You express your psychic abilities in innovative, often eccentric ways. Your spiritual beliefs may be just as eccentric and unusual as your other talents. You idealize personal freedom and equality for all. To embrace spiritual communication, it must appeal first and foremost to your intellect.

Shadow: Your blind spot is being so fixed and stubborn in your beliefs that you cease to grow.

Pisces. With Neptune in the sign that it rules, psychic and intuitive attunement is as natural as breathing. Your psychic abilities flow from the deepest parts of your soul. Your spiritual values are intimately linked with your imagination. You idealize compassion. Spirit communication is your domain.

Shadow: Your blind spot is that when you lose touch with reality, you lose yourself in illusion.

NEPTUNE IN THE HOUSES

If you have your birth chart, read on. If not, turn to Appendix 3 to figure out your Rising sign.

1st House. Your sensitivity is both a blessing and a curse. You're so attuned to other people that you inadvertently absorb their moods and emotions. It's easy for you to read people. But this can become confusing because you don't know which feelings and moods belong to you and which ones belong to other people.

There's usually something mysterious about people who have this placement. You have an odd effect on others; they often see you as something you aren't. To some extent, you're an actor assuming roles to fit the situation or the person you're with. You may have musical, artistic, or dramatic talent. You may be drop-dead gorgeous, with a kind of Greta Garbo allure.

You're innately kind. It's so easy for you to walk in someone else's shoes that you can't be otherwise. Your compassion extends to strangers, too, of both the human and animal variety. Your inner life is rich and wonderful, often better than real life, and you retreat to this inner world to replenish yourself. The danger, of course, is that you may find you prefer the inner world to the external world, then you use this place to hide from and avoid life.

Your spiritual beliefs aren't something you really think about consciously. They are simply part of who you are, of your identity. It's likely that you've had inexplicable experiences since you were very young, perceiving what other people did not.

You may be blind to your own faults and shortcomings.

2nd House. You're able to use your intuitive abilities, skills, and talent to earn money. You instinctively know how to earn money. You may even earn your living doing something related to your spiritual values.

Neptune in the 2nd house can make you susceptible to get-rich-quick schemes. You're presented with an idea that at the time looks so good you simply can't pass it up. Six months down the road, the whole thing caves in and you lose a bundle. One of the lessons attached to Neptune in the 2nd house is to act responsibly toward finances and possessions.

Another way this placement is expressed is through nonattachment to money and possessions. You may be so casual about money that you give away money and possessions and readily share what you have with others. For Neptune to function smoothly in the 2nd house, you must be completely honest in your financial dealings.

3rd House. You shine when it comes to communication. You're able to use your intuitive abilities and your imagination in some facet of communication—through writing, speaking, perhaps acting. Your imagination is so active at times that you may be prone to exaggerating the truth. This isn't conscious lying; you actually believe your version of events. This propensity is best funneled through creativity, as in fiction writing.

With Neptune in the 3rd house, your intellectual clarity may be foggy and confused at times. Or you may be fearful about saying what you think. The fear itself is the problem. Get rid of the fear, be forthright about what you think and believe, and the problem itself dissipates. This is especially true when dealing with your siblings and relatives. Clarify your relationships with these people, and life moves more smoothly.

If you can find a creative outlet for your spiritual insights and beliefs, everything else will fall into place naturally.

4th House. Your intuitive abilities are so strong that you usually know what's going on inside other people, especially people in your own family and within your personal environment. But these feelings are difficult to express verbally.

Your family life may not be ideal, but you're not aware of it. You idealize your family life and one of your parents. But if something happens that strips away that illusion, you feel bereft, adrift, uncertain. The best remedy is to create a sense of security within yourself, a place to which you can retreat when life overwhelms you.

Your spiritual beliefs are deeply rooted in your early childhood and home life. When your imagination takes flight, it returns to these deep roots. To release these spiritual insights, you may delve into mythology, psychology, anything that is unknown and mysterious, seeking the common thread.

5th House. Your intuitive abilities and spiritual interests bring you enormous pleasure, especially when you can use them to help other people. Your imagination is so rich and broad that with little effort you can tap into spiritual currents that elude others. Your artistic abilities are impressive—music, writing, art, dramatic talent. The challenge is to discipline yourself so that you can hone these talents.

With Neptune in the 5th house, you idealize love and romance, which may blind you to the true nature of the people you love. This can get confusing at times, so it's best if you approach love and romance slowly, cautiously.

Be aware that you can easily place yourself in the role of nurturer and rescuer with Neptune here. It's part of the "victimization" that rides tandem with Neptune.

One of the lessons you have to learn with Neptune in the 5th house is to distinguish between people who are worth helping and those who are not. It sounds harsh, but it's only self-preservation.

Psychic Millie Gemondo has Neptune in Virgo in the 5th house. The sign of Virgo gives her a sense of duty and responsibility about her intuitive abilities, and also makes her precise and detailed in imparting psychic information to others. One of the manifestations of Neptune in Virgo in the 5th house is the offering of a service without thought of compensation. An example of this is when Millie told a coworker that she felt the woman had a growth in her breast and should see a doctor. Millie didn't charge her for this information; the idea of financial recompense for this spontaneous reading probably never crossed her mind. It was simply the *right* thing to do. The information turned out to be accurate and probably saved that woman's life.

6th House. Since this house symbolizes health and daily work, Neptune's placement here indicates that your body may be very sensitive to external influences. It's important to avoid drugs, to live in an area where the temperature is comfortable for you, and to be aware of how various foods affect you physically. You may have odd allergies.

It's likely that any health problems you have will be difficult to diagnose and that mainstream medical practitioners may think it's all in your head. Be assured that it isn't. Your health problems are *not* psychosomatic. However, to get to the root of the problem, whatever it is, you must delve into yourself to find its emotional and/or spiritual source.

With Neptune in the 6th house, you may earn your daily living through your intuitive and artistic abilities. You may also find yourself in jobs that provide a service for others. You have deep compassion and sympathy for people, but must be careful that you don't "take on" their difficulties.

Psychic Renie Wiley, who passed away shortly after this book was written, had Neptune in Virgo in the 6th house. Before she began her work as a professional psychic, she was a commercial artist. At one point in her psychic career, she worked with the police. Her fee for this service was a cup of fresh coffee. Like Millie, whose Neptune is also in Virgo, Renie *performed a service without compensation.* Since Virgo is connected to health and physical issues, Renie often picked up on physical problems when she did readings. This was one of the things that made police work difficult for her.

During the early 1980s, she and a policeman for a small town in South Florida decided to see what Renie could pick up on the Adam Walsh kidnapping. Adam had disappeared one day while he and his mother were at the Hollywood, Florida, mall. The publicity surrounding the kidnapping was considerable. No ransom demands had been made, and no clues had been uncovered as to the kidnapper or Adam's whereabouts.

Renie and the cop were driving around the Hollywood area where the kidnapping had occurred and, suddenly, Renie had trouble breathing. Her hands flew to her throat, she started to gasp for breath, and images flashed through her head. She realized the sensations were connected to the Walsh kidnapping and quickly shut down her intuition. Gradually, the sensations ceased. She told the cop that Adam Walsh was dead and that he'd been decapitated.

Not long afterward, the boy's torso was found in Indian River County, several hours north, confirming her impressions.

In psychic and spiritual work with this placement of Neptune, your body often acts as the vehicle for your impressions. It's vital to learn how to detach or separate those impressions from your emotions.

7th House. Your psychic and artistic abilities work well in partnership with another person. At its highest expression, this placement for Neptune leads to partnerships, marriages, and relationships that are spiritual and psychic in nature. You idealize partnership, however, which can result in your seeing only what you want to see in another person. This is fine as long as the illusion holds together. But when it's stripped away, you're like the emperor who discovers he isn't wearing clothes made of golden threads, that he is, in fact, wearing nothing at all.

One of the manifestations of Neptune in the 7th house is that you may project your own weaknesses and flaws onto the people you love. Or you may choose partners to whom you feel superior, people with alcohol or drug addictions whom you feel you can rescue or change.

The secret to navigating this placement successfully is to know who you are. It sounds simple, and most of us manage to do this to one degree or another over the course of our lives. But for you, it's important to begin this journey of self-discovery early so you can avoid heartache later on.

8th House. This placement is loaded. Your intuitive and artistic abilities focus on everything the 8th house represents—reincarnation, life after death, astral travel, ghosts and hauntings, precognitive dreams, Spiritualism . . . it's a long list. You have the innate ability to enter higher realms of consciousness by drawing on the psychic energy this placement symbolizes.

You're good at figuring out what makes people tick and at investigating larger mysteries. When something seizes your interest, you absolutely have to get to the bottom of it.

Because the 8th house also represents death and joint resources, there may be mysterious circumstances surrounding your death or that of your partner. You and your partner may share a deep spiritual bond that originated in other lives, and you may work together in a spiritual or investigative capacity.

Jane Roberts's Neptune in Leo was in the 8th house. She used this energy in a dramatic way—through channeling—and spent twenty years of her life investigating and living with the Seth phenomenon, right in line with the fixed nature of Leo. For anyone acquainted with the Seth material, it's obvious that the spiritual bond between Roberts and her husband, Rob Butts, was strong and that their lives centered around their "investigation" of the Seth material.

From her earliest years, Roberts was mystically inclined. She used her artistic skills—poetry, art—to explore this side of her nature. Later in life, as the Seth material became her focus, the influence of the earth signs in her chart (Taurus Sun and Moon, Capricorn Rising) compelled her to question the material, scrutinize it, and to channel it in a practical way—all very earthy characteristics.

The circumstances of her death were somewhat mysterious. In the September 1984 issue of *Fate Magazine,* her death was reported as "complications from rheumatoid arthritis." Although this was factually true, the whole truth came out with the posthumous publication of several books that described her illness and the excruciatingly difficult final year of her life. In her memoir about Roberts, author Sue Watkins, who knew Roberts for more than sixteen years, reported that toward the end of her life, Roberts could move only her fingers and her lips. Her legs were "frozen" up against her chest.

9th House. This is one of the most psychic placements for Neptune. You may have a deep interest in Eastern thought and belief systems, Spiritualism, reincarnation, and mysticism. You are constantly seeking to expand and broaden your spiritual beliefs.

Your idealism may interfere with your daily reality; you aren't the most practical person who ever walked the face of the earth. Higher education may not be high on your list of priorities. You may have strange experiences overseas. But you have deep compassion for people and animals, and you readily perceive that we are all connected. Your kindness is fundamental to your nature.

Edgar Cayce had his Neptune in the 9th house, in the sign of Taurus. As his biographers reveal, Cayce wasn't the most practical man. He had money problems for much of his life, no more than an eighth-grade education, and yet was known as a kind, gentle man. Cayce was a Pisces, so Neptune, the ruler of Pisces, was instrumental in his life. His deep faith sustained him through many tribulations and was the cornerstone of who he was and who he became. As the "sleeping prophet," he was able to reach the highest energy to obtain the psychic and spiritual information that comprised the more than 14,000 readings that he conducted in his lifetime.

Hazel West, a medium whom you'll meet in the Cassadaga chapter (Chapter 21), also has Neptune in the 9th house, in Virgo. Hazel is a soft-spoken woman who radiates kindness. She came to Cassadaga through a series of coincidences and studied under Wilbur Hull, one of Cassadaga's renowned mediums. She has spent most of her adult life honing and perfecting her skills, provides detailed information in her readings, and also teaches spiritual awareness, another facet of Neptune in the 9th house.

10th House. This mystical placement of Neptune indicates that you may gain recognition for something you achieve related to spirituality or your artistic talents. Artists, writers, and musicians with this placement of Neptune often feel as if they are plugging into a higher source when they are working. Your work is connected, in some capacity, to service to others. This Neptune placement is good for a career in medicine or for caring for others in some way. It's a good placement for mediums.

The placement can create difficulties, however, until you decide on what you want to do with your life. Even once you've decided, your choice may change. You must *feel right* about the career path you choose, otherwise it will dissatisfy you.

James Van Praagh has Neptune in Scorpio in the 10th house. True to the placement, he went into the seminary, had a stint in Hollywood where he aspired to writing, and eventually arrived on his present path through a "chance" meeting with a medium. By following his instincts and his need to penetrate to the core of the strange experiences he had as a child, he's able to combine his mediumship with writing, which has produced several bestsellers on the topic. He gives seminars and talks worldwide on his work and is a sought-after guest on TV talk shows.

11th House. Neptune in the 11th house can work in several ways. You may attract friends who are unreliable, with various types of addictions or problems. Or you may attract friends who are highly evolved artists, musicians, actors, and writers. In the former category, these people may expect you to solve their problems or to constantly bail them out of trouble. In the latter category, these people may be part of some group to which you belong.

You're very idealistic about your goals and your direction in life. This idealism can play havoc with the reality of your situation. So you must be able to distinguish between realistic goals and those that are sheer fantasy.

Your artistic abilities and spiritual beliefs may unfold best within a group of individuals who share your goals, interests, and beliefs.

12th House. Neptune is actually at home in the 12th house. It's a wonderful placement for the development of psychic ability. You benefit, in fact, from any type of psychic activity or artistic work done behind the scenes. Your imagination is able to embrace large concepts and to delve deeply into your own unconscious to find whatever it is that you need.

One of the ways that Neptune in the 12th house can manifest is through caring for individuals in institutions such as a prison, nursing home, or hospital. But it can indicate that at some point in your life you may care for someone personally in that capacity—an aging parent, for instance.

You're very sensitive to other people's moods and thoughts. If the people you're around are primarily negative individuals, then get away from them fast. Their moods and thoughts can too easily become your own. You're usually good at dream recall, and you receive much psychic and spiritual information and guidance through your dreams.

19. Neptune Aspects

> Knowledge has three degrees—opinion, science, and illumination.
>
> —Plotinus

Aspects to Neptune

One facet of astrology that we haven't touched on is aspects. Aspects are geometric angles that planets form to each other and to the four critical angles of a birth chart. On the Star Charts in the Appendices, you'll find aspects in the grid in the lower left-hand corner.

A lengthy explanation of aspects is beyond the scope of this book. But in case you do have your birth chart drawn up, it's a good idea to know a little something about aspects and—for the purpose of this book—about aspects that your natal Neptune makes to other planets or to angles in your chart.

When astrologers talk about major aspects, they're usually referring to five configurations: conjunctions, sextiles, squares, trines, and oppositions. They also talk about *orbs,* the acceptable number of degrees for each aspect. A *conjunction,* for instance, is two or more planets in the same sign and degree. But an acceptable orb for a conjunction may be anywhere from three to ten degrees, depending on the astrologer and the planets involved.

In James Van Praagh's chart, for example, his Neptune lies at two degrees and twenty-six minutes of Scorpio (02♏26) and his Jupiter is at twenty-seven degrees and thirty-one minutes of Libra (27♎31). Depending on the orbs an astrologer uses, this could be considered a five-degree conjunction.

Table 5 provides an overview of the major aspects.

Table 5: Aspects		
Aspect	*Separating Distance/Orb*	*Significance*
Conjunction ☌	0° (5° orb)	Major hard aspect. Intensifies energy of planets in same degree or within 4 degrees of each other.
Sextile ⚹	60° (3° orb)	Major soft aspect. Free flow of energy between planets involved. Ease, lack of tension.
Square □	90° (3° orb)	Major hard aspect. Friction between planets involved. Dynamic energy. Galvanizes individual into action.
Trine △	120° (3° orb)	Major soft aspect. Harmonious functioning. Buffer against turmoil.
Opposition	180° (3° orb)	Major hard aspect. Forces change through conflict. May involve polarities.

Conjunctions to Neptune

Neptune Conjunct Sun. People consider you mysterious, puzzling. Your mystical talents can trigger great creativity when used constructively, and that creativity can serve as the structure for spiritual communication. Learn to separate illusion from reality.

Neptune Conjunct the Moon. You're psychically attuned to other people and to their emotional lives. Your intuitive abilities lead you into the collective mind with utter ease. You're a proficient dreamer who receives considerable spiritual guidance through your dreams. Idealism may be connected to the parent who nurtured you. Edgar Cayce had this aspect, and it provided him with help from women in his work.

Neptune Conjunct Mercury. Your imagination leads you into realms that aren't available to the rest of us. Your psychic receptivity is connected to the ways in which you communicate. Poetry, mystical fiction, psychic art can be expressed with this aspect.

Neptune Conjunct Venus. Your gentle nature is attractive to other people. You enjoy music and art that has a spiritual or mystical undercurrent. You may idealize your romantic partners. Healing ability and spiritual self-awareness come with this aspect.

Neptune Conjunct Mars. This aspect unites physical and spiritual energy, and has been considered one of the most magnetic aspects in a horoscope. Healing ability can be evident with this aspect. Spirit may be channeled through the body.

Neptune Conjunct Jupiter. This conjunction comes along about every thirteen years. It confers imagination and a distinct spiritual basis to your personality. Your philosophy expands as a result of your spiritual awareness.

Van Praagh has this conjunction in his 10th house of profession and career.

Neptune Conjunct Saturn. This aspect can indicate clairvoyance and tremendous spiritual insight. The two aren't particularly compatible, however, because where Neptune is nebulous, Saturn seeks structure and parameters. If psychic abilities and spiritual insight can be channeled into a creative pursuit, however, the mix works well. This aspect can support other indications in a chart that mean fame and prominence.

Neptune Conjunct Uranus. This conjunction comes around about every 171 years. The most recent conjunction happened in 1994. Kids born under this aspect will make significant strides in psychic and spiritual development.

Neptune Conjunct Pluto. Spiritual revolution and rebirth are indicated by this conjunction. This aspect won't happen again until the twenty-fourth century.

SEXTILES & TRINES TO NEPTUNE

These two aspects are combined because they are so similar.

Neptune Sextile/Trine Sun. Your intuitive abilities are impressive. They flow effortlessly from some deep place inside you, right into your conscious mind. You need to express yourself in some creative way. If you can do this by being self-employed, that would be ideal. You don't work well under a boss.

Your sleeping mind is psychically active, and it's possible to receive spiritual guidance through your dreams. Van Praagh's Neptune is sextile his Sun.

Neptune Sextile/Trine Moon. Your imagination is fueled by your psychic abilities. This placement is great for fiction writers, poets, dancers, anyone in the arts. Your spiritual beliefs are deeply rooted in your unconscious and early childhood.

Van Praagh and psychic Renie Wiley both have this aspect.

Neptune Sextile/Trine Mercury. This aspect is often found in the charts of spiritual speakers as well as poets, novelists, shamans, mystics, and composers. You have deep access to spiritual realms. The information and guidance you need come to you effortlessly.

Van Praagh has this aspect.

Neptune Sextile/Trine Venus. Artistic talent, compassion, and spiritual depth characterize this aspect. It also may indicate clairvoyant ability.

Hazel West, Jane Roberts, and Renie Wiley all have this aspect in their birth charts.

Neptune Sextile/Trine Mars. This is primarily an aspect that affects the physical body through strength and a muscular physique. But it does indicate that you can achieve success in your chosen field.

Neptune Sextile/Trine Jupiter. The mystical side of this aspect seeks continual expansion through studying and the accumulation of knowledge that broadens spiritual wisdom. Your spiritual interests may be unorthodox, but you readily share them with others.

Edgar Cayce and Millie Gemondo both have this aspect. It's one of marked compassion.

Neptune Sextile/Trine Saturn. This aspect brings the dreamy, ethereal qualities of Neptune down to earth, to everyday reality. You instinctively realize that every species is here to realize its fullest potential.

Jane Roberts had this aspect in her chart. It explains her insistence on proving who Seth was and keeping the material couched in everyday, practical terms.

Neptune Sextile/Trine Uranus. You're spiritually aware and able to penetrate to the deeper levels of reality. Your imagination may be your greatest ally.

Neptune Sextile/Trine Pluto. Intense spiritual involvement is indicated by this aspect.

Van Praagh has this aspect.

SQUARES TO NEPTUNE

Neptune Square Sun. At various times in your life, you may feel that you aren't as good or as smart or as beautiful as everyone else. So, to compensate, you will polish skills in some area where you know you have talent.

Your empathy for the underdog gives you deep compassion and sympathy for people less fortunate than you. Your insight into other people is nothing short of remarkable.

Psychic Millie Gemondo has this aspect.

Neptune Square Moon. The challenge here is to be open about what you feel and why you feel it and to do it while you're feeling it. You easily put yourself in other people's shoes, feeling what they feel. This stirs your compassion but also may make you want to retreat from the world.

Neptune Square Mercury. At times, you find your dealings in the everyday world so confusing that all you want to do is go to bed and pull the covers over your head. Instead, use your imagination and creativity as your retreat. Your mind is able to grasp broad concepts, but you may have trouble verbalizing those concepts. So find an artistic mode in which you can express what you know.

Medium Hazel West and psychic Millie Gemondo have this aspect.

Neptune Square Venus. You're a romantic who idealizes your friends, your romantic partners, even love itself. Your artistic abilities are strong and pervasive in your life and can provide a needed outlet for the friction caused by this square. Once you come to terms with your life emotionally, everything else seems to fall into place.

Neptune Square Mars. Your insight into people's motives is excellent. You're able to pinpoint deep psychological patterns in other people and, to some extent, within yourself. Your self-insight comes through your creativity and imagination.

Neptune Square Jupiter. This aspect often manifests as wanderlust, especially when you're younger. But as you mature, it's wanderlust with a purpose, to sate some deep spiritual hunger.

Your nature is giving and generous, sometimes to a fault. You spend money like there's no tomorrow.

Neptune Square Saturn. A lot of unconscious fear is inherent in this aspect. Part of the problem is that your ideals don't seem to have much to do with physical reality. Somehow, reality always disappoints you. There's a tendency toward escapism with this aspect. The best way to overcome this is to find something that really fires your passions.

Neptune Square Uranus. Rebellion! Revolution! Freedom! Idealism! Think before you act. You're wonderfully inventive and have a terrific imagination. Put them to work for you.

Neptune Square Pluto. This powerful aspect is disruptive and not very pretty, no matter how you look at it. It last occurred in the 1800s and won't come around again until late this century. It signals the collapse of old paradigms.

OPPOSITIONS TO NEPTUNE

Neptune Opposite the Sun. This aspect takes focus to overcome. You need objectivity in your dealings with other people. You may be confused about your spiritual beliefs.

Neptune Opposite the Moon. Psychic sponge! You take on other people's negativity and can also project your negativity onto others. Make unconscious patterns conscious. One way to do this is through spiritual and creative work.

Psychic Millie Gemondo has this aspect.

Neptune Opposite Mercury. Be direct in your communication with others even when it seems they are trying to pin you down or hem you in.

Neptune Opposite Venus. You have idealized notions about money, beauty, the arts, that prevent you from seeing how things really are. Strive for realism in your relationships.

Neptune Opposite Mars. Avoidance is the key here. Avoid alcohol, drugs, food addictions, anything that smacks of escapism. The more grounded you are, the better off you'll be. If you explore spiritual communication, do it with a grounded partner.

Neptune Opposite Jupiter. Spiritual conflicts surface with this aspect. Your idealism has difficulty finding a practical outlet. Ground yourself through physical exercise or practices like yoga and meditation.

Neptune Opposite Saturn. None of the Neptune oppositions are easy, but this one may be more difficult than most. Your sense of reality is flawed, and you need to honestly appraise where you stand in your life.

Neptune Opposite Uranus. Deception and delusion mark this aspect. But unless Neptune or Uranus plays an important role in your birth chart, this aspect has little personal significance.

Neptune Opposite Pluto. Like the previous aspect, this is primarily an aspect that affects generations.

20. Animals as Guides

Take care of your pets . . . They are the closest thing to
God that we will ever find on earth.

—GEORGE ANDERSON

Many native cultures have elaborate initiation rituals
for finding the animal spirit that will become your
guardian and guide as you travel through the spirit world.
Shamans call on animal spirits in their healing rituals,
their divination work, and for general wisdom. In daily
Western life, many of us are closer to our animal com-
panions than we are to our own families. As author Ted
Andrews puts it, "Everyone has been touched by animals
in some way, either in life or in dreams, and always the
difficulty is determining what it means."

When you begin your attempts at spirit communication, you may find that animals appear more frequently
in your dreams and in your waking life. When it happens,
think of the animal as a symbol and try to interpret what
its appearance means. If, for instance, a snake figures
prominently in a dream, your first step in interpreting
the symbol is to define what snakes mean to *you*. Do
they horrify you? Scare you? Or do you feel some sort
of kinship for them?

Note the details of the dream. What was the snake
doing? Did it threaten you? Hurt you? Protect you? How

large was the snake? Was it poisonous? Was it shedding its skin?

Through this process of peeling away the layers of the symbol within the dream, you should be able to figure out what it means.

But suppose a snake appears in your waking life. Can its appearance be construed as guidance? For Lea, a teacher, a snake's appearance in her waking life portended an event. "I have a sliding glass door in my den that opens onto an atrium where I have a lush garden of various types of plants. I often leave the screen door open so my cats can wander in and out. One afternoon I was working at my computer when my tiger cat suddenly leaped through the open screen door, obviously chasing something. I didn't see whatever it was she was chasing, so I pushed back from the desk and looked under it, where she was.

"That's when I saw the snake, slithering along between the edge of the carpet and the wall. I shot to my feet, grabbed the cat, and ran out of the room shouting for my husband. He grabbed the broom, I put the cat in the bathroom, and found some shoes, then we ran back into my den.

"The snake hadn't moved. We didn't want to kill it, so the best option seemed to be to drive it back toward the open door to the atrium. At one point, it got trapped between the two sliding glass doors and we had to maneuver the doors to give it space to escape. We finally got the snake back outside and watched it slither off into the brush. I don't know whether it was poisonous, I never got that good a look at it. But it was definitely shedding its skin because I found part of the skin under my desk.

"I happened to mention the incident on a message board, just as an example of the kinds of things that happened with critters in Florida. Another woman on the board sent me an e-mail in which she interpreted the incident as a warning. 'Snakes are often symbolic of the men in our lives, especially the men who represent authority,' she wrote. 'The fact that the snake was shedding its skin may indicate a major change of some kind related to a man in your life who is an authority figure—your father, an uncle, maybe a grandfather. It didn't harm you or even threaten you in any way. Instead, it sought refuge in your room. My gut feeling is that this man, whoever he is, may be ill in the near future and you will have to tend to his care in some way.'

"This was the first time I'd ever thought of animals as symbolic of events in our lives. I sort of shrugged off her interpretation and didn't think any more about it until a week or so later, when my father went into the hospital for emergency surgery. Now I pay attention when an animal appears in my life."

If you have an affinity for a particular animal, then that animal may play some sort of guidance role for you, particularly as you undertake your exploration of spirit communication. Scorpio Janet, a graduate student, had begun exploring the area of spirit communication, but hadn't had any experiences yet. Then, one weekend, she visited her parents and happened to be standing under a tree in their yard when a baby bird fell out of its nest and landed on the ground in front of her.

"It was a mockingbird. I hesitated about picking it up because I'd heard that once you touch a baby bird, the mother won't come near it. But it was just lying there at my feet, chirping and trying to fly. I couldn't just leave it. I picked it up and tried to get it back into the nest, but the nest was too high for me to reach. I ended up caring for it that weekend, feeding it with an eye dropper. And then I couldn't just abandon it, so I took it back to school with me."

When she got back to school, she had a friend in the veterinary department check the bird over. It appeared to be okay despite its long fall from the tree, and her friend believed it would be flying and on its own within a few weeks. He recommended a particular food to feed it, and Janet decided to keep the bird until it could live on its own.

"This little bird brought out my nurturing instincts. I became less distrustful of people, less suspicious, more trusting in the process of life. And on the day I released him, I felt that I had also released the parts of myself that had grown hard over the years. Now, whenever I have an encounter with a mockingbird, I know there's a message in it for me."

Ted Andrews, in his book *Animal-Wise: The Spirit Language and Signs of Nature,* believes there are four lessons every animal can teach us, "lessons that are the animal's blessings to us and can serve as a mirror to show us what we need to do to be more successful. If we study and learn nothing else about the animal other than these four things, we will find our lives greatly enhanced."

1. By studying the life cycle and rhythm of any animal that appears in our lives, we learn something about what rhythms we should be following at that time. If, for example, frogs repeatedly appear in your life, then perhaps it's time to initiate new projects, look for a new job, or embrace change.

2. Be aware of the animal's adaptive behaviors. What behaviors or physical attributes allow it to survive in its environment? Chameleons, for instance, change

colors to blend in with your environment. If a chameleon has appeared in your life, perhaps the message is that you must do whatever you have to do to camouflage yourself.

3. Notice the skills the animal has. Spiders weave their intricately beautiful webs, then sit back and wait for the prey to come to them. "If spiders have shown up in your life, spin your web and weave your plans; be patient and let things come to you," writes Andrews.

4. Study the relationships of animals that appear in your life, advises Andrews, because their relationships to other animals may have a lot to say about your relationships with the people in your own life. Also, take note of the animal's environment. It, too, will hold a message for you.

If, after you do all this, you're still confused about the significance of this particular animal for you, look to mythology or ask other people what they think the meaning might be. Quite often, other people have insights that escape us because we're too close to the situation or because we're looking too hard or not looking in the right way. If these methods fail to shed light on the significance, then ask for guidance in a dream.

OTHER METHODS

The best meanings for animal appearances come from *you.* But when you're stuck, there are a couple of invaluable resources. Ted Andrews's *Animal-Wise* doesn't include every animal that walks the planet, but there are enough in here to head you in the right direction. The book is conveniently divided into birds, mammals, insects and arachnids, reptiles and amphibians, and sea life. Even if you don't find mockingbirds as one of the listings, reading some of the other bird entries will shed light on the significance of a bird that has shown up in your life.

Medicine Cards, which is actually a divination tool, comes with a set of cards and a slender volume for reference. There aren't a lot of animals listed in the book, but the entries for the ones that are included are insightful.

Here's a short list of animals and what their appearance may mean:

Ant. These busy little devils are among the most efficient workers in the insect kingdom. If ants appear in your life, the message may be that you need to use your energy more efficiently and to simply go about your business without concern for what other people think.

Bird. Birds often act as messengers. The type of bird, however, seems to be important. Owls, for instance, are considered to be messengers between the dead and the living. Hawks—depending, again, on the type of hawk— may indicate spirit messages. A vulture may indicate that a message will arrive concerning life, death, or some type of transformative event.

Butterfly. The call of beauty and freedom.

Caterpillar. Rebirth or a new birth. Time to shed what no longer works in your life.

Dolphin. A spiritual awakening.

Dragonfly. Messages.

Earthworm. It's time to burrow into your experiences and take stock of what works and doesn't work. Can indicate a period of solitude.

Firefly. Like Diogenes, they light up the dark. Can indicate some type of spiritual illumination.

Fox. Be wily, keep your own counsel.

Frog. From water breather to air breather, the frog usually indicates that it's time to embrace the new, that we shouldn't fear change. Because frogs are so sensitive to the environment, a frog's appearance in your life may also indicate that something in your immediate environment should be changed.

Slug. These incredibly ugly bugs were actually tools for divination in ancient cultures. A slug's appearance in your life may be referring to the success of a spiritual path or endeavor.

Snake. Male energy, transformation, shedding of the old.

Spider. Do what you have to do, then be patient and trust.

PART FOUR

✽

Cassadaga:
A Spiritualist
Community

21. Where the Living & the Dead Meet

It starts with empathy and compassion.

—HAZEL WEST

Just thirty minutes north of Disney World lies another world altogether. As soon as you turn off Interstate 4, memories of Dumbo and Epcot, Universal and MGM, give way to southern pine forests. A kind of presence infuses the still air. You can't help but feel that nothing is what it appears to be.

From I-4, in fact, there's not even a sign for Cassadaga. It's almost as if the people who are supposed to find their way here do it despite the lack of directions. Even on a map, Cassadaga is little more than a black dot, a punctuation point in the vastness of the pine forest. The only sign is for Lake Helen, the nearest town. The ramp for Lake Helen curves gently onto a country road that leads through pine and towering live oaks draped in Spanish moss. This road feeds into Volusia County Road 430A and brings you straight into Lake Helen.

Blink, and Lake Helen is already a memory. Just beyond the outer edge of the town, the road climbs and dips through a series of low hills and shallow valleys. The trees seem thicker and darker here, the Spanish moss sways in the breeze, and shapes eddy across the shadowed road. A hush lingers in the air. Stop your car, lower your windows, and you probably won't hear a sound.

About half a mile outside of Lake Helen, you'll see a sign announcing that you're now in Cassadaga. But it isn't until you come around the next sharp curve that you know you're there. A large two-story stucco building looms in front of you, the Cassadaga Hotel. Its Mediterranean architecture dates back to the 1920s, during the heyday of Spiritualism. Along the right side of the building stretches a wide porch filled with rocking chairs. At dusk some evenings, when the light plays tricks with perception, some of the empty chairs rock, creaking softly in the quiet.

Spirits enjoying the evening? One never knows for sure. But perhaps that's part of the lure and the mystique of Cassadaga.

Cassadaga is actually composed of two distinct areas. The part of the town that's known as the Spiritualist camp lies to the south of 430A, behind and to the west of the hotel. This is where the mediums live and work, on thirty-five acres of land owned by the Southern Cassadaga Spiritualist Camp Meeting Association, otherwise known as Camp Cassadaga.

The camp area is filled with old houses, some of which look like they belong on Cape Cod or in a child's fairy tale. Some seem to list to one side, as if the wind has blown them that way, and others have sagging front porches. They are different colors, these crooked homes, and many have porches where elderly people often sit in the evening, rocking in their chairs, smoking, gossiping, and watching the strangers pass by. What distinguishes these little houses from similar houses elsewhere are the signs out in front.

The signs that say, CERTIFIED MEDIUM.

Outside of the Andrew Jackson Davis Educational Building—otherwise known as a meeting hall—stands a bulletin board with a list of the mediums in town who are available for readings. In one sense, this bulletin board says it all for Cassadaga. *Here's what we do,* that list seems to say. *Here's what we're about. We've got nothing to hide. Like it or leave.*

Cassadaga also has a bookstore, a gift shop and restaurant located in the hotel, and two lakes. These lakes, at least on the surface, aren't unusual for central Florida. But as you approach Lake Colby and Spirit Pond, that strangeness returns to the air. You feel it in your bones, an alien chill, and a pall of unreality clamps down over you. Is it the whir of insects that you hear or the soft beating of drums from some distant past? If you shut your eyes for a moment, the past moves in around you like mist, down there by Spirit Pond, in all the impossible greens, the startling blues. And that's the thing about this town. The border between reality and illusion blurs. To an astrologer, it's pure Neptunian energy.

Even Cassadaga's origins strain credulity. Story has it that back in 1875, out there in Iowa cornfields, a medium named George Colby was holding a séance at the home of a local resident, a fellow named Wadsworth. Nothing extraordinary had happened so far that night. Colby was already a successful medium, and he'd done the usual things that night—passed on messages from the dead to the living.

Then, suddenly, Colby received a message from his Indian guide, Seneca, instructing him to travel immediately to Eau Claire, Wisconsin, where he was to hook up with T. D. Giddings, a Spiritualist. Once he was in

Wisconsin, Seneca said, further instructions would be given.

Colby, being a product of a time when the Spiritualist movement was sweeping across the country, did the expected thing. The next morning, he packed up and left for Wisconsin. He met up with Giddings. At a séance shortly afterward, Colby and Giddings were given instructions to leave Wisconsin and head to Florida.

Colby was only twenty-seven years old at the time, a single man ready for adventure. Giddings, however, had a family and took them along. Back then, steamboats and trains were the only route south, and this odd little entourage took both. They rode a train to Jacksonville, Florida, then traveled by steamboat down the St. John's River to a place called Blue Springs. This frontier town was supposedly in the general vicinity of their final destination.

Seneca had described the place they were going to settle as having hills and a chain of lakes. The only thing that lay beyond the borders of Blue Springs looked like dense, subtropical forest. But when Seneca made contact and told the two men to begin their trek into the woods and to follow his directions, they did so.

They made their way through dense growth, and after several miles arrived at the spot where Seneca said the Spiritualist camp would be created. Everything—from the high bluffs to the lakes and the lay of the land— looked exactly as Seneca had described.

Colby built a house on the shores of Lake Colby, and Giddings and his family built a home nearby. Colby eventually obtained a government deed for seventy-four acres that adjoined the area where he and Giddings had settled. They were apparently the only people for miles around.

For eighteen years, Colby apparently didn't do much of anything about establishing a Spiritualist community in the area. He adopted several orphans, however, and raised them. He also operated a dairy.

In 1893, a Spiritualist named Rowley showed up and decided to establish a Spiritualist center in either De Leon Springs or Winter Park. He invited a number of prominent Spiritualists from the North to travel to Florida to check out the area. Two of these Spiritualists were women who were prominent in the Lily Dale Spiritualist camp in New York. They didn't particularly care for Rowley, but Colby won them over and they decided to create a Spiritualist camp on his property.

In October 1894, twelve mediums signed the charter for the Southern Cassadaga Spiritualist Camp. According to the charter, the association was to be a nonprofit organization that would promote the Spiritualist beliefs in the soul's immortality, "the nearness of the Spirit World, the guardianship of Spirit friends, and the possibility of communion with them."

Seneca, Colby's guide, apparently advised him to remain in the background during this time, so his name doesn't appear on the charter and he didn't have much to do with the organization of the camp. However, in 1895, he deeded the association thirty-five acres of his land. The first meeting was held in late 1895 and lasted three days. A hundred people attended the event to meet and sit with the mediums who had been invited to the meeting.

Within three years of that first meeting, eight cottages, a dancing pavilion, a lodging hall, and a library had been built on the association grounds. Wealthy mediums from the North were being enticed to move to Cassadaga on a more or less permanent basis. From the late 1800s to the early part of the twentieth century, not much is written about the town. The camp apparently flourished, however, because the Cassadaga Hotel was built in 1922 and so were most of the cottages that still stand today.

By the late 1930s, as the rest of the country was emerging from the depression, life in Cassadaga was booming. Thirty to forty mediums were now living there year round and many wealthy Spiritualists from the North were visiting during the winter season. They packed the Cassadaga Hotel for weeks at a time and even spilled over into hotels in nearby towns.

There was great fanfare and drama in the séances in those days, not unlike séances in the heyday of Spiritualism. Flamboyance was at its height: materialization of spirits, apports, physical manifestations. By the 1960s, however, most of this had died down, spurred in part by reports of fraudulence.

CASSADAGA IN THE 21ST CENTURY

Today there isn't much flamboyance in Cassadaga. You won't find anyone using cabinets or trumpets, favorite tools in the old days. If there are séances, they aren't for public view. Some people, upon arriving in Cassadaga for the first time, seem surprised by what they find. If they were expecting something similar to an Amish village, this isn't it. There are no historical reenactments of the good ole days, Williamsburg style, either. In fact, if you happened to drive through town without knowing mediums lived there, you might mistake it for a retirement community.

Church services are held in the Colby Memorial Building. Every Sunday, healings and readings are part of the services and are open to the public. If you've never had a reading before, this might be a place to start because the readings are free, spontaneous, and done by camp mediums and their students.

The Cassadaga Hotel has been refurbished several times over the years since it was built. It supposedly is haunted by a ghost named George who makes his presence known by the smell of his cigars. An outfit called Ghost Tracker has photos on the Web of some of the spirits that hang out around Cassadaga and the hotel. Even if you don't believe in spirit photography, check out the Web site: www.ghostracker.com.

MARIE'S STORY

In 1973, Marie, a graduate student at the time, went to Cassadaga with her roommate "to see what was there." She'd heard about the town from people on campus and thought it would be interesting to have a reading with a medium. She and her roommate arrived around noon, on a warm day in May. "Back then, central Florida was very rural, a virtual wasteland of scrub brush and pines. When I first saw the town, it reminded me of a movie set that had been built in the middle of nowhere: the little houses that belonged somewhere on Cape Cod, the porches with rocking chairs on them, the signs out in front that stated whether the resident was a medium or an astrologer or a palmist . . . It was all wonderfully strange."

Marie and her roommate walked around town for a while, getting a feel for the place, trying to decide which psychic to see. They finally chose one of the first houses in town. The man who lived there was a quadriplegic, bedridden, and did the reading in his bedroom, with Marie sitting next to the bed.

"He asked for something he could hold—a ring, a necklace, something personal and preferably metal. I was wearing a ring, I can't even remember what kind of ring, except that it was silver and had some sort of stone in it. I handed it to him and he closed his fingers around it and shut his eyes for a few moments. In those moments, something changed in the room, I could *feel* it, an almost electrical energy permeated the air. And then he started to speak.

"I can't remember anymore what he said. I can't remember the specifics. But I was so shocked I didn't even take notes. I just stood there, listening, astonished that this guy I'd never seen before was reading me like the Sunday funnies."

Eight years later, Marie returned to Cassadaga with a man she was dating at the time. She looked for the house of the handicapped man who had read for her, but discovered he had passed away. She and the man she was with walked around town for a while and finally decided to try a two-story house set back off one of the roads, in the shadows of some huge banyan trees.

"The man who lived in this house was named Don. He had lived in Cassadaga for a long time. That's all I remember about him personally. We sat out on his screened porch for the reading. He didn't ask for any personal objects, didn't pull out a deck of tarot cards, didn't even ask our birth dates. He sat down across from us, we chatted for a few minutes about the weather or whatever, then he shut his eyes for a moment and started talking.

"This reading was much different than the first one I'd had. Don talked rapidly and much of what he said seemed broadly symbolic and could have applied to anyone. 'I see a large, blank table in front of you both.

In time, as your lives together unfold, this table will begin to fill up . . .' Yeah, right, I thought. But then, as he went on, he started saying things that felt right somehow. For instance, the man I was with, Bob, had refused to go to Vietnam. He didn't run off to Canada to avoid the draft, he didn't look for any kind of physical deferment. He just flatly refused to go and went to jail for it.

"Don told Bob that in several of his lives, he had been killed in war and his relationship with me was incomplete. In this life, he'd refused to go to war and now he and I would be able to complete a relationship begun many lifetimes ago. I was now listening very carefully. So was Bob. The reading went on for about an hour. Unfortunately, neither Bob nor I took notes. But there were many specific references to work we were involved in at the time, to work we would do in the future. In the end, I left impressed by his ability to pull this stuff out of what seemed like thin air."

A number of years later, Marie returned with Bob, to whom she was now married, and her infant daughter. "We stayed on the top floor of the Cassadaga Hotel. We were the only guests because the hotel was undergoing renovations. It was cold that weekend, I remember, in the low forties, and around midnight that night, I woke from a sound sleep to the sound of heavy footsteps on the stairs. It frightened me and I woke Bob.

"We both hurried over to the door and listened with our ears pressed to the wood. We didn't hear voices, just this loud, terrible *thump thump thump*. At times, it almost sounded as if a body were being pulled up or dragged down the stairs. We knew we were the only people staying in the hotel and it seemed unlikely that the manager would make so much racket at such a late hour."

When the sounds paused outside their door, they nearly panicked. "We pushed the heavy wooden dresser in front of the door, then I ran over to one of the windows, opened it, and started looking for a way down. That's how terrified we were. We did *not* want to open that door.

"Then the footfalls resumed, but sounded as if they were moving away from our door. They simply faded away. The next morning, I mentioned the incident to the woman at the desk and she just smiled. We've never stayed there again."

GETTING A READING IN CASSADAGA

More than a hundred psychics and mediums live in this town. You don't have to call ahead to get a reading. In fact, part of the adventure is to simply walk through Cassadaga, up and down the narrow, shaded streets, and allow your intuition to guide you about which door to knock on.

No psychic is legally bound to read for people who come to the door. In fact, when intuitive Millie Gemondo was visiting her niece in Daytona, they drove over to Cassadaga one afternoon to get readings. "No one would read for me. They thought I was an investigator or something," she laughs.

During the winter, many of the psychics are fully booked, thanks to the influx of tourists. But from shortly after Easter, when the snowbirds go home, to just after Halloween, you can usually find someone to read for you just by knocking on a few doors. Or you can walk up to the hotel and ask whoever is working the desk for a recommendation.

If it's Sunday, you can walk to the other side of 430A, into the part of Cassadaga that doesn't belong to the association, and attend a nondenominational service in one of the several churches. Here, at the end of the service, a medium will do spot readings for the audience. In many ways, this is about as close as you'll get to the heyday of Spiritualism. An on-the-spot reading goes something like this: *I'm receiving the name June. She passed over when she was in her late sixties and has a daughter whose name starts with an S. Does that pertain to anyone in this room?* Invariably, people glance around, looking for S whose mother's name was June. If no hands shoot up, the medium offers a little more information. *She passed from an injury to the head . . .*

And then a hand rises into the air.

This process is similar to what happens when medium John Edward works an audience on television or when James Van Praagh or Char Margolis or Sylvia Browne takes calls from strangers on TV talk shows. You have the sense that information is flowing so rapidly into the medium that he or she can't speak rapidly enough to keep up with it. This type of reading rarely lasts more than sixty seconds. But the information conveyed can blow your socks off.

A CASSADAGA RESIDENT

Hazel West, like Jane Roberts, is a triple earth sign. Her Sun is in Capricorn, her Moon—like that of Roberts—is in Taurus, and her Rising, like Roberts's, is in Capricorn. To an astrologer, this isn't the chart of someone who speaks to the dead. This is the chart of someone so grounded, so completely in the here and now of physical life, that she might be a CEO, a financial analyst, a master gardener, an artist.

But her Neptune in Virgo lies in the 9th house—just like Cayce's Neptune in Taurus in the 9th house—and it all begins to make sense. The earth is there, rooting and holding her to physical reality, precisely because she speaks to the dead. Her Sun sign's polarity, Cancer, is the Hazel that you see when you come to her for a reading. It's the Hazel who is nurturing, caring, compassionate. It's the Hazel who always answers her door with a smile and a softly spoken, "Hi, may I help you?"

She's an attractive woman, a brunette who, at sixty-two, doesn't have a gray hair on her head. And it's her natural color, which she has maintained through a regimen of vitamins, diet, and, as she says, laughing, "with pure will."

Hazel has lived in Cassadaga for so many years that, in many ways, her identity is inseparable from the town's identity. She's married to another Spiritualist, Art Burley, has several children from her first marriage, and a grandson on whom she dotes. The room where she conducts her spiritual work is rectangular, small, very tidy. One wall is lined with books, most of them related to her work, health, and other interests. The wall against which the couch sits is glass and overlooks an outside patio bright with flowers. On a spring day, when the windows are open to the fresh air, there is no place more pleasant to while away a couple of hours than in Hazel's company, in her den.

Hazel came to Cassadaga as the result of a dream she had in 1963. She was then living in Merritt Island, Florida, where she and her first husband were both students. In the dream, she saw herself with an older man who was in a wheelchair. He asked her to help him with a book, and, in the dream, she told him she would be delighted to do so but first she had to do two things. At the time of the dream, Hazel had never heard of Cassadaga. She didn't have any idea who the elderly man in her dream was, but understood that the dream was leading her to what would become her life's work. "I had been asking for guidance about what to do with my life. Although I was happily married, I sensed there was something else I was going to be doing."

Seven months after this dream, a friend of Hazel's who ran a health food store brought her to Cassadaga to have a reading with a medium named Anne Gehman. "At that point, when I had that reading, I understood all the strange experiences I'd had throughout my life—voices, dreams, the knowing."

Gehman became Hazel's first teacher, and every three months or so over the course of the next year, Hazel returned to Cassadaga to study with her. About a year after that first reading, Gehman urged Hazel to meet her at a Spiritualist community in Wisconsin. Despite the fact that there were a million reasons not to go, Hazel went. There, she met the elderly white-haired gentleman in the wheelchair who had appeared in her dream. His name was Wilbur Hull, and he was one of the finest mediums Cassadaga has ever known. "He was thirty-five years older than me, a very private person, and I was too intimidated to tell him about my dream. But we became good friends."

In the spring of 1968, Hazel returned again to Cassadaga to study with Hull. During that stay, he asked her to help him with a book. "Just like in my dream. Wilbur had muscular dystrophy and although he could move his upper body, he needed legs for research. I had legs."

Hazel then told him about her dream. "I remembered from the dream that I had two things I had to do before I helped Wilbur with the book, but I didn't have any idea what those two things were. But I knew I wanted children. My husband and I had been married almost six years by then. We wanted a family. Yet, a gynecologist had told me I couldn't have children. Even so, I had this recurring vision—a very strong vision—of a little girl and then I began to have visions about two kids, a girl and a boy. I knew they were 'the two things' I had to do before I could help Wilbur with his book."

On the last night of Hazel's visit, Wilbur went into trance and his guides spoke directly to Hazel. They described how she had been guided to Cassadaga, how certain events and meetings had been arranged for her to arrive at that precise place, at that precise time. "That night, I asked for healing so that I could have children. Wilbur's guides told me it was improbable but not impossible and that they would do everything they could to heal me."

In 1974, Hazel's marriage ended. Her husband realized that she didn't belong in Atlanta, that her destiny lay in Cassadaga, and he urged her to follow that dream. "We split without so much as a harsh word. By then, I had my two children, a boy and a girl, and I knew it was time."

She traveled to Cassadaga to look for a place to live. There was nothing available in the camp at the time, so she made an offer on a house outside the camp. She wasn't crazy about the place, but at least it was near to the other mediums she knew. "That night, I stopped by Wilbur's and he went into trance and Spirit said I was going to have the opportunity to buy the house I really wanted. I thought they were referring to the place I'd made the offer on. That was around ten o'clock at night. The next morning, Anne Gehman and her husband called Wilbur and told him their house was for sale and was he or anyone else interested?"

Hazel laughs softly at the recollection. "This is how Spirit works. When Wilbur asked Anne when she and her husband decided to sell, Anne said around ten o'clock the previous night—at exactly the time Wilbur's guides were telling me I'd have the opportunity to buy the house I wanted."

The following year, Hazel moved to Cassadaga, into the very house where she'd had her first reading. "I was leaving a five thousand square foot house north of Atlanta for a cottage in the Florida hills. Spirit told me, 'Don't look at the wood, the mortar. The house in Cassadaga is made of the vibration that holds it together. It's created out of the love and the spirituality that you put into it and which others bring to it.'"

Hazel advises that anyone with a desire to work as a medium must have empathy and compassion for other people. She uses handwriting to attune to the individual during a reading. "To me, handwriting is the picture of the soul. It gives me the picture of who that person really is. And of course I use the mediumship. I ask those in Spirit to help. Well, I don't really have to ask anymore. They know when to start!"

Sometimes she hears inner voices (clairaudience) and sometimes she receives images, pictures, impressions (clairvoyance). But mostly, she's clairsentient. "You have to be very courageous to do this kind of work. By that, I mean that it requires courage to tell people things that may be hurtful or which may not make sense or not seem reasonable or obvious."

She relates a funny story about her husband, Art, that

happened during a church service where mediums give on-the-spot readings for people attending the service. "There was a woman in the audience whom Spirit had selected for him to read. He told her he was picking up on a gentleman who had died of some sort of rodent bite. I thought, oh no, Art, not here, not in a church. That isn't an appropriate thing to mention in a church. I was so sure he was wrong. But sure enough, the woman's father had worked in a research lab and he had died of a rat bite."

Those in Spirit, Hazel says, work in mysterious ways. Quite often, her guides will give her information on people who show up unexpectedly several days later. Sometimes she'll jot the information down, along with the name of the individual to whom the information pertains. But more often than not, she files it away in her head and when she hears the individual's name, the rest of the information falls into place.

"I don't just give predictions. I try to help people understand how they can use their free will to create the life they want. In most instances, we create the life we want through our thoughts and actions, and those in Spirit get behind our efforts. My readings are always a teaching in helping people to help themselves."

Those in Spirit, says Hazel, work with the medium's knowledge and interests to bring through information. "That's why it's so important for someone in this line of work to constantly be learning, reading, studying. The more evolved the medium, the more evolved are those in Spirit who come through to help."

In recent years, she has learned a lot about Alzheimer's patients, perhaps because many of the clients who come to her have aging parents. In one reading, a woman had come to Hazel in the hopes that she would be able to tell her where her mother had put some important financial papers.

"I thought the woman's mother was dead, that she was in Spirit. That's how my communication with her felt like to me. To my surprise, the woman told me her mother had Alzheimer's and was in a facility. This and subsequent readings in which Alzheimer's patients have come through have led me to believe that the consciousness of people with this disease are already in Spirit."

And those financial papers? "The mother showed me an old trunk in a dusty attic. The daughter called me the next day and said they'd found the papers in an old trunk in the attic of her mother's former home, where she'd been living when she was in the early stages of the disease. With Alzheimer's, both Art and I feel that the Spirit is already in the next dimension of life."

Due to Hazel's compassion and empathy, she often picks up information about the physical condition that led to someone's death, and it can be quite specific. For a woman whose editor had died of AIDS-related pneumonia, Hazel described a "blood disorder, an immune deficiency disease. I feel congestion in my lungs, as if I'm suffocating."

She also picks up on health problems for her clients, in much the same way that a medical intuitive does. "Those in Spirit have a great desire to assist."

On occasion, Hazel asks Spirit to help in the healing of someone, just as she once requested to be healed so that she could have children. "There have been instances of people being healed of chronic illnesses. *I'm* not the healer. Spirit works through me."

When Hazel does readings over the phone, she asks that the client send her a photograph and a sample of his or her handwriting. These are the tools she uses to attune herself to the individual. "It doesn't matter whether the client is in front of me or on the phone. The energy is the same either way. Spirit works either way."

Quite often in readings, animals and pets come through. "They feel like human spirits to me and express the same kind of love for the people they have left behind."

This echoes what George Anderson writes in *Lessons from the Light*. "Some people come only for communication with their beloved pet, and the communication is filled with the same emotion as those of the human kind."

Hazel believes we are all psychic and mediumistic, some of us more than others, but only because they work at it. "It requires focus and discipline," says the triple earth sign. "And it requires love of the world. You must have the ability and willingness to enter into another person's world, their life, to feel their pain, to go through with them what they're going through."

Sounds like a triple earth sign!

In addition to the guidelines and suggestions mentioned here, Hazel has these pointers for developing your intuitive and mediumistic skills:

1. Trust what you're receiving. Don't repress or block information just because it doesn't seem reasonable or logical.
2. Be sincere in your search.
3. Be open and receptive.
4. Remember that "like attracts like." The more knowledgeable you are, the more you work at the spiritual side of your life, the greater the chances of attracting evolved Spirit helpers.

5. Success comes from hard work. From persistence. It's the old adage: "God helps those who help themselves."
6. Be free of dogma, fears, and defenses.
7. Be compassionate.

What to Expect from a Reading

Every psychic and medium has an individual way of working with clients. But regardless of how they work— and whether they live in Cassadaga or elsewhere—there are certain things you should and shouldn't expect from a reading.

1. No psychic should tell you what to do with your life, whom you should marry, or what job you should take or leave or apply for. If they do, get up and leave because this psychic may have an agenda.
2. If a psychic informs you that you have a lot of negative energy around you or that a spirit has attached itself to you and says you would benefit from additional psychic work—for an extra and sometimes exorbitant fee—get up and leave.
3. Allow your intuition to guide you in the choice of a psychic. If you resonate with the person, if the individual's energy feels good to you, then chances are you won't get taken.
4. Have your questions in mind when you go to the reading. Sometimes it's helpful to write down the questions before you go. This helps fix them in your own consciousness. A good psychic usually will answer all those questions in the course of the reading, without you having to guide him or her in the right direction.

5. Psychics and mediums work with probability patterns. They probably don't think of it that way, but it's the same type of probability pattern that operates when you toss I Ching coins, pull tarot cards, or do any other sort of divination.

   A psychic or medium tunes in on you—with the aid of spirit or just raw intuitive ability—and sees the events and situations that are *most probable for you given where you are at the moment of the reading.* If you don't like what you hear, take steps to change the circumstances in your life that pertain to the issue. *Nothing in a reading is preordained.*

6. Always weigh psychic information against your own intuition. In the end, *you* are the expert on your own life.

7. The best readings often occur when your life is in transition, when you're really seeking answers and guidance. Then, it's as if everything about you is right there on the surface, and for the psychic or medium it's like skimming the cream off milk.

8. You don't have to pay outrageous sums to get a good reading. Cayce, even at the height of his reputation, kept his fees reasonable. Just because a psychic or medium charges a thousand bucks for a reading doesn't mean that the information you'll get is any better than that from a psychic or medium who charges $35. They have to make a living, of course, just like anyone else, but for a thousand bucks the information better be so accurate that it seems to come from God.

9. Understand your own motives. Why do you want a reading?

10. Psychics and mediums aren't omniscient. They aren't always right.

11. Timing is a challenge for most of them. Some psychics and mediums can provide a range of time—two to six weeks, three to five years—but don't hold them to it. Neptune knows no time. You're the scriptwriter of your life.

12. Maintain an open mind. Don't pass judgment in the middle of your reading. Remember, psychics and mediums are only human beings.

Appendices

Appendix 1.
Neptune's Signs

Locate the range of dates that includes your birth date and note which sign Neptune was in when you were born.

Dates	Neptune's Sign
1889–5/21/1902	Gemini
5/22/1902–7/15/1915	Cancer
7/16/1915–9/21/1928	Leo
9/22/1928–8/2/1943	Virgo
8/3/1943–8/5/1957	Libra
8/6/1957–1/4/1970	Scorpio
1/5/1970–1/18/1984	Sagittarius
1/19/1984–11/27/1998	Capricorn
11/28/1998–4/4/2011	Aquarius

Appendix 2.
Books & Other Resources

Anderson, George. *Lessons from the Light.*

Andrews, Ted. *Animal-Wise: The Spirit Language and Signs of Nature.*

Bowman, Carol. *Children's Past Lives; Return from Heaven.*

Day, Laura. *Practical Intuition; Practical Intuition for Success.*

Edward, John. *One Last Time.*

Einstein, Patricia. *Intuition.*

Hay, Louise. *You Can Heal Your Life.*

Jung, C. G. *Memories, Dreams and Reflections.*

Margolis, Char. *Questions from Earth, Answers from Heaven.*

Matheson, Richard. *What Dreams May Come* (fiction).

Moen, Bruce. *Voyages into the Unknown; Voyage Beyond Doubt; Voyages into the Afterlife.*

Moody, Raymond. *Life After Life.*

Myss, Caroline. *Anatomy of the Spirit.*

Orloff, Judith. *Second Sight; Intuitive Healing.*

Roberts, Jane. *Seth Speaks; The Nature of Personal Reality; The Seth Material; The Unknown Reality; The*

Way of Health; Dreams, Evolution & Value Fulfillment.

Schultz, Mona Lisa. *Awakening Intuition.*

Van Praagh, James. *Talking to Heaven; Reaching to Heaven.*

Weiss, Brian. *Many Lives, Many Masters; Through Time into Healing; Messages from the Masters.*

Psychics & Mediums

The psychics and mediums listed in this section have graciously allowed the author to use their names and contact information.

Millie Gemondo. Call in advance to schedule a reading by phone or in person: 304-584-4233. P.O. Box 63, Lumberport, West Virginia 26386.

James Van Praagh. Contact him through his Web site: vanpraagh.com.

Noreen Renier. Call in advance to schedule a reading by phone or in person: 352-336-9362. Get in touch with Noreen through her Web site: atlantic.net~nrenier.

Hazel West. Call in advance to schedule a reading by phone or in person: 904-228-3826. E-mail: aburley@yahoo.com. Or by snail mail: P.O. Box 92, Cassadaga, Florida 32706.

Web Sites of Interest

afterlifecodes.com—home page for author and psychic Suzy Smith.

astrology.com—for a free chart.

brianweiss.com—home page for past-life researcher and author Brian Weiss.

childpastlives.org—home page for author and past-life researcher Carol Bowman.

georgeanderson.com—home page for medium George Anderson.

hayhouse.com—home page for author and medical intuitive Louise Hay and for her publishing house.

johnedward.com—home page for author and medium John Edward.

judithorloff.com—home page for author and medical intuitive Judith Orloff.

Psychicchar.com—home page for psychic and author Char Margolis.

sylvia.org—home page for author and psychic Sylvia Browne.

Other Information

All the birth data for charts in this book were provided by the individuals. The charts were generated with Matrix's Winstar Plus, version 2.

Appendix 3. How to Determine Your Rising Sign—the Ascendant

Using the blank chart at the back of the book, locate the horizontal line that cuts through the center of the chart. Label the left-hand side east; this is where the Sun rises. Label the right-hand side west; this is where the Sun sets. At the top of the vertical line, jot Midheaven; here, it's high noon. At the bottom of that line, write Nadir or IC; here, it's midnight.

The Ascendant changes about every two hours. To make it easier, place 6 a.m. at the left side of the chart, indicating the time the Sun rises. If you're an Aries born between 4 and 6 a.m., you're an Aries with Aries Rising. If you were born between 6 and 8 a.m., then you're an Aries with Taurus Rising. If you were born between 8 and 10 a.m., then you would be an Aries with Gemini Rising. This method doesn't take into account the degree of the sign that was rising at your birth, but it should give you a close enough approximation to figure out into which house your Neptune falls.

Suppose you're a Gemini, born between 2 to 4 p.m., with a Neptune in Libra. What would your Rising sign be? Where would your Neptune fall?

The easiest way to figure this out is to jot 6 a.m. at the east, 6 p.m. at the west, noon at the top, midnight at the bottom. Now, in the 1st house, jot down 4–6 a.m. and, moving clockwise, jot 6–8 a.m. in the 12th house, 8–10 a.m. in the 11th, 10 a.m. to 12 noon in the 10th house, and so on around the circle.

Having done that, you see your Gemini Sun would fall in the 8th house (2–4 p.m.), so Gemini would be on the cusp of the 8th house. This puts Taurus on the cusp of the 7th, to the west, Aries on the cusp of the 6th, and around the chart toward the east until you end up with Scorpio Rising on the cusp of the 1st house. Your Libra Neptune falls in the 12th house.

Now calculate your own chart!

Star Charts

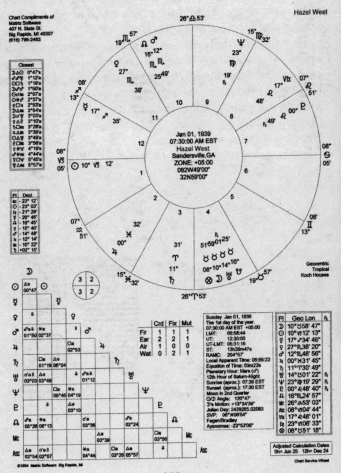

Chart Compliments of
Matrix Software
407 N. State St.
Big Rapids, MI 49307
(616) 796-2483

Hazel West

Closest	
☽△☉	0°47's
♂☍♅	1°12'a
☉□♄	1°19'a
☽☍♂	1°50'a
☉☌Asc	2°07'a
☉✶♂	2°37'a
♀□♃	2°53'a
☽△Asc	2°54'a
☽☌♅	3°03'a
♀△♇	3°10'a
♄□Asc	3°26'a
♃△Mc	3°39'a
☉△♅	3°49'a
♇□Mc	3°56'a
♀✶♆	4°19's
♂✶Asc	4°44'a
☿□♆	5°45'a
♅△Asc	5°57'a

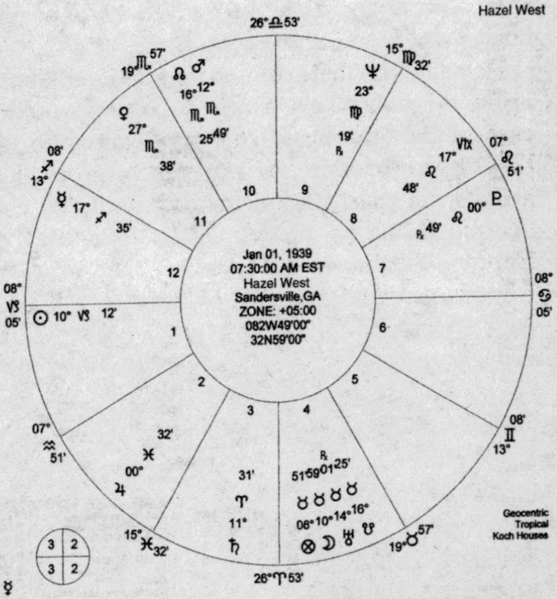

Jan 01, 1939
07:30:00 AM EST
Hazel West
Sandersville,GA
ZONE: +05:00
082W49'00"
32N59'00"

Pl	Decl
Asc	- 23° 12'
☉	- 23° 03'
Eq	- 21° 28'
☿	- 20° 46'
☊	- 16° 45'
♀	- 15° 40'
♂	- 14° 48'
♃	- 12° 14'
Mc	- 10° 22'
♄	+02° 15'

Geocentric
Tropical
Koch Houses

	☽	☉	☿	♀	♂	♃	♄	♅	♆	♇	☊	Mc
☉	△s 00°47											
☿												
♀	#											
♂	☍a# 01°50	✶a 02°37		∥								
♃				□a 02°53								
♄		□a 01°19	△s 06°04									
♅	☌a∥ 03°03	△a 03°49		#	☍a# 01°12							
♆			□a 05°45	✶s 04°19								
♇		#		△a 03°10								
☊	☍a 05°26	✶a 06°13			☌a 03°36			☍s 02°24				
Mc						△a 03°39				□a 03°56		
Asc	△a 02°54	☌a∥ 02°07			✶a 04°44		□a 03°26	△a 05°57		#		

	Crd	Fix	Mut
Fir	1	1	1
Ear	2	2	1
Air	1	0	0
Wat	0	2	1

Sunday Jan 01, 1939
The 1st day of the year.
07:30:00 AM EST +05:00
LMT: 06:58:44
UT: 12:30:00
UT-LMT: 05:31:16
ST: 13h39m47s
RAMC: 204°57'
Local Apparent Time: 06:55:22
Equation of Time: 03m22s
Planetary Hour: Mars (♂)
12th Hour of Saturn-Night
Sunrise (aprox.): 07:39 EST
Sunset (aprox.): 17:30 EST
Moon in 2nd Quarter
☉/☽ Angle: 120°47'
☽'s Motion: +13°34'39"
Julian Day: 2429265.02063
SVP: 06°♓06'54"
Fagan/Bradley
Ayanamsa: -23°53'06"

Pl	Geo Lon	℞
☽	10°♉58' 47"	
☉	10°♑12' 13"	
☿	17°♐34' 46"	
♀	27°♏38' 20"	
♂	12°♏48' 56"	
♃	00°♓31' 45"	
♄	11°♈30' 49"	
♅	14°♉01' 22"	℞
♆	23°♍19' 29"	℞
♇	00°♌48' 40"	℞
☊	16°♏24' 57"	
Mc	26°♎53' 03"	
Asc	08°♑04' 44"	
Vtx	17°♌48' 01"	
Eq	23°♑06' 33"	
⊗	08°♉51' 18"	

Adjusted Calculation Dates
0h= Jun 25 12h= Dec 24

Chart Service Wheel

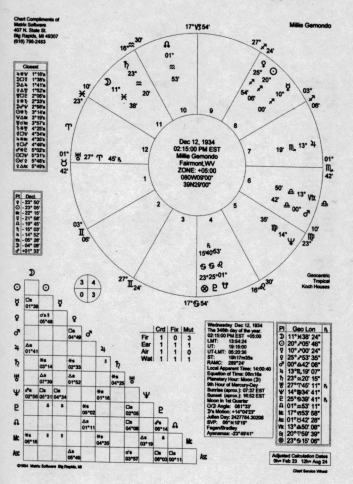

Chart Compliments of
Matrix Software
407 N. State St.
Big Rapids, MI 49307
(616) 796-2483

Millie Gemondo

Closest	
♃✱♆	1°16'a
☽□☿	1°38's
☽△♃	1°41'a
♀△♅	1°52'a
♅□♇	2°05'a
♀✱♄	2°33's
☽☍♆	2°56'a
☉✱♄	3°14'a
♆△Mc	3°19's
♅☌Asc	3°57's
♄✱♅	4°25'a
☿□♆	4°34'a
♃✱Mc	4°35's
♀□♂	4°49'a
♂✱♇	5°02's
☉□♆	5°31's
☉☌♀	5°48's
♀△Asc	5°49's

Pl	Decl.
♀	- 23° 50'
☉	- 23° 05'
Mc	- 22° 15'
☿	- 21° 58'
☊	- 19° 45'
♄	- 15° 03'
♃	- 14° 52'
Vx	- 05° 28'
☽	- 04° 08'
♂	+01° 33'

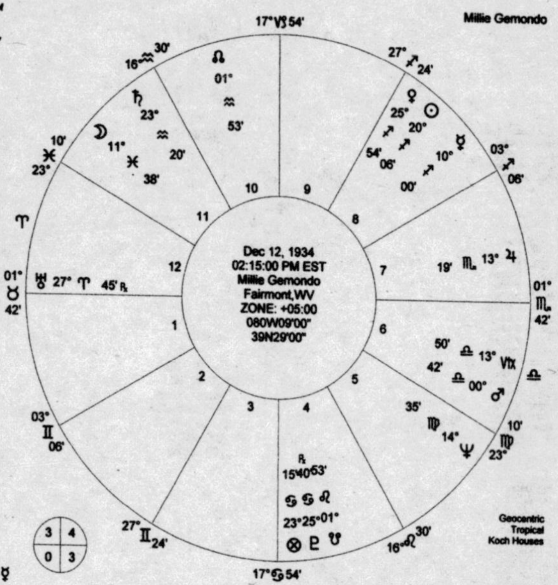
17° ♑ 54'
27° ♐ 24'
03° ♐ 06'
01° ♏ 42'
10' ♍ 23°
16° ♌ 30'
17° ♋ 54'
27° ♊ 24'
03° ♊ 06'
01° ♉ 42'
10' ♓ 23°
16° ♒ 30'
☊ 01° ♒ 53'
♄ 23° ♒ 20'
☽ 11° ♓ 38'
♀ 25° ♐ 54'
☉ 20° ♐ 06'
☿ 10° ♐ 00'
19' ♏ 13° ♃
50' ♎ 13° Vx
42' ♎ 00° ♂
35' ♍ 14° ♆
♅ 27° ♈ 45' ℞
℞ 15 40 53'
♋ ♋ ♌
23° 25° 01°
⊗ ♇ ☋
Dec 12, 1934
02:15:00 PM EST
Millie Gemondo
Fairmont,WV
ZONE: +05:00
080W09'00"
39N29'00"

Geocentric
Tropical
Koch Houses

3	4
0	3

	☽	☉	☿	♀	♂	♃	♄	♅	♆	♇	☊	Mc
☉												
☿	□s 01°38											
♀		☌s ∥ 05°48										
♂				□a 04°49								
♃	△a 01°41											
♄		✱s 03°14		✱s 02°33		∥						
♅		△a 07°39		△a 01°52			✱a 04°25					
♆	☍a 02°56	□s 05°31	□a 04°34			✱a 01°16						
♇		#	#		✱s 05°02			□a 02°05				
☊					△s 01°11			□s 04°06		☍s 06°14		
Mc	✱s 06°16	∥	∥			✱s 04°35			△s 03°19	#		
Asc				△s 05°49				☌s 03°57		□s 06°03	□a 00°11	

	Crd	Fix	Mut
Fir	1	0	3
Ear	1	1	1
Air	1	1	0
Wat	1	1	1

Wednesday Dec 12, 1934
The 346th day of the year.
02:15:00 PM EST +05:00
LMT: 13:54:24
UT: 19:15:00
UT-LMT: 05:20:36
ST: 19h17m35s
RAMC: 289°24'
Local Apparent Time: 14:00:40
Equation of Time: 06m16s
Planetary Hour: Moon (☽)
9th Hour of Mercury-Day
Sunrise (aprox.): 07:37 EST
Sunset (aprox.): 16:52 EST
Moon in 1st Quarter
☉/☽ Angle: 081°33'
☽'s Motion: +14°04'23"
Julian Day: 2427784.30208
SVP: 06°♓10'19"
Fagan/Bradley
Ayanamsa: -23°49'41"

Pl	Geo Lon	℞
☽	11°♓38' 24"	
☉	20°♐05' 46"	
☿	10°♐00' 24"	
♀	25°♐53' 35"	
♂	00°♎42' 06"	
♃	13°♏19' 07"	
♄	23°♒20' 15"	
♅	27°♈45' 11"	℞
♆	14°♍34' 41"	
♇	25°♋39' 41"	℞
☊	01°♒53' 11"	
Mc	17°♑53' 58"	
Asc	01°♉42' 28"	
Vx	13°♎50' 08"	
Eq	20°♈59' 39"	
⊗	23°♋15' 06"	

Adjusted Calculation Dates
0h= Feb 23 12h= Aug 24

Chart Service Wheel

Chart Compliments of
Matrix Software
407 N. State St.
Big Rapids, MI 49307
(616) 796-2483

Jane Roberts

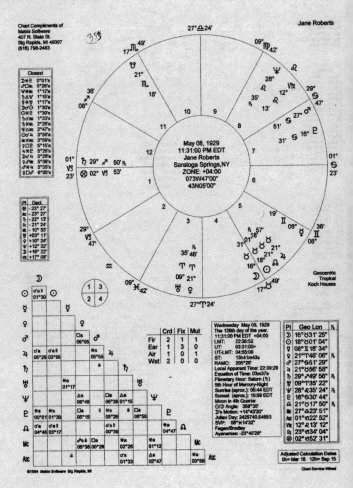

May 08, 1929
11:31:00 PM EDT
Jane Roberts
Saratoga Springs, NY
ZONE: +04:00
073W47'00"
43N05'00"

Geocentric
Tropical
Koch Houses

Closest

☽⚹❋	0°01'a
♂☊⚷	0°28'a
♇⚹❋	1°12'a
♆☊⚷	1°15'a
♀♄♃	1°17'a
☽☊⊙	1°30'a
⊙☊❋	1°30's
♄♃⚹	1°33's
♆♃⚹	2°26'a
♆☊❋	2°47's
⊙♂⚹	3°56's
♀♄⚷	3°59's
♀☊♇	5°15'a
♃♇⚹	5°26's
♀♇⚹	5°26'a
♀♇⚷	5°38's
♂♆♃	5°55's
♀☊♇	6°05's

Pl | Decl.

☽	- 23° 27'
Asc	- 23° 27'
♄	- 22° 13'
⊙	- 21° 24'
♅	- 10° 33'
♃	+03° 11'
♆	+12° 32'
♇	+16° 22'
Vtx	+17° 08'

Wednesday May 08, 1929
The 128th day of the year.
11:31:00 PM EDT +04:00
LMT: 22:36:52
UT: 03:31:00ν
UT-LMT: 04:55:08
ST: 13h41m43s
RAMC: 205°28'
Local Apparent Time: 22:39:29
Equation of Time: 03m37s
Planetary Hour: Saturn (♄)
5th Hour of Mercury-Night
Sunrise (aprox.): 05:44 EDT
Sunset (aprox.): 19:59 EDT
Moon in 4th Quarter
☉☽ Angle: 359°30'
☽'s Motion: +14°43'20"
Julian Day: 2425740.64653
SVP: 06°❋14'32"
Fagan/Bradley
Ayanamsa: -23°45'28"

Pl | Geo Lon

☽	16°♑31' 25"
⊙	18°♉01' 04"
☿	08°♉18' 34"
♀	21°♈46' 06' ℞
♂	27°♋51' 29"
♃	21°♉56' 53' ℞
♄	29°♐49' 56' ℞
♅	09°♈35' 22"
♆	28°♌35' 24' ℞
♇	16°♋30' 44" ℞
Asc	01°♑22' 52"
Vtx	12°♌13' 12"
Ɛ	23°♏34' 04"
⊗	02°♑52' 31"

Adjusted Calculation Dates
0h= Mar 18 12h= Sep 15

©1994 Matrix Software Big Rapids, MI

Chart Service Wheel

			Crd	Fix	Mut
Fir			2	1	1
Ear			1	3	0
Air			1	0	1
Wat			2	0	0

Chart Compliments of
Matrix Software
407 N. State St.
Big Rapids, MI 49307
(616) 796-2483

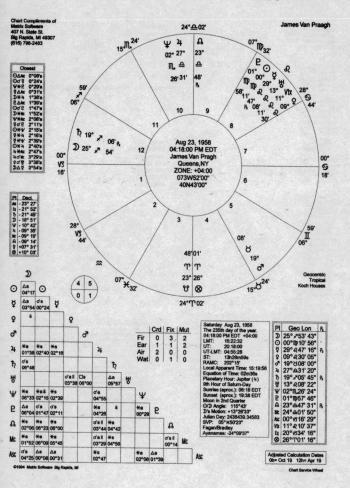

James Van Praagh

Closest	
☉△Asc	0°08's
☉☌☿	0°24's
♆✱♇	0°29'a
☿△Asc	0°31's
☽✱♃	1°38'a
♇△Asc	1°39'a
☉☌♇	1°47'a
☽✱Mc	1°52'a
♆✱Asc	2°08'a
☿☌♇	2°11's
☉✱♆	2°15'a
☿✱♃	2°16'a
☿✱♆	2°39's
☉✱♃	2°40's
♃✱Asc	2°47's
♃☌Mc	3°29'a
♀☌♅	3°38'a
☽△☿	3°54'a

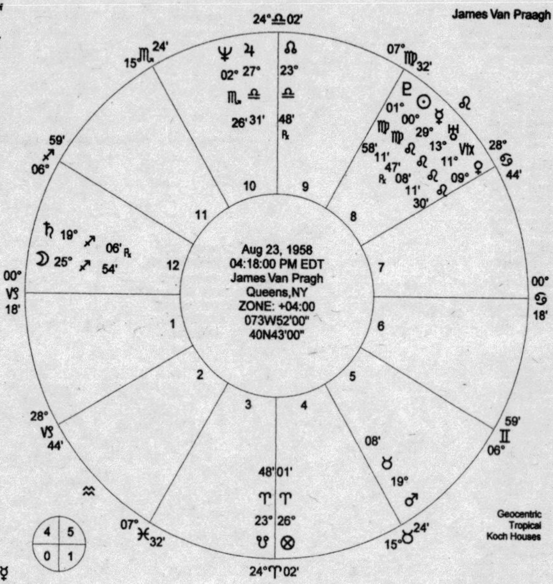
24°♎02'
15°♏24'
07°♍32'
06°♐59'
28°♋44'
00°♑18'
00°♋18'
28°♑44'
06°♊59'
07°♓32'
15°♉24'
24°♈02'
♆ 02° ♏ 26'
♃ 27° ♎ 31'
☊ 23° ♎ 48' ℞
♇ 01° ♍ 58'
☉ 00° ♍ 11'
☿ 29° ♌ 47' ℞
♅ 13° ♌ 08'
Vtx 11° ♌ 11'
♀ 09° ♌ 30'
♄ 19° ♐ 06' ℞
☽ 25° ♐ 54'
♂ 19° ♉ 08'
☋ 23° ♈ 48'
⊗ 26° ♈ 01'
Aug 23, 1958
04:18:00 PM EDT
James Van Pragh
Queens,NY
ZONE: +04:00
073W52'00"
40N43'00"
4
5
0
1

Geocentric
Tropical
Koch Houses

Pl	Decl.
Asc	-23° 27'
Eq	-21° 52'
♄	-21° 45'
☽	-18° 51'
♆	-10° 42'
♃	-09° 35'
Mc	-09° 19'
☊	-09° 14'
☿	+07° 31'
⊗	+10° 03'

	☽	☉	☿	♀	♂	♃	♄	♅	♆	♇	☊	Mc
☉	△a 04°17											
☿	△a 03°54	☌s 00°24										
♀	#											
♂												
♃	✱a 01°38	✱s 02°40	✱a 02°16									
♄	☌s 06°48											
♅				☌a ∥ 03°38	□s 06°00		△a 05°57					
♆	✱a 06°33	✱a # 02°15	✱s 02°39			☌a 04°55						
♇	△a 06°04	☌a 01°47	☌s 02°11			✱a 04°26	#		✱a 00°29			
☊	✱s 02°06	✱s 06°23	✱s 06°00			☌s ∥ 03°44	✱a 04°42					
Mc	✱a 01°52	✱a 06°09	✱a 05°45			☌a ∥ 03°29	✱s 04°56				☌s ∥ 00°14	
Asc	☌s 04°25	△s 00°08	△s 00°31			✱s 02°47			✱a 02°08	△a 01°39		

	Crd	Fix	Mut
Fir	0	3	2
Ear	1	1	2
Air	2	0	0
Wat	0	1	0

Saturday Aug 23, 1958
The 235th day of the year.
04:18:00 PM EDT +04:00
LMT: 15:22:32
UT: 20:18:00
UT-LMT: 04:55:28
ST: 13h28m59s
RAMC: 202°15'
Local Apparent Time: 15:19:56
Equation of Time: 02m36s
Planetary Hour: Jupiter (♃)
9th Hour of Saturn-Day
Sunrise (aprox.): 06:18 EDT
Sunset (aprox.): 19:38 EDT
Moon in 2nd Quarter
☉/☽ Angle: 115°43'
☽'s Motion: +13°26'33"
Julian Day: 2436439.34583
SVP: 05°♓50'23"
Fagan/Bradley
Ayanamsa: -24°09'37"

Pl	Geo Lon	℞
☽	25°♐53' 43"	
☉	00°♍10' 56"	-
☿	29°♌47' 16"	℞
♀	09°♌30' 05"	
♂	19°♉08' 00"	
♃	27°♎31' 20"	
♄	19°♐05' 45"	℞
♅	13°♌08' 22"	
♆	02°♏26' 24"	
♇	01°♍57' 46"	
☊	23°♎47' 31"	℞
Mc	24°♎01' 50"	
Asc	00°♑18' 29"	
Vtx	11°♌10' 37"	
Eq	20°♑34' 16"	
⊗	26°♈01' 16"	

Adjusted Calculation Dates
0h= Oct 19 12h= Apr 19

Chart Service Wheel

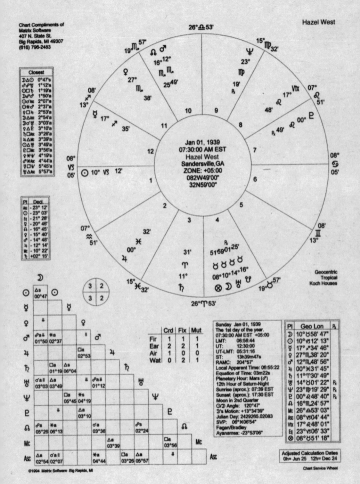

Chart Compliments of
Matrix Software
407 N. State St.
Big Rapids, MI 49307
(616) 796-2483

Hazel West

Jan 01, 1939
07:30:00 AM EST
Hazel West
Sandersville, GA
ZONE: +05:00
082W49'00"
32N59'00"

Geocentric
Tropical
Koch Houses

Sunday Jan 01, 1939
The 1st day of the year.
07:30:00 AM EST +05:00
LMT: 06:58:44
UT: 12:30:00
UT-LMT: 05:31:16
ST: 13h39m47s
RAMC: 204°57'
Local Apparent Time: 06:55:22
Equation of Time: 03m22s
12h Hour of Saturn-Night
Sunrise (aprox.): 07:39 EST
Sunset (aprox.): 17:30 EST
Moon in 2nd Quarter
☉☽ Angle: 120°47'
☽'s Motion: +13°34'39"
Julian Day: 2429265.02083
SVP: 06°X06'54"
Fagan/Bradley
Ayanamsa: -23°53'06"

Closest		
☽△☉	0°47's
♂♂△	1°12'a
☉☐♄	1°19's
☽♂☉	1°50's
☉♂△	2°07's
☉⚹♂	2°37'a
♀☐♄	2°54's
☽△△	2°54'a
♂♂⚹	3°03's
♀△☍	3°10'a
♄△△	3°26'a
☽△☍	3°39'a
☉△☍	3°49'a
☌△△	3°56'a
♀⚹♀	4°19's
♂☍☍	4°44'a
♀☐♀	5°45's
☿△△	5°57's

Pl	Decl.
Mc	- 23° 12'
☉	- 23° 03'
♂	- 21° 28'
♀	- 20° 46'
♀	- 16° 45'
♀	- 15° 40'
☿	- 14° 48'
♃	- 12° 14'
☽	- 10° 22'
♄	+02° 16'

Pl	Geo Lon	℞
☽	10°♊58' 47"	
☉	10°♑12' 13"	
☿	17°♐34' 46"	
♀	27°♏38' 20"	
♂	12°♏48' 56"	
♃	00°X31' 45"	
♄	11°♈30' 49"	
♅	14°♉01' 22"	℞
♆	23°♍19' 29"	℞
♇	00°♌48' 40"	℞
☊	16°♏24' 57"	
Mc	26°♎53' 03"	
Asc	08°♒04' 44"	
Vtx	17°♌48' 01"	
Eq	23°♍06' 33"	
⊗	08°♉51' 18"	

Adjusted Calculation Dates
0h= Jun 25   12h= Dec 24

Chart Service Wheel

	Crd	Fix	Mut
Fir	1	1	1
Ear	2	2	1
Air	1	0	1
Wat	0	2	1

©1994 Matrix Software Big Rapids, MI

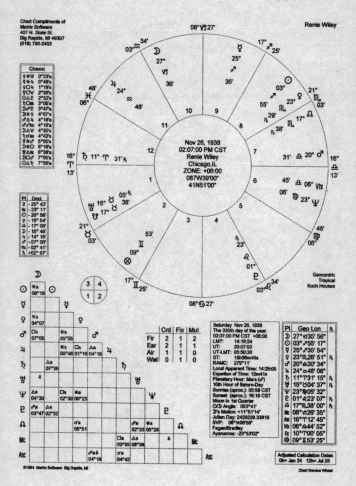

Renie Wiley

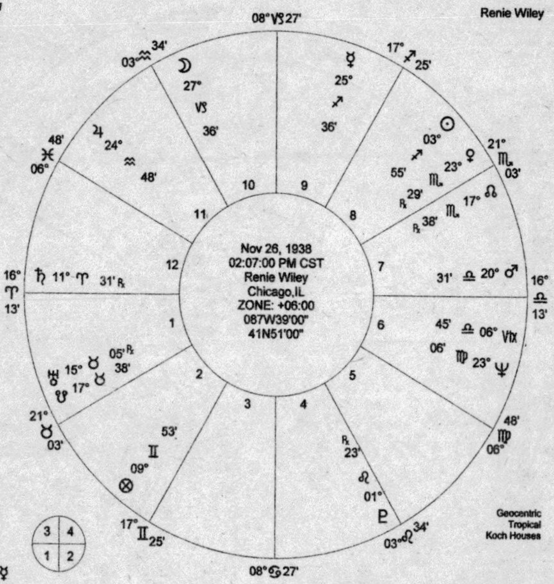
Nov 26, 1938
02:07:00 PM CST
Renie Wiley
Chicago,IL
ZONE: +06:00
087W39'00"
41N51'00"
08°♑27'
08°♋27'
16° ♈ 13'
16° ♎ 13'

Geocentric
Tropical
Koch Houses

Closest	
♀✶♆	0°23'a
☿✶♃	0°48's
♀□♃	1°19's
☿□♆	2°30's
☉△♇	2°32's
♄□Mc	3°05'a
☽☍♇	3°47'a
☽✶♀	4°07's
♂△♃	4°18'a
♂☍Asc	4°18'a
☽△♆	4°30's
♄☌Asc	4°42's
☿✶♂	5°05's
☽✶☉	6°19's
♅△Mc	6°38'a
☽□♂	7°05's
☉△♄	7°36'a

Pl	Decl.
☿	-25° 43'
Mc	-23° 11'
☉	-20° 56'
♀	-19° 54'
☊	-17° 06'
☽	-15° 48'
♃	-14° 16'
♂	-07° 00'
Vx	-02° 41'
♄	+02° 07'

	☽	☉	☿	♀	♂	♃	♄	♅	♆	♇	☊	Mc
☉	✶a 06°19											
☿												
♀	✶s 04°07											
♂	□s 07°05		✶s 05°05									
♃			✶s 00°48	□s 01°19	△a 04°18							
♄		△a 07°36										
♅	#											
♆	△s 04°30		□s 02°30	✶a 00°23								
♇	☍a 03°47	△s 02°32										
☊				☌s 05°51				☍a 02°33	✶s 05°28			
Mc							□a 03°05	△a 06°38		#		
Asc					☍a# 04°18		☌s 04°42					

	Crd	Fix	Mut
Fir	2	1	2
Ear	2	1	1
Air	1	1	0
Wat	0	1	0

Saturday Nov 26, 1938
The 330th day of the year.
02:07:00 PM CST +06:00
LMT: 14:18:24
UT: 20:07:00
UT-LMT: 05:50:36
ST: 18h36m46s
RAMC: 279°11'
Local Apparent Time: 14:29:05
Equation of Time: 12m41s
Planetary Hour: Mars (♂)
10th Hour of Saturn-Day
Sunrise (aprox.): 06:58 CST
Sunset (aprox.): 16:18 CST
Moon in 1st Quarter
☉/☽ Angle: 053°41'
☽'s Motion: +11°51'14"
Julian Day: 2429229.33819
SVP: 06°♓06'58"
Fagan/Bradley
Ayanamsa: -23°53'02"

Pl	Geo Lon	℞
☽	27°♑35' 56"	
☉	03°♐55' 17"	
☿	25°♐35' 54"	
♀	23°♏28' 51"	℞
♂	20°♎30' 34"	
♃	24°♒48' 06"	
♄	11°♈31' 15"	℞
♅	15°♉04' 37"	℞
♆	23°♍05' 32"	
♇	01°♌23' 07"	℞
☊	17°♏38' 00"	℞
Mc	08°♑26' 35"	
Asc	16°♈12' 45"	
Vtx	06°♎44' 52"	
Eq	10°♈00' 05"	
⊗	09°♊53' 25"	

Adjusted Calculation Dates
0h= Jan 24 12h= Jul 26

Chart Service Wheel

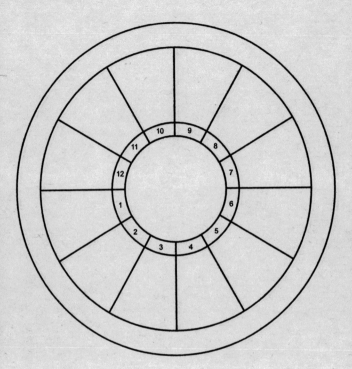

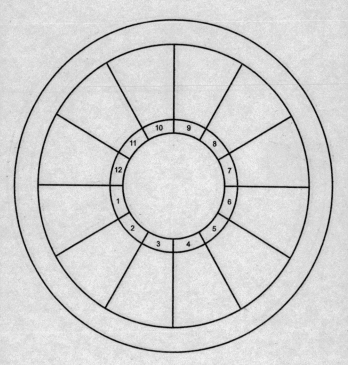

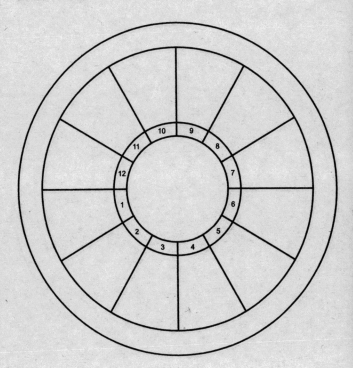

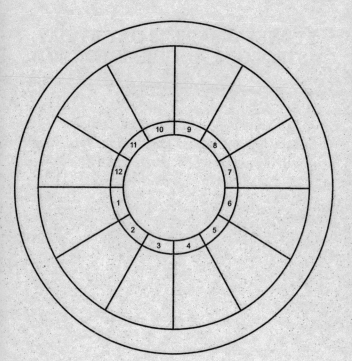

SYDNEY OMARR®'S DAY-BY-DAY ASTROLOGICAL GUIDES FOR 2004

SYDNEY OMARR®

Nationally syndicated astrologer
Sydney Omarr® guides fans into the new year
with his amazingly accurate predictions—
available for every sign.

Aquarius	208770
Aries	208897
Taurus	208900
Pisces	208889
Gemini	208919
Cancer	208927
Leo	208935
Virgo	208934
Libra	209095
Scorpio	208951
Sagittarius	20896X
Capricorn	208978

Available wherever books are sold, or
to order call: 1-800-788-6262

The Ultimate Guide to Love, Sex,
and Romance

SYDNEY OMARR'S® ASTROLOGY, LOVE, SEX, AND YOU

Whether your goal is a sexy seduction, finding your
soulmate, or spicing up a current relationship, this
all-in-one volume will guide you every step of the
way—with a little help from the stars.

Includes:

- An in-depth description of each sign for men and women
- Compatibilty forecasts
- A fantastic section on romantic dinners for two, featuring
a complete kitchen-tested menu for each sign
- Myths and symbols associated with each sign
- An introduction to each sign's shadow
- Ratings on which signs are the most passionate
- and much more

206932

Available wherever books are sold, or
to order call: 1-800-788-6262